REFORM
AND
REACTION
IN
POST-MAO
CHINA

REFORM
AND
REACTION
IN
POST-MAO
CHINA

THE ROAD
TO TIANANMEN

EDITED BY RICHARD BAUM

ROUTLEDGE
New York • London

Published in 1991 by

Routledge
An imprint of Routledge, Chapman and Hall, Inc.
29 West 35 Street
New York, NY 10001

Published in Great Britain by

Routledge
11 New Fetter Lane
London EC4P 4EE

Library of Congress Cataloging in Publication Data

Reform and reaction in post-Mao China : The road to Tianamen / edited
  by Richard Baum.
        p.   cm.
    Includes bibliographical references.
    ISBN 0-415-90317-3 —ISBN 0-415-90318-1 (pbk.) :
      1. China—Politics and government—1976– 2. China—Economic
policy—1976– I. Baum, Richard
JQ1502.S78   1990
951.05'7—dc20   89-70082

British Library Cataloguing in Publication Data

Reform and reaction in post-Mao China : the road to
  Tianamen.
    1. China. Economic development   2. China politics
    I. Baum, Richard
    320. 951

ISBN 0-415-90317-3
ISBN 0-415-90318-1 (pbk)

Contents

Preface

The idea for a collection of essays examining the effects of the first decade of China's post-Mao reforms was originally suggested to me by Stanley Rosen. The product of our collaboration—a special double issue of the journal *Studies in Comparative Communism* (Summer/Autumn 1989)— went to press several weeks before the Tiananmen crisis reached its violent climax on the weekend of June 3–4, 1989.

In the aftermath of the crackdown in Beijing, Jay Wilson, then my editor at Routledge, Chapman and Hall, encouraged me to revise and update the various essays in the original collection for inclusion in a new, post-Tiananmen volume. David Cattell, editor of *Studies in Comparative Communism*, generously consented to permit reproduction of portions of the original articles in a new and expanded format. The authors then rewrote their individual essays to incorporate analysis of the forces shaping the Tiananmen tragedy; and new introductory and concluding chapters were added relating the events of the Beijing Spring to the extraordinary "gentle revolution" that swept through Eastern Europe and the Soviet Union in the autumn and winter of 1989–90.

Throughout the production process, Karen Sullivan and Jayne Fargnoli of Routledge, Chapman and Hall were extremely helpful and supportive. Jody Kennedy provided valuable research and wordprocessing assistance at U.C.L.A. Steve Futterman, correspondent for NBC/Mutual radio news, generously shared with me his personal collection of photographs from the Tiananmen crisis, one of which adorns the front cover of this book.

Richard Baum
Los Angeles
August 1990

1

Introduction:
The Perils of Partial Reform

Richard Baum

The decade of the 1980s ended in crisis for communist regimes everywhere, as shock waves of citizen unrest and rebellion spread from Beijing to Bucharest, from Baku to Ulan Bator. Whipped by winds of *glasnost* and triggered by tremors from the Tiananmen crisis, the upheaval was for the most part peaceful, though spasmodic political and communal violence broke out at several points.

In the course of the cascading "gentle revolution" of 1989–90, Leninist regimes underwent a series of profound transformations. Some were swept away altogether; others survived only by renouncing their own recent history, replacing their leaders, and redesigning their institutions; still others dug in their heels and resisted the rising tide of popular unrest. Whatever the local regime response, the overall effect was unmistakable: the core doctrines and institutions of Marxism-Leninism-Stalinism were decisively repudiated by those most directly subject to their hegemony. In their place a variety of localized experiments in political and socioeconomic pluralism were launched—with varying degrees of efficacy and varying prospects for long-term success.[1]

In a remarkable display of political initiative, early in 1990 the Soviet Communist Party Central Committee voted to terminate its seventy-two-year monopoly on political power, scrapping Article 6 of the Soviet constitution, legitimating multiparty competition, and thereby signaling the demise of Leninism as the guiding doctrine of the Soviet state. Throughout Eastern Europe and in several Soviet republics, popular elections in the spring of 1990 ratified the momentous transformations of the gentle revolution, formally inaugurating a new era of political pluralization—albeit a highly volatile and uncertain one. The overall pattern of cascading communist dissolution was so striking that one observer was moved to suggest, in a burst of hyperbolic enthusiasm, that the exhaustion of world communism marked not merely the end of the Cold War, but the end of history itself.[2]

Notwithstanding such euphoria, there were notable exceptions to the rule of Leninist dissolution. The most important was China—ironically, the place where the revolution of 1989 got its start. At the beginning of that year China stood among the most progressive and globally engaged of the reform-oriented communist states, with a ten-year history of economic reform and "openness" to the outside world; by year's end, however, it had become isolated and embattled, its educated youth demoralized and disillusioned, its reforms in limbo, and its leaders stubbornly clinging to power through a combination of political repression and ideological revivalism. As the first decade of post-Mao reform ended, the nation's shoulders sagged visibly under the weight of the Tiananmen tragedy.

The immediate sources of China's political crisis have been well documented: mounting popular alienation, stemming from runaway urban inflation, official corruption, and profiteering; endemic student political unrest, centering on demands for enhanced democratic rights and freedoms; the sudden death of pro-reform party leader Hu Yaobang, catalyzing student demonstrations; and a series of heavy-handed government attempts, spearheaded by a small group of conservative, semiretired octogenarians, to delegitimize the country's budding pro-democracy movement and discredit its leadership.[3]

While the immediate antecedents of the crisis are thus clear, it is more difficult to isolate and elucidate the deeper, systemic sources of tension and conflict. To a considerable extent, these underlying sources are to be found in the dynamics of the reform process itself—its convolutions, its contradictions, and ultimately its convulsions.

Reform and Retreat:
China's First Decade Without Mao

In China, the process of systemic reform began earlier than in most other communist countries. By the time Mao Zedong died in September 1976, fallout from his tumultuous Cultural Revolution had produced a severe and widespread "crisis of confidence" that affected China's political institutions, values, and leadership. With the economy deeply mired in allocational inefficiency and bureaucratic stagnation, with countless victims of Red Guard abuse and "Gang of Four" persecution calling for "reversal of verdicts" and an end to the arbitrary lawlessness of Maoist "feudal autocracy," the situation demanded urgent attention.

At this critical juncture, Deng Xiaoping and a small group of reform-oriented pragmatists within the CCP leadership rejected major elements of the Maoist legacy—including the late Chairman's unremitting emphasis on class struggle—and initiated a series of sweeping economic and political-legal reforms.[4] Among the more prominent early reforms were the adoption of various market-oriented "production responsibility systems" in agriculture;[5] the creation of "special economic zones" and "open door" policies to attract foreign investment, commerce, technology, and tourism;[6] the restoration and expansion of citizens' basic constitutional and legal rights;[7] the revamping of local electoral mechanisms and the strengthening of popular representation in the political arena;[8] the introduction of limited terms of office and mandatory retirement for senior, veteran cadres; and a related drive to prohibit party leaders from holding concurrent posts in state administration.[9]

Additional reforms were introduced in the mid-1980s. The most important of these were price deregulation, designed to reduce allocational distortions caused by a state-imposed pricing system that reflected neither actual production costs nor relative scarcities; and the structural reform of urban enterprises, designed to increase managerial autonomy, initiative, and responsibility in state-owned factories and commercial establishments.[10]

Although these reforms were introduced amid great fanfare, stimulating high public hopes and expectations, their actual implementation was slow and halting due to a combination of factors that included mounting conservative political resistance and a series of unanticipated economic imbalances. Among the latter, the most serious were a dangerously high rate of urban inflation (approaching 30 percent in 1988); a runaway money supply; a "get rich quick" mentality among young people; and an epidemic of cadre-centered profiteering and corruption. Taken together, these difficulties highlighted the fragility of the reform program and the inadequacy of existing mechanisms of economic readjustment, shock absorption, and burden sharing.

Responding to rising public alarm over these developments—and to a sudden wave of panic-buying among nervous urban consumers who feared the destabilizing effects of further price deregulation—party leaders in the late summer of 1988 declared a two-year moratorium on the introduction of further reforms. This had the effect of leaving China's partially restructured economy in a frozen, hybrid state, its internal contradictions perpetuated rather than resolved.

If economic reform was thus halting and incomplete, the course of China's post-Mao political reform was no less fitful. Following a brief flurry of liberal institutional innovation in 1978–80, the CCP in 1981 reasserted its "four cardinal principles"—an ideological litmus test that defined the acceptable limits of political thought and behavior;[11] there followed a five-year hiatus on political reform, during which time little meaningful political debate took place in China and official support for democratization and human rights all but ceased.

In 1986, hopes for a new round of political reform were raised when the state-controlled mass media reissued a report written in 1980 by Deng Xiaoping, "On the Reform of the System of Party and State Leadership." Noting that problems in the political sphere had "reached intolerable proportions," the report called for a thorough overhaul of the Chinese leadership system, which was said to be dominated by "bureaucratism, over-concentration of power, patriarchal methods, life tenure in leading posts, and privileges of various kinds."[12]

Emboldened by the publication of Deng's report, university students and political activists throughout China pushed the twin issues of democracy and human rights to the forefront of attention in the fall and early winter of 1986–87 in a series of well-publicized campus demonstrations. The protests ceased, however, when party conservatives, with Deng Xiaoping's concurrence, launched a campaign to oppose "bourgeois liberalization." In the course of the new campaign a number of the CCP's most prominent democratic activists, including astrophysicist Fang Lizhi and journalist Liu Binyan, were expelled from the party; at the same time, CCP General Secretary Hu Yaobang—an outspoken supporter of liberal reform—was removed from office.[13]

The Road to Tiananmen:
What Went Wrong?

China's reform movement, inaugurated in the late 1970s amid expectations of rapid modernization and change, thus encountered a debilitating series of delays, diversions, and distractions. By the late 1980s there had emerged an uneven—and in many respects incoherent—pattern of patchwork-quilt reforms and half-way institutional adaptations. Partial measures served, in turn, both to intensify existing structural stresses and to create new ones. The result was a deepening crisis.[14]

The very incompleteness of the reforms meant, for example, that disparate elements of old (centrally planned) and new (market-oriented) economic institutions and policies continued to coexist in uneasy—and often mutually disruptive—juxtaposition. One result was a dramatic rise in levels of income inequality and a skewing of opportunities for upward social mobility. While some occupational groups and individuals (e.g., rural cadres, suburban peasant entrepreneurs, urban taxi drivers, private merchants, and lawyers) were able to prosper in the partially deregulated, partially marketized reform environment, others (including contract workers, clerks, teachers, and students, *inter alia*) were poorly placed to take advantage of the new market mechanism.[15]

Compounding the problem of unequal opportunity was the persistence of a two- (and sometimes three-) tiered pricing system that created strong incentives (as well as manifold opportunities) for party and government officials and their families to capture windfall profits by engaging in such illicit activities as speculation, profiteering, and commercial brokering. Other reform-related stresses included runaway urban inflation (fueled by uncontrolled growth in the country's money supply and partial government decontrol of consumer prices) and a loss of central government control over local investment and construction.Caught between spiralling consumer prices, rampant corruption, and the limited availability of opportunities for upward mobility, many social groups experienced a growing sense of relative deprivation, downward mobility, and status envy (known in China as "red-eye disease").[16]

Such structurally induced stresses and contradictions, far from being isolated exceptions, eventually came to dominate and define the basic contours of China's reform system; indeed, in some respects they *were* the system. By the spring of 1989 the social frictions produced by these contradictions could no longer be contained by a party leadership that was itself deeply divided over the pace and direction of reform—and over its political and spiritual implications. To the accompaniment first of marching students, then of government ultimatums, and finally of machine-gun fire, the contradictions played themselves out at Tiananmen Square, in full view of a dismayed, disbelieving world.

The Anatomy of Incomplete Reform:
An Overview

In this volume, nine specialists on contemporary China offer an assessment of the socioeconomic and political effects of the first decade of post-Mao reform in China. Originally drafted prior to the Tiananmen crisis, each of the essays in the volume has been rewritten with a view to offering fresh insight into the deeper forces that shaped—and the implications that flowed from—the crisis.[17] The authors adopt an explicitly comparative perspective, bringing to bear on China's recent history lessons drawn from contemporaneous events and developments in other communist systems. Their focus ranges from analysis of the long-term macro-historical forces governing the evolution (and dissolution) of Leninist regimes to the short-term microsocietal effects of incomplete structural reform upon the incidence of corruption and clientelism in urban enterprises and rural villages. In between these extremes of macro/micro analysis the authors address a variety of issues of central concern to students of reform in communist systems.

Several of the essays in this book deal directly or indirectly with the relationship between structural reform and emergent forces of political pluralism and democratization. In the first essay, **Lowell Dittmer** compares the reform experiences of China under Deng and the Soviet Union under Gorbachev in an attempt to shed light on the question of the possible long-term co-evolution and structural confluence (i.e., "convergence") of reform-oriented Leninist systems. Tracing the history and mutual impact of reform efforts in the two countries, Dittmer notes that there have been two distinct phases and patterns of reciprocal Sino-Soviet influence since the late 1970s. In the first phase (1978–86), the initiative belonged to China, as Deng Xiaoping introduced a series of radical innovations to jump-start China's stalled, stagnant command economy. Examining several of the most important reforms of this period, Dittmer notes that China's early experiences were carefully monitored by Soviet leaders, who subsequently modeled many of their own reform proposals upon Chinese prototypes.

In the second phase of interactive reform (1986–90), the Chinese reform program became bogged down in a series of economic difficulties stemming, *inter alia,* from the unsettling effects of partial urban industrial and commercial restructuring. In this period Gorbachev regained the initiative for the Soviet Union, implementing a series of sweeping political reforms designed to ease the way for structural renovation of the Soviet economy. Thus, Dittmer notes, the late 1980s brought a visible shift from the previous pattern of Chinese reform initiative and cautious Soviet response to a new pattern of bold Soviet initiative and Chinese caution—culminating in the violent repression of spring 1989.

In an attempt to account for this shift, Dittmer suggests that a common problem giving rise to both patterns may have been "the premature exhaustion of economic reform"—i.e., its tendency to run aground before achieving its intended results. In the Soviet case, he argues, early efforts at economic reform made little headway before running up against insuperable bureaucratic obstacles, thus necessitating political reform in order to effect a breakthrough. In the Chinese case, on the other hand, economic reform achieved significant gains before political reform became an urgent priority. Whereas Soviet bureaucratic elites tended to passively resist economic reforms while grudgingly accepting political change, Chinese elites were far more receptive to economic reforms, remaining firmly opposed to any political reforms that might undermine their position. Thus, Dittmer argues, the correlation between economic and political reform has been quite dissynchronous in the two cases; and it is for this reason that the seemingly convergent trajectories of reform in the two countries paradoxically began to diverge sharply at precisely the moment of anticipated consummation—i.e., during Gorbachev's May 1989 "renormalization" visit to Beijing. Nevertheless, and despite China's hostile reaction to subsequent Soviet political initiatives in Eastern Europe, Dittmer believes that the long-term prospects for renewed Sino-Soviet convergence seem reasonably favorable. Lest such a prospect evoke undue complacency, however, he cautions that the final victory of convergence theory could well bring with it a violent, implosive disintegration of the socialist world—a prospect whose full implications cannot yet be readily grasped or assimilated.

In the next essay, **Nina P. Halpern** examines more closely the relationship between economic reform and political democratization in China. Rejecting some of the more mechanistic assumptions of convergence theory, she postulates the contingent nature of the interaction between economic and political factors in the process of reform. That is, instead of seeing the impetus for political democratization springing inexorably from the pluralizing socioeconomic effects of structural reform, as implied in convergence theory, she suggests that localized political, historical, and attitudinal variables and contingencies ultimately play a major role in shaping the outcome of reform in Leninist systems; and she argues that democracy is only one among several possible outcomes of the Chinese reform movement—and not necessarily the most likely one.

Analyzing the Chinese reform movement from its inception in 1978 to the crackdown at Tiananmen Square, Halpern argues that the major impetus behind Deng Xiaoping's initial efforts to modify China's political system came not from any quest for economic rationality or modernity, but rather from two localized political factors: a strong popular backlash against the arbitrary cruelty, hardship, and lawlessness of the Cultural Revolution; and an intense post-Mao succession crisis, in the course of which Deng and his allies employed the rhetoric of democratic reform—including calls for intellectual liberalization, "seeking truth from facts," and a systemic critique of the institutions and practices of "feudal autocracy"—as a tactic in their struggle to dislodge Mao's chosen successor, Hua Guofeng. Once Hua had been ousted, China's new leaders conveniently pulled the plug on further democratic reform, substituting instead a less radical and disruptive program of institutional rationalization and enhanced intellectual tolerance.

Having sanctioned the values of political liberty and mass participation, however, Deng discovered that he could not easily stuff the democratic genie back into its prereform jar. Halpern suggests that a key reason for this lay in the fact that the Cultural Revolution had legitimated participatory values for a large segment of the Chinese population, inclining them more strongly than ever to take political action to achieve their goals. And when, beginning in the mid-1980s, mass political mobilization began to exceed the limits prescribed by the party's "four cardinal principles," China's top leaders, rather than grant an additional measure of democratization, became more firmly convinced of the need for tightened central authority, stability, and control. Therein, Halpern argues, lay the wellsprings of the government's violent crackdown during the Tiananmen crisis. And she concludes that similar crises will recur in the future—in amplified form—if and when the party again decides to move ahead with economic and political reform; when that happens, she predicts, China's leaders are likely to discover that those social groups which participated actively in the 1989 demonstrations will become even more readily mobilized to demand democratic change the next time around.

Linking the political dynamics of reform at the elite level with an assessment of the impact of reform at the mass level, **Stanley Rosen** next examines the role of public opinion research in the Chinese reform process. Noting that a common denominator of reform in communist systems everywhere has been increased elite attentiveness to the *vox populi,* Rosen suggests that such attentiveness stems partly from a systemic need to obtain accurate societal feedback during periods of rapid socio-economic change, and partly from the regime's desire to mobilize public support for its own agenda and policies. These two objectives—opinion *measurement* and opinion *manipulation*—frequently work at cross purposes, however; as a result, there is often profound elite ambivalence toward public opinion polling and survey research—even in the most reform-oriented communist systems.

Comparing China's experience with that of the Soviet Union and Eastern Europe, Rosen observes that survey research got off to a relatively slow start in post-Mao China. This was due, in large measure, to the residual legacy of the CCP's traditional preference for "mass line"-style methods of assessing popular attitudes. Systematic, quantitative scientific survey research was not encouraged until the Chinese Academy of Social Sciences underwent a period of rapid institutional expansion from 1979 to 1981. By the latter half of the 1980s a plethora of opinion research institutes and centers had sprung up in China. Some of these were privately run; others were either affiliated with or funded by various organs of the Chinese government.

Rosen documents the Chinese government's growing discomfort with the results of a series of public opinion polls conducted in the late 1980s—polls which showed the Chinese population becoming increasingly restive over the failed promises of reform, increasingly inclined to pursue narrow self-interest at the expense of societal goals, and increasingly cynical about their political leaders and their own personal futures. Against this background of rising public alienation and discontent, by 1988 different political factions and leadership groups were using their own "friendly" public opinion polls as partisan weapons against rival groups and factions in a surrogate struggle of "dueling surveys."

Both before and during the Beijing Spring of 1989, Rosen notes, Chinese opinion surveys revealed a mass public that was both alienated and increasingly sympathetic to student demands. Because of this, and because the opinion pollsters themselves tended to be located at the extreme liberal end of the reform spectrum, China's hardliners targeted several leading public opinion centers for closure—and their leaders for arrest—soon after the crackdown began on June 3–4. Rosen informs us that as of the end of 1989 eleven members of one leading opinion research institute—the privately run Chinese Economic System Reform Research Institute (CESRRI)—remained under detention, while two leading members of another group, the Beijing Social and Economic Research Center, were arrested after four months on the run.[18]

Rosen suggests that although opinion polling is slowly being resumed, new official guidelines make it clear that both the pollsters and their surveys will henceforth be subjected to much tighter political and ideological scrutiny. In such a controlled milieu, Rosen argues, one likely result will be a repoliticization and ideological skewing of opinion surveys, along with a corresponding degradation in the quality and social utility of the information contained therein—an ironic outcome in view of the fact that the rise of opinion research in China was driven in the first instance by reform leaders' growing need to obtain accurate, unbiased societal feedback.

A similar irony is evident in the Chinese government's treatment of its newly emergent private business sector. Assessing the renaissance of China's urban private sector under Deng Xiaoping, **Thomas B. Gold** documents the profound ambivalence of China's post-Mao leaders toward this erstwhile "tail of capitalism." Desiring to take advantage of the incentive and productivity-enhancing effects of autonomous individual and small collective-based economic exchange, but fearful of the political and ideological consequences of such autonomous activity, party planners sought to steer a middle course—a stratagem that Gold (following CCP elder statesman Chen Yun) refers to as the "bird in cage" approach, i.e., "giving people a roomier birdcage but not removing the cage altogether."

From 1981 to 1988 the private sector expanded greatly as China's reformers, under the prevailing theory of the "primary stage of socialism," emphasized rapid development of the material forces of production above all other considerations. This period witnessed a tenfold increase in the total number of people employed in private business (from 2.3 million to 23 million) and a fourteenfold increase in the volume of retail trade conducted in free markets (from RMB 2.4 billion yuan to 34.7 billion). Urban private enterprise accounted for about one-fourth of these totals.

Noting that China's reformers appeared to lack a clear, coherent, and well-articulated plan for managing the effects of market-oriented reforms, Gold documents the worsening urban socioeconomic stresses and contradictions that accompanied the rise of China's *getihu* (private households) in the mid- and late 1980s. Mounting inflation, budget deficits, rampant corruption, gross inequalities in income distribution, and macroeconomic chaos were some of the more damaging by-products of partial, incoherent reform. Equally distressing—especially to conservative party elders—was the emergence of a new economic ethos of "everyone for himself" and a pervasive "get rich quick" mentality that threatened to seriously corrode the social values and priorities of Chinese youth.

Things came to a head in the late summer and fall of 1988, when CCP conservatives, reacting to mounting public fears of economic chaos, put the brakes on further economic reform in an effort to cool down the overheated Chinese economy and rein in the free-wheeling private sector. By this time, however, the seeds of incipient crisis had already been deeply sown.

Gold notes that during the tumultuous days of April–June 1989, Beijing's
getihu played a generally supportive role vis-à-vis the emerging student
protest movement. Many private households supplied food, blankets, and
other provisions to demonstrators. Still others, utilizing private motorcycles
(a symbol of nouveau-riche status among urban youth), served as messen-
gers, pickets, and sentries for the students. One prominent private businessman, Wan Runnan, chief of the controversial Stone Company, reportedly
donated US$25,000 to the Tiananmen demonstrators as well as providing
them with electronic broadcasting equipment. Still other urban entrepreneurs were active in petitioning the Standing Committee of the National
People's Congress to hold an emergency session to end the declared state of
martial law in Beijing.

In the immediate aftermath of June 3–4, several leading *getihu* supporters
of the democracy movement were arrested or fled the country. Shortly
thereafter, the government began to crack down on some of the more flagrant
economic abuses of *getihu,* such as tax evasion, operating without a license,
illicit hiring practices (including employment of child labor), bribery, and
profiteering. Gold reports that by early November 1989 more than 2.2
million private enterprises—roughly 15 percent of the total—had been
forced out of business in the government's drive to strengthen its control
over business operations.

Despite the post-Tiananmen crackdown on illegal practices, Gold observes
that private business *per se* has not been attacked or outlawed; indeed,
the "positive contributions" of the private sector have been reaffirmed by
government officials. This suggests, in Gold's view, that China's leaders
remain deeply divided over just how far to go in loosening up, or how to
channel and control the forces unleashed by economic reform. And this, in
turn, suggests that there will continue to be considerable ambivalence in
government policy toward the private sector.

Turning from the private commercial sector to the public sector, **Dorothy
J. Solinger** examines the effects of urban economic reforms, introduced
in 1984, on the commercial behavior of China's state-owned enterprises.
Although the 1984 reforms were clearly intended to strengthen the operation
of market forces in the urban economy, Solinger finds that nothing approaching the neoclassical model of free market exchange has emerged in
Chinese industry. Using case studies drawn from a series of interviews in the
central Chinese city of Wuhan, she traces this failure to the persistence of
three traditional weaknesses in the Chinese economy: *extreme scarcity*
(which forces enterprise managers to confront recurrent shortages of vital
productive inputs and capital goods); *lack of design standardization* (which
reduces managers' confidence in their ability to secure, on open or spot

markets, inputs that meet their required technical specifications and quality standards); and *weak channels of market information* (which increases managerial uncertainty concerning the availability of inputs and the reliability of particular products and suppliers encountered on the open market).

Due to the persistence of these three endemic problems—none of which is unique either to China or to socialist command economies—the "transaction costs" of Chinese enterprise managers seeking to operate on the open market tend to be prohibitively high; consequently, Solinger observes, factory purchasing and sales agents frequently resort to the device of "relational contracting;" that is, they stay with their established, prereform suppliers and customers, preferring to deal with known quantities rather than risk confronting the vagaries and uncertainties of the market. The result is that the actual economic behavior of urban enterprises has been far less market-oriented—and far closer to the behavior patterns mandated under the old system of centralized state planning—than anyone anticipated.

Solinger suggests that the economic conditions that give rise to managerial preferences for relational contracting—viz., inadequate transportation and communications, endemic industrial quality control problems, and recurrent commodity shortages—are encountered in a wide variety of institutional settings; and she thus finds important parallels between the rise of relational contracting in China and the appearance of such phenomena as "sheltered markets" and "mutually obligated trading relationships" in other developing economies.

Although not confined to socialist command economies, Solinger's observations have special relevance for students of reform in communist systems. In recent years we have been led—by socialist planners and neoclassical economists alike—to expect that "pure" market-oriented commercial relations would simply displace plan-mandated relations once structural reform was effected. Solinger demonstrates that there are good reasons to question this assumption; and she concludes that so long as infrastructural and informational weaknesses persist in socialist systems undergoing reform, preexisting commercial relationships will tend to exhibit a certain "stickiness" that will continue to confound the expectations of reformers and economic theorists alike.

Echoing Solinger's argument that economic reform has failed to create a true market in China, **Connie Squires Meaney** notes that enormous structural gaps and contradictions have been engendered by the partial, incomplete reform of China's urban economy since 1984. Such gaps—e.g., between a newly decentralized, weakened state economic apparatus and a newly strengthened, semiautonomous local cadre corps, as well as between state-fixed commodity prices and deregulated market prices—have been readily exploited by opportunistic enterprise managers and local government officials, who have been among the prime beneficiaries of economic deregulation and decentralization. One result has been an alarming rise in reports of economic crime and corruption in urban Chinese industry and commerce.

Noting that the issue of cadre corruption was the single most prominent issue uniting student demonstrators and the citizens of Beijing in the spring of 1989, Meaney asks whether the reforms themselves actually generated a quantum leap in the incidence of corruption, or whether corruption merely assumed new, more politically explosive forms under the reformist regime. Following Michael Johnston, she draws an analytical distinction between "integrative" and "disintegrative" forms of corruption. Integrative corruption serves to link people and groups into lasting networks of exchange and shared interest, and includes such traditional practices as clientelism and the customary dispensing of small favors as a routine cost of doing business. Disintegrative corruption, by contrast, is less routinized, involves higher stakes, and generally produces tension and conflict with those who are excluded from sharing in the preferential benefits of participation. Examples of disintegrative corruption include nepotism, windfall profiteering, and market speculation.

Analyzing numerous cases of urban economic impropriety as reported in the Chinese media, Meaney suggests that disintegrative forms of corruption have increased markedly relative to other varieties since 1984, and that it is this fact that accounts for the rising public alienation and outrage manifested in the 1989 Tiananmen demonstrations. Documenting the myriad ways in which partial economic reform has enabled people with official connections to reap huge windfall profits from disparities in prices, inside information, and access to goods, Meaney argues that what emerged in the wake of market reform was a plethora of insider networks protected by cadres and bureaucrats acting in collusive secrecy. In the rush to make quick financial killings, cadres frequently appropriated official organizations and routinely placed their own offspring (or other family members) in financially advantageous positions.

Meaney notes the existence of a paradox in the fact that Leninist systems, for reasons having to do with their ideological intolerance toward particularistic loyalties and familistic relationships, tend to be more vulnerable to abuses of nepotism and clientelism than most other systems. The existence of particularistic ties must routinely be denied and hidden from view in Leninist systems. Such deception and denial has the effect of increasing both the general public awareness of elite hypocrisy and the level of public cynicism toward politics—an effect which, if reinforced by a sudden upsurge in windfall profiteering by greedy, opportunistic cadres and their families, may result in a crisis of political legitimacy for the Leninist regime. In exploring these questions, Meaney advances our understanding of economic corruption in post-Mao China and sheds valuable new light on the origins and implications of China's recent political upheavals.

Jean C. Oi extends the analysis of post-Mao clientelism and corruption from China's cities to the surrounding countryside, where she too finds evidence of increasing concern over the incidence of illegal economic activity since the introduction of production and marketing reforms in the late 1970s. Discounting cultural explanations of rural corruption, Oi argues instead for a systemic, structural interpretation. Like Meaney, she traces the increasing magnitude of corrupt behavior to the partial deregulation of rural economic activity under the reform program. Partial deregulation, she notes, has had the paradoxical effect of weakening the central government's control over the local economy while at the same time giving individual village cadres enhanced discretionary power over the allocation of local resources and economic opportunities. As a result, individual Chinese peasant households are actually more dependent on the goodwill and patronage of local officials today than they were before the reforms; consequently, peasants have become highly vulnerable to systematic predation by greedy, opportunistic cadres and their local networks of clients and cronies. Far from removing the structural sources of corruption, partial reform has thus actually exacerbated them.

Noting that the costs and gains, burdens and benefits of official patronage, cronyism, and corruption have been distributed unevenly throughout the countryside, Oi suggests that rising inequalities in economic opportunity under the reforms have contributed to the growth of new class distinctions in rural China—and to a rising perception of distributive injustice that could, if allowed to go unchecked, seriously impair peasant enthusiasm for reform. In this connection, she notes that public outrage against *guandao*—illegal or preferential profiteering by the offspring of party and government cadres—played a major role in precipitating the 1989 Tiananmen crisis.

Whereas in the past local corruption was seen by many as "necessary grease" to keep the system running smoothly, Oi suggests that corruption is now increasingly perceived as the byproduct of an inefficient, inequitable system run by (and for the benefit of) a small, privileged group of officials. Such a situation is not likely to change, she concludes, so long as local cadres remain the primary fulcrum of the new, partially-reformed rural economy.

In the penultimate essay, **Edward Friedman** places China's post-Mao reforms in macro-historical, macro-systemic perspective. Examining the relationship between global economic forces and the local political dynamics and vicissitudes of communist reform, Friedman posits the notion of a worldwide "crisis of permanent technological revolution" that confronts

Leninist regimes in the late twentieth century. Arguing that openness to
international advances in science and technology is an essential prerequisite
for Leninist systems to compete successfully in the modern world, he suggests
that technological openness is unlikely to be sustained without a concurrent
opening to political democratization. This is true, he argues, because the
economic and political institutions of Leninism-Stalinism have become so
over-sized, over-centralized, and ossified that they are wholly unsuited to a
contemporary era that demands flexible institutions and competitive trade
as conditions of economic progress; and it is only through democratization—
the political empowerment of the common man—that such flexibility and
competitiveness can be optimized.

While thus postulating the techno-economic obsolescence of Leninism-
Stalinism, Friedman, echoing Halpern, does not foresee the necessary or
inevitable victory of democracy in China. Instead, he proposes the notion
of a "democratic moment." Though global technological and economic
challenges may provide an *opening* for democratization, they do not constitute an *imperative*. It is politics, he argues, that ultimately determines
whether the opening will be grasped and permitted to develop into fully
democratic political forms. Political elites have options; and they may choose
reactionary as well as progressive solutions to the technologically induced
crisis of institutional obsolescence. In support of this proposition, Friedman
adduces evidence from the earlier modernizing experiences of Japan, Germany, Russia, Holland, and England, *inter alia*.

One possible alternative to democratization involves reactionary populistic appeals to the latent xenophobic sentiments of the masses—such as earlier
occurred in Bismarck's Germany and in prewar Japan. Noting the occurrence
of a series of anti-foreign riots in China in 1985, 1986, and 1988, and
the appearance of a spate of anti-Western propaganda in the government-
controlled mass media in the aftermath of the Tiananmen crackdown of
1989, Friedman suggests that China's elderly, embattled leaders may find it
increasingly convenient to play upon the nativistic fears and hostilities of the
Chinese people, whose modern history of repeated humiliation at the hands
of foreigners and whose lost dignity as a result of two millennia of predatory,
feudal-autocratic rule have rendered them susceptible to chauvinistic appeals.

In the end, however, Friedman remains cautiously optimistic. "Conservatives may win for a while," he declares, and "naked coercion can be employed
to suppress democrats"—as occurred at Tiananmen. Nevertheless, "the historical forces that gave rise to the democratic impulse are undiminished; and
the issue of democratization cannot but remain high on a basic and continuing political agenda."

In his concluding epilogue, **Richard Baum** revisits some of the central
themes and controversies raised in previous chapters. Casting his commen-

tary within the framework of a newly revived debate over the relevance of convergence theory, occasioned by the gentle revolution of 1989–90, he finds that there is much of value in the notion of a globalized, techno-economically driven process of structural and normative convergence. While acknowledging that the course of the gentle revolution was inevitably influenced by a great many localized vicissitudes and variations, he suggests that there are three interrelated macro-historical forces driving convergent processes in the Communist world: the *globalization of commerce* (which has served to break down systemic barriers to the intersocietal flow of ideas, products, and people), the *marketization of exchange relations* (which has constrained would-be economic competitors to improve the efficiency of their productive processes and feedback mechanisms), and the *technological acceleration of information diffusion* (which, by multiplying and extending communications links both within and between countries, has dramatically reduced the capacity of political elites to willfully control and manipulate the flow and content of ideas and information).

Examining the series of unprecedented political convulsions that shook the Communist world in 1989–90, Baum highlights the interconnections between events in China, Eastern Europe, and the Soviet Union. He points out the considerable irony of China's descent, in the space of less than a year, from being the boldest, most innovative Leninist system to being the most conservative; and he suggests that the extreme violence that marked the Chinese government's globally televised, faxized, and VOAized response to the turmoils at Tiananmen demonstrably served to deter similar state-induced violence elsewhere. Deng's crackdown thus had the paradoxical effect of hastening the spread of liberal political reforms throughout the rest of the Communist world—except in Romania, where the violent overthrow of the regime of Nicolae Ceausescu in December 1989 served as a painful reminder to Chinese leaders of the substantial risks involved in becoming excessively isolated and alienated from their own people.

Observing that the Chinese government, in the aftermath of the Romanian upheaval, severely tightened its political and ideological controls over society rather than relaxing them, Baum suggests that such defensive behavior can only prove counterproductive in the long run, making it more (rather than less) difficult for the regime to accommodate the interests and aspirations of its citizens. And he thus predicts renewed political instability in the People's Republic.

Collectively, the ten essays in this volume clearly illuminate both the compelling logic of systemic reform and its many pitfalls and perils. The authors do not share a single, uniform set of attitudes or expectations on such issues as the reversibility of reforms, the inevitability of democracy, or the efficacy of political repression; nor do they always agree among themselves on the precise importance to be attached to specific causal factors or on the implications of particular events. They do, however, share a common belief that by placing China's post-Mao political and economic developments in comparative perspective, a significant contribution can be made to the emerging dialogue on the social dynamics and future prospects of reform in Leninist systems—a dialogue made all the more urgent by the phenomenal, cascading changes that have taken place throughout the Communist world, from Tiananmen to Timisoara.

Notes and References

1. For a comprehensive account of the key events and developments affecting communist regimes in the late 1980s, see Bernard Gwertzman and Michael T. Kaufman, eds., *The Collapse of Communism* (New York: Random House, 1989).

2. See Francis Fukuyama, "The End of History?" *The National Interest* 16 (Summer 1989), pp. 3–18.

3. For analysis of the origins and development of the Chinese upheaval of April–June 1989, see Yi Mu and Mark V. Thompson, *Crisis at Tiananmen* (San Francisco: China Books and Periodicals, 1989); *Massacre in Beijing: China's Struggle for Democracy* (New York: Warner Books, 1989); Scott Simmie and Bob Nixon, *Tiananmen Square* (Seattle: University of Washington Press, 1989); and Michael Fathers and Andrew Higgins, *Tiananmen: The Rape of Peking* (London: The Independent/Doubleday, 1989).

4. For a general review of China's post-Mao reforms, see Harry Harding, *China's Second Revolution: Reform after Mao* (Washington, D.C.: The Brookings Institution, 1987).

5. See Nicholas Lardy, "Agricultural Reforms in China," *Journal of International Affairs* 39 (Winter 1986), pp. 91–104; and Vivienne Shue, "New Course in Chinese Agriculture," *Annals* 476 (November 1984), pp. 74–89.

6. See Samuel P.S. Ho and Ralph W. Huenemann, *China's Open Door Policy: The Quest for Foreign Technology and Capital* (Vancouver: University of British Columbia Press, 1984); and Jonathan Woetzel, *China's Economic Opening to the Outside World* (New York, Westport and London: Praeger, 1989).

7. See Richard Baum, "Modernization and Legal Reform in Post-Mao China: The Rebirth of Socialist Legality," *Studies in Comparative Communism* 19, no. 2 (Summer 1986), pp. 69–103.

8. See Brantly Womack, "Modernization and Democratic Reform in China," *Journal of Asian Studies* 43 no. 3 (May 1984), pp. 417–39; also Kevin J. O'Brien, "China's National People's Congress: Reform and Its Limits," *Legislative Studies Quarterly* 13, no. 3 (August 1988), pp. 343–67.

9. See Benedict Stavis, *China's Political Reforms: An Interim Report* (New York: Praeger, 1988); also Harding, note 4, chapters 7–8.

10. On price reform, see Dong Fureng, "China's Price Reform," *Cambridge Journal of Economics* 10 (1986), pp. 291–300; on enterprise reform, see Sukhan Jackson, "Reform of State Enterprise Management in China," *The China Quarterly* 107 (September 1986), pp. 405–32; also, Gene Tidrick and Chen Jiyuan, eds., *China's Industrial Reform* (New York: Oxford University Press, 1987).

11. First articulated in 1978, the "four cardinal principles" mandated support for party leadership, for socialism, for the people's democratic dictatorship, and for Marxism-Leninism-Mao Zedong Thought.

12. Deng Xiaoping, *Selected Works of Deng Xiaoping (1975–82)* (Beijing: Foreign Languages Press, 1984), pp. 302–25.

13. For analysis of these events and their implications, see Stanley Rosen, "China in 1987: The Year of the 13th Party Congress," *Asian Survey* 28, no. 1 (January 1988), pp. 35–51.

14. On the stressful consequences of partial, incoherent reform see, *inter alia*, Susan Shirk and James B. Stepanek, "The Problem of Partial Reform," *The China Business Review* 10, no. 6 (November–December 1983); Susan Shirk, "The Politics of Chinese Industrial Reform," in Victor Nee and David Stark, eds., *Remaking the Institutions of Socialism: China and Eastern Europe* (Stanford: Stanford University Press, 1989); Jan Prybyla, "Why China's Economic Reforms Fail," *Asian Survey* 29, no. 11 (November 1989), pp. 1017–32; and Deborah Davis and Ezra Vogel, eds., *Chinese Society on the Eve of Tiananmen: The Impact of Reform* (Cambridge: Harvard University Council on East Asian Studies, 1990).

15. On the social impact of rising economic inequality see Kang Chen, "China's Economic Reform and Social Unrest," *China Report* 1, no. 1 (March 1990), pp. 1–12.

16. *Ibid.* See also Andrew G. Walder, "The Political Sociology of the Beijing Upheaval of 1989," *Problems of Communism* 38, no. 5 (September–October 1989), pp. 30–40.

17. Pre-Tiananmen versions of the essays in this volume appeared in a special double issue of *Studies in Comparative Communism* 22, nos. 2–3 (Summer-Autumn 1989).

18. At least one prominent opinion pollster, Cao Siyuan of the Stone Company's Social Development Research Institute, was included in a group of 211 political prisoners released from detention in May 1990.

2

Socialist Reform and Sino-Soviet Convergence

Lowell Dittmer

The theory of convergence, which had its heyday in the early 1960s, postulated that the logic of economic development was so compelling that in the course of industrialization, capitalist and socialist systems would become more and more alike, overriding the disparate political structures that had hitherto rendered them incompatible.[1] Implicit in this projection was the assumption that the structural isomorphism engendered by economic modernization would have positive political spinoffs; for if conflict between the two rival socioeconomic systems could be attributed to their antithetical organizing principles and sharply contrasting social structures, then any significant diminution of those differences should facilitate mutual accommodation. Convergence, in short, implied community.[2]

How has history dealt with this hypothesis? As Richard Baum shows in his epilogue to the present volume, from its inception in the early 1960s to the mid-1980s, convergence theory failed to be supported by evidence of any substantial weakening of centralized party control over political and economic life in Leninist systems. Over the same span of two decades, despite periodic efforts at detente, there was little if any net diminution in Cold War tensions between the two superpowers. More recently, however, the advent of *perestroika* and *glasnost* in the Soviet Union under Gorbachev and the sudden, domino-like collapse of communist regimes throughout Eastern Europe have served to reopen the convergence debate, with the result that the theory has enjoyed a strong renaissance. The Cold War has ended, we are now told; liberal democracy has triumphed over Leninism.[3] Or has it?

We do not propose to offer a definitive answer to the question of the final triumph of liberalism. Rather, this chapter seeks to explore a less obvious facet of convergence theory, viz., its implications for the co-evolution and structural confluence of socialist systems. If convergence theory originally foundered on the intractability of the political structures in which socioeconomic systems were imbedded, the theory would appear to have a better chance of confirmation if the cases under examination exhibited similar political structures. That is, while convergence between Leninist and non-

I wish to thank the Center for Chinese Studies at the University of California/Berkeley and the Woodrow Wilson Center in Washington, D.C., for financial support in writing this paper.

18

Leninist systems might be problematic, convergence among Leninist systems might be expected to have a higher degree of probability.

Convergence and Co-evolution

Certain basic similarities mark the political culture and institutions of the two communist giants. In the People's Republic of China (PRC), not only did the revolution emerge from a traditional sociocultural system broadly analogous to the Russian (both were large, economically underdeveloped agrarian empires administered by centralized bureaucracies and led by hereditary autocrats), but the post-revolutionary political apparatus superimposed following liberation was essentially identical to the Soviet structure upon which it was patterned. The elites who led these revolutions shared the same general ideological outlooks as well as the specific objective of modernization without the putative inequities of capitalism. They fully expected their duplicate structures to assure a sense of socialist community between them, and they further expected their developmental paths to converge in the course of socialist modernization and the eventual realization of communism.

One assumption of this chapter is that if two countries have convergent political systems they are more likely, *ceteris paribus*, to have amicable bilateral relations than if they do not. This assumption might appear to be belied by the fact that within a decade of the signing of the Sino-Soviet Treaty of Friendship in 1950, bilateral relations had begun to deteriorate, first into polemical rivalry and eventually into border conflicts and nuclear threats; and this was true in spite of China's conscious modelling of Soviet ideology and political institutions. However, this apparent anomaly dissolves if we bear in mind that the Sino-Soviet isomorphism was in the first instance artificially imposed—a Galatea-Pygmalion relationship in which modeling implied dependency and emulation implied self-abnegating subordination. Surely a convergence voluntarily arrived at, between nearly equal partners, without sacrifice of sovereignty, would in contrast facilitate mutual understanding and accommodation?

The following discussion will focus on two questions. First, what has been the reciprocal impact of recent reform efforts in both countries? Second, what are the implications of convergent reforms on the newly emerging Sino-Soviet relationship, with special reference to the extraordinary sequence of events that shook the Communist world beginning in the spring of 1989?

In view of the fact that the initiation of Chinese reforms under Deng Xiaoping predated Mikhail Gorbachev's Soviet reform effort by more than half a decade, it is not surprising that the Chinese impact on Soviet reforms was initially stronger than the reverse. However, by 1986 the Chinese reforms had become stalled, while the Soviet reform program began to gather momentum. Thus we see two distinct stages and patterns of reciprocal impact. In the first stage (1978–86) the dominant pattern of influence was the diffusive demonstration effect of China's sweeping economic reforms; in the second stage (1987–90), feedback from Soviet political and cultural reforms dominated the flow of influence, as China backed away from further structural reform. In the following discussion, we first examine the primary impact of China's post-Mao economic reforms on the Soviet Union; we then turn to an analysis of the secondary, reciprocal impact of Gorbachev's political reforms upon the PRC.

Economic Reform:
The Chinese Model

The post-Mao CCP leadership under Deng Xiaoping inaugurated economic reform at the watershed Third Plenum in December 1978, at a time when analogous impulses had expired in Brezhnev's Soviet Union and had long been languishing in Eastern Europe. The demonstration effect of these reforms on the Soviet Union and the rest of the socialist world was considerable, as China for the following decade became one of the fastest growing economies in the world. Although the Chinese set out without a comprehensive plan or theoretical precept beyond "seeking truth from facts" and "crossing the river by moving from stone to stone," in retrospect their progress may be seen to have focused around three programs: the so-called *production responsibility system*, the shift from *central planning to markets*, and the policy of *opening to the outside world*. The production responsibility system (PRS) involved separating property into two components, ownership and control, with a redistribution of the latter being effected without any substantial alteration of the former. The shift from plan to market entailed a transition from *command* planning to *guidance* planning, giving the market substantial autonomy while using fiscal and monetary levers to correct undue volatility or distributive imbalance. The policy of opening to the outside world was designed to facilitate China's integration into international commodity, capital, technology, and even service markets, primarily through the promotion of foreign trade and investment.

Chinese agricultural reforms were the first and remain the most conspicuously successful of their entire effort. Under the PRS, *de facto* decollectivization occurred, as the fifty-five thousand people's communes—organizational backbone of Chinese agriculture for more than two decades—were eliminated outright and individual family households were permitted to lease farmland with extensive use rights. Under this new regime, Chinese peasant income doubled in less than a decade (1978–84); over the same period, grain production increased by 4.9 percent per annum (compared to 2.1 percent per annum during the previous twenty years). Output of other crops grew even more rapidly; and by 1987 statistics released by the State Statistical

Bureau indicated that the gross value of China's agricultural output was the highest (in absolute terms) of any country in the world.

Until early 1986 Soviet commentators focused mainly on the drawbacks of the PRS; since that time its success has been conceded, but the Soviets have been hesitant in emulating it. One of the first to refer favorably to the Chinese agricultural reforms was pro-reform sociologist Tat'iana Zaslavskaia, who referred to the "collective responsibility family contract system" as a model of what might be done when discussing reforms in Soviet agriculture.[4] Soviet peasants have been encouraged to expand their private plots, which account for less than 4 percent of total farm acreage but produce up to half its potatoes and a third of its meat and dairy products. There has been no move as yet to phase out state or collective farms (*sovkhoz, kholkhoz*), though their financial independence has been expanded (e.g., they may now sell up to 30 percent of their harvest to urban markets and cooperatives rather than to the state). Experiments have been launched with the brigade system and a contract responsibility system popularly known as the "link" (*beznaryadnoye zveno,* similar to an early cooperative progenitor of China's PRS), consisting of a team of farm households who agree to produce a given output while the collective supplies the needed material inputs; in 1988 the Gosagroprom approved new regulations authorizing land to be leased to private groups and individuals for up to fifty years. Agricultural machinery, now owned by state and collective farms, will be either leased or sold to new private entrepreneurs. Farmers may hire labor, so long as wages are not lower than those paid by adjoining state enterprises.

It is to early to say how widely these new regulations will be implemented, but they seem likely to be opposed by existing *raion* (district) party secretaries, whose power bases are directly threatened. As indicated by the prior history of the "link," the Soviet bureaucracy has become highly effective at thwarting policies perceived to be inimical to its corporate interests.[5] In this connection, the appointment of the relatively conservative Yegor Ligachev to the Agricultural Ministry was not particularly encouraging.

Although the PRS has been the jewel in the crown of Chinese agricultural reform, there are several reasons for Soviet misgivings about plunging in more boldly. Nationality issues are much more salient in a nation in which the dominant nationality has dwindled to less than 52 percent of the population (in China minorities constitute only about 7 percent). *De facto* decollectivization may well be avoided because of fear of loss of political control in non-Russian republics, where latent nationalism remains extremely potent. In traditional agricultural regions, Russian family farms (*kulaks*) had barely been established following dissolution of the prerevolutionary estates when Stalin collectivized the land, and several generations have since grown accustomed to collective institutions. In those areas in which large-scale resettlement has taken place, on the other hand—about 140 million acres of "virgin lands" were added to cultivation between 1950 and 1960, increasing total Soviet croplands by more than 38 percent—the farmers had no original title to the land, so to redistribute land into family responsibility plots would be as artificial as the current organization of ownership. Agricultural machinery is extensively used in these vast and marginally productive regions, and the subdivision of fields might adversely affect economies of scale. Finally, the CPSU's cumulative success in socializing the Soviet citizenry to "socialist" values should not be underestimated. Public opinion polls (as well as other less systematic indicators) do show, in contrast to the climate of opinion in the Chinese countryside, a lack of enthusiasm for any major shift in the agricultural incentive system in the USSR, suggesting that Gorbachev cannot count on popular pressure to bolster his calls for change.[6]

Marketization may or may not entail political liberalization,[7] but it does presuppose two essential freedoms: the freedom of prices to fluctuate according to supply and demand, and the freedom of agents to purchase, own, and market commodities (i.e., some measure of privatization). Both countries have undergone an evolution in their approach to the realization of these two prerequisites. Concerning the first, in addition to the semiprivatization of agricultural (and, more recently, industrial) property in the form of leaseholds, the PRC has given formal legitimacy to private enterprise (denounced and curtailed as the "tail of capitalism" under Mao) in the service, commercial, and even industrial sectors.[8] The private sector quickly became the most rapidly expanding of the three forms of ownership (state, collective, and private), followed by the collective sector.[9] China's collectively owned industries, employing about 15 percent of China's labor force but representing some 30.5 percent of total industrial output, grew by almost one-third in 1985, another 16.7 percent in 1986, and 22 percent in 1987—well ahead of the state sector. More than 80 percent of the restaurants, repair shops, and service outlets set up since the Cultural Revolution are privately owned; although most are small in scale, they have grown in size from an initial limit of seven or eight employees to several hundred. As these collective and private ventures rely on their own sources of finance capital and set their own prices, their vigorous expansion has eroded the state's ability to control the economy.[10]

Price reform in the still-dominant public sector was however postponed until the "second stage" of urban reform was introduced in October 1984. The freeing of retail prices then snowballed (many price hikes were unauthorized), triggering inflation, which had the effect of reducing living standards for a fifth of China's two hundred million urban dwellers;[11] this in turn induced a restoration of price controls, and in early 1987 China temporarily suspended efforts to free prices. In June 1988 a more determined effort was made to free urban food and commodity prices, but this set off an inflation unprecedented since before Liberation (the official estimate for the year was

17 percent, but unofficial estimates put it closer to 40 percent). The inflation precipitated bank runs and stockpiling of consumer commodities. As a result, price reform for China has been postponed indefinitely. Still, the Chinese theoretical commitment to marketization has not diminished over time: whereas in the early 1980s the theoretical ideal was an economy in which the plan would remain dominant, supplemented by markets (Chen Yun's "bird in cage" model), the formulation at the Thirteenth Party Congress (October–November 1987) was that the state would manage the market (through various fiscal and monetary levers), while the market would guide the individual firm—a formulation tantamount to market socialism. Although the sponsor of this formulation, Zhao Ziyang, has fallen from power, the formulation itself has not yet been repudiated.

With regard to privatization, from an initial position of explicit hostility to the market,[12] Gorbachev's position has undergone considerable evolution. Beginning May 1, 1987, the Soviet Union has permitted citizens to operate small restaurants, tailor shops, taxis and other small businesses (a total of twenty-nine kinds of enterprises are included), thereby bringing this segment of the underground economy into the moonlight of legality. Private enterprise has not yet gained legitimacy, however; the preferred form of non-state unit continues to be the cooperative, an autonomous unit of up to fifty farmers (or workers in the industrial or service sector) who share the proceeds from their work. First authorized in August 1986, some fourteen thousand coops (most of them relatively small-scale) were set up within the first year; a law passed in May 1988 extends to them multiple new rights.[13] At this writing, regulation remains relatively stringent—the owners must register with local authorities, quit their jobs in state enterprises, cannot hire labor, and must obtain their supplies from Gossnab (the official state supplier) and not from other private traders. In October 1989 the Supreme Soviet adopted additional amendments setting ceiling prices for coops and disqualifying cadres from participating.

With respect to price reform, Gorbachev has been uncharacteristically circumspect. In the "Basic Principles" adopted at the June 1987 Central Committee Plenum, the Soviets resolved to encourage private and cooperative activity, a labor market, the abandonment of annual plans, and a shift from command to indicative planning (in which central authorities control only variables of national importance, leaving operational decisions to lower levels). But after announcing at the plenum that "a radical reform of the pricing system is a most important part of the economic overhaul," Gorbachev was dismayed to see evidence of consumer stockpiling. The problem of price reform was hence postponed until after 1991.

The PRC's "open door" policy (*kaifang zhengce*) is designed to facilitate China's integration into world markets, and has had a quite dramatic impact on both trade[14] and investment.[15] The policy of opening has been subject to spontaneous broadening to include cultural as well as commercial opening (as in the out-migration of more than seventy thousand Chinese students for study abroad, or the internal penetration of tourists, electronic media, and "spiritual pollution") and to include domestic as well as international opening (as in recurrent attempts to revive a "hundred flowers" atmosphere in the cultural and political arenas). The authorities have tended to react ambivalently—but on the whole restrictively—to such tendencies.

Entering the Global Marketplace

Like the Chinese, the Soviets have expressed interest in integrating their economy into the world market, increasingly lauding "interdependence" and an "international division of labor." The ratio of Soviet imports to GNP, less than one percent in the 1930s and about 3 percent in the mid-1960s, had climbed to roughly 5 percent by the beginning of the 1980s. In September 1986 it was decided to facilitate trade by vesting more than twenty central ministries and departments as well as seventy large enterprises with the power to deal directly with foreign traders, thereby removing monopoly control from the Ministry of Foreign Trade. Since that time the Soviet Union has voluntarily begun to cooperate with the Organization of Petroleum Exporting Countries (OPEC), and has applied for membership in the General Agreement on Tariffs and Trade (GATT), the International Monetary Fund, the World Bank, and other international financial organizations. Anticipating typical prerequisites imposed by these organizations, the Soviets have committed themselves to make the ruble convertible with other East bloc currencies by 1991, and with Western currencies by the late 1990s.

To attract foreign technology and earn hard currency, the Soviet Union has offered Western investors up to 49 percent ownership of joint ventures, a form of cooperation previously rejected in principle. By April 1988, some three hundred offers from Western concerns had been received (only about twenty of which were seriously considered by the Soviets), signaling an interest comparable to that in the opening of the China market. In his Vladivostok speech Gorbachev proposed to take a leaf from the Chinese special economic zone experience and open that closed city to international investment and trade; the same proposal has been eagerly taken up by the Baltic republics, which are also seeking greater political autonomy. From refusing to recognize the European Community (EC), the Soviet Union has switched to a position of encouraging formal relations between EC and the East bloc ; in 1988 most of the Eastern European states established direct bilateral trade relations with the EC.[16]

Just how successful Soviet overtures for inclusion in the world market will be under current circumstances remains an open question. The import demand is there, given Soviet interest in Western technology (as indicated by their intense involvement in industrial espionage), not to mention continuing agricultural shortfalls. But balance of payment constraints may impinge fairly sharply, even if the upward surge in arms sales to the Third World (the USSR's most lucrative source of foreign exchange) continues. Soviet hard currency earnings, their preferred way of financing imports, surged with world oil and gold prices after 1973, only to level off in the early 1980s when prices sagged; the prognosis is that the Soviets will do well to hold hard currency earnings at their present level over the next decade, using natural gas exports to offset a drop in oil exports. In case of an imbalance of trade, it is possible that the Soviets might turn to Western credit markets. Faced with an enormous internal deficit, they would perhaps not be well advised to entertain the prospect of a large foreign debt. In the past, the Soviets were put off by American failure to deliver most favored nation status (or rather, by linkage of this concession to unacceptable demands on Soviet emigration policy), and by recurrent embargoes in response to Soviet military initiatives in the Third World.[17] These sticking points have diminished since 1989, however.

Although the Soviet bid for inclusion in the international economy is expected to fare better under Gorbachev than during the Brezhnev era of detente, the Soviets may still have to compete with other newly reformed socialist systems under their nominal patronage. Since the early 1980s, Soviet subsidies to Eastern Europe have steadily declined, and there has been a concurrent deterioration of terms of trade with the Soviet Union, likely motivating these countries to look elsewhere for trade partners.[18] The Eastern European countries—most of whom are already affiliated in some way with GATT and the IMF—have always been closely linked to Western markets, although several of them were burned by petrodollar loans in the 1970s and are saddled with large debts. Now that Soviet interest in joint ventures has legitimated such undertakings, East European countries are beginning to compete for a limited pool of Western investment capital. On January 1, 1989, Poland put into effect a new law permitting joint ventures wholly owned by the foreign partner, going well beyond terms the Soviets were prepared to offer.

While it is fair to say that theory has followed rather than led reform in both countries, both have endeavored to revise Marxism-Leninism to facilitate modernization. The Chinese again seem to have a substantial head start, with the concept of a "socialist commodity economy" that does not borrow from the sparse prognoses of classical Marxist texts concerning the future socialist economy, but places Chinese socialism in the category of commodity economies along with capitalism, therefore subject to the same universally valid laws (as outlined in *Capital*) governing any economy under conditions of shortage. Thus Chinese reform theory envisages an economy of independent but interacting commodity producers (be they private, semiprivate, or public) who decide in relative autonomy on the production and exchange of commodities and who are subject to pressure to improve efficiency via the "law of value." State planning regulates not the firm but the market, through various fiscal and monetary mechanisms; the party's role is to be limited to ideological suasion.

Gorbachev's *Perestroika* Initiatives

The Soviets, after a long period of macrotheoretical underdevelopment, have also begun recently to reconceptualize the framework of socialism. Despite opposition from conservatives such as E. Bugaev, a movement has been afoot to reevaluate the New Economic Policy of the early 1920s, with its legitimation of the market and small private enterprise, and in this connection Bukharin and Rykov, two prominent Bolshevik supporters of the NEP later executed in the purge trials, were politically rehabilitated in January 1988. In a speech to the Central Committee the following month, Gorbachev called for updating those elements of communist doctrine that were outdated and calcified.[19] Whether such rethinking would draw China and the Soviet Union closer together was uncertain; but it is noteworthy that until the exacerbation of Sino-Soviet relations that occurred in the immediate aftermath of the December 1989 popular rebellion in Romania, key Soviet reformers seemed confident that it would. "I am deeply convinced that Gorbachev has already launched the country on a path of reform comparable to that of the Chinese," said Feodor Burlatskii of the Soviet Academy of Social Sciences. "But here the obstacles will be greater because there is a group within the political leadership who will struggle against the reform."

Although *perestroika* was inspired in part by China's post-Mao reforms, there are several limiting conditions that seem likely to inhibit wholesale application of China's reforms to the Soviet Union. First is the distinctive Soviet national experience. Soviet leaders have been molded by a past in which hurried reforms, from Khrushchev's thaw to the Prague Spring, led inevitably to loss of party control. Whereas the Chinese revolution arose in a country victimized by Western imperialism, the Soviet Bolsheviks inherited a successful European imperialist tradition, which they (after some lofty rhetorical flights) have not only perpetuated but extended; now, that unconquered past is returning to haunt them, as ethnic unrest in Armenia/Azerbaijan, Khazakstan, the Baltic republics, and elsewhere has raised the prospect that history may repeat itself. Gorbachev's repudiation of the Brezhnev Doctrine has opened the door to the "Finlandization" of Eastern Europe; this, in turn, has served to exacerbate domestic ethnic tensions, raising the twin spectres of secession and the possible dismemberment of COMECON and the Warsaw Pact. A second factor that militates against Soviet imitation of China's reforms is the fact that the Soviet party-state apparatus and "military-industrial complex" are proportionately larger and more deeply entrenched than their Chinese counterparts. This creates problems of bureaucratic obstruction and resistance by powerful vested interests—problems far more serious than those encountered by Chinese reform leaders in their effort to break the "iron rice bowl." Finally, there is the question of national pride. To "learn from China" would involve an implicit reversal of the Sino-Soviet relationship of the 1950s, with painfully ironic overtones that the Soviets may prefer not to advertise. Although the USSR may have an objective interest in emulating those Chinese innovations that would help stimulate its own economic revival, it also has a commitment to maintaining its traditional hegemonic claim to vanguard status vis-à-vis other socialist countries—a status which Gorbachev now makes bold to reclaim by leaping to the forefront of the reform wave.

Despite these historical and institutional barriers to Soviet emulation of the Chinese reforms, Soviet reformers have begun encouraging such innovations as the PRS, special economic zones, and joint ventures—without any effort to conceal their Chinese provenance. This suggests that the barriers are now less imposing than before. Ironically, this comes at a time—i.e., in the aftermath of the Romanian revolution—when China has begun to partially reverse the reform process and denounce Soviet leaders for fanning the flames of "bourgeois counterrevolution" in Eastern Europe.

The Dissynchronous Dynamics of Political Reform

Contrary to initial expectations, the Chinese delayed the onset of political reform, preferring to maintain the unchallenged hegemony of their Leninist party-state throughout the process of economic reform. By contrast, Soviet efforts to promote legally regulated mass participation in politics go back several decades, paralleling similar Eastern European initiatives. Several Eastern European polities have carried out multicandidate elections (under single-party auspices) for decades; although the USSR did not adopt this particular innovation until recently, they have had a good deal of experience with standing committees, interpellation, and other innovations designed to strengthen the legislative branch.[20] The Chinese did not adopt multicandidate elections until 1980, for local and district elections, and the results so upset local party organizations that the scope of popular participation in the nominating process has since been sharply curtailed. Within China's national legislature, the first seven standing committees were established, with their own separate staffs, at the Fourth NPC in 1982; by this time the Supreme Soviet, which had first established standing commissions in 1965, already had twenty-six such bodies.[21]

Thus it is perhaps not surprising that the major initiatives in the reform of European communism have come in the political and cultural arenas, and at a time when economic reforms seemed to be blocked. From the time of his contested accession to power in March 1985 through the end of 1986, Gorbachev was preoccupied with the consolidation of his own position, primarily through the time-honored mechanism of the purge. In his first year in office, Gorbachev removed 47 of 121 regional party secretaries and replaced more than half of the CPSU Central Committee; by the end of 1986 half the membership of the Council of Ministers (42 ministers) had been removed. The Twenty-seventh CPSU Congress, held in the spring of 1986, demonstrated his control of the party apparatus, formalizing his removal of former rivals Georgii Romanov and Viktor Grishin (among other personnel changes), but otherwise signaled no policy departures. Then, with the convention of the January 1987 Central Committee Plenum (which had been postponed three times), Gorbachev adopted a far more critical posture toward the Brezhnev legacy and began to advance his own agenda. He introduced the notion that economic reform presupposed political reform, calling for "democratization" of the political system by instituting multiple candidacy elections for local soviets and party posts, involving more nonparty personnel in the government and the economy, and expanding the sphere of private economic activity. In the realm of culture and propaganda, he inaugurated a policy of "openness" (glasnost), leading to a thaw redolent of, but more far-reaching than, Khrushchev's. Long-suppressed literary works such as Pasternak's Doctor Zhivago and Rybakov's Children of the Arbat, and the anti-Stalinist movie Repentance, were approved for release. Beginning with the pardon of Sakharov in the summer of 1986 Gorbachev adopted a more tolerant stance toward intellectual dissidents. The June 1987 Central Committee Plenum in Moscow sought to extend the spirit of perestroika to the economy, aiming to reduce central planning and give more independence to managers of enterprises, promote competition, and improve the level of services. Albeit ambitiously conceived, Gorbachev's economic reforms failed to catch fire, and from the fall of 1987 to April 1988 he faced a series of setbacks, including the Yeltsin affair and the outbreak of interethnic strife in Transcaucasia.

Gorbachev managed to recover momentum only when he returned to the political arena. He convened a massive all-union party conference in June 1988 (the first since 1941); this was followed a month later by a Central Committee Plenum. A series of reforms was introduced, including limited tenure for all elective party and government officials (two five-year terms), the right to a multiple-candidate slate for every elective office, the right of recall, and, most importantly, preparations for an ambitious restructuring of the Soviet legislative apparatus. Constitutional reforms were introduced by the Supreme Soviet in November 1988 to clear the way for a general election in March 1989 to a new and more powerful Congress of People's Deputies, involving contests between candidates in single-seat constituencies.

This election was held on schedule, and although not all candidacies were contested, the number of upsets that occurred testifies to its general validity as a free election. The Congress of People's Deputies held its first session in April to select a working parliament and elect the country's first executive president, Mikhail Gorbachev.

Following closely upon these reforms, the Supreme Soviet has become the first standing parliament in Soviet history, convening each year for three to four months each fall and spring; it is also a smaller forum than the Congress of People's Deputies, consisting of a total of 542 legislators, divided into a Council of the Union and a Council of Nationalities; because of its smaller size and standing nature, the Supreme Soviet is likely to become a serious deliberative legislature, rather a mere "rubber stamp," as before.[22] A fledgling opposition, the so-called interregional deputies group, has formed within the Supreme Soviet. The CPSU, too, is scheduled to have an election campaign to reelect all party committees, from shop-floor level to CC, also in multicandidate elections. Finally, in a startling departure from Leninist precedent, President Gorbachev announced in early January 1990 that the door was open to multiparty pluralism in the Soviet Union.

These spectacular Soviet political reforms contrast starkly with China's very cautious and conservative response to mounting pressures for expanded political rights and freedoms. Whereas the Chinese have in the past introduced periodic relaxations in the political and intellectual spheres (e.g., "Let a hundred flowers blossom" and the concept of "nonantagonistic contradictions," both introduced in the mid-1950s), implementation has been sporadic and uneven, oriented toward the goal of "continuing the revolution under the dictatorship of the proletariat," which worked to inhibit institutionalization of a politically tolerant or pluralistic polity.[23] Although the Deng leadership did introduce a series of political reforms beginning in August 1980, these were modest in conception and were carried out without a great deal of conviction.[24] Since the mid-1980s, when Chinese reform efforts began to be complicated by the more unsettling consequences of urban industrial reform and became intertwined with the struggle to succeed Deng Xiaoping, the CCP's response to political reform has been even more sensitive. Thus for example, when Chinese public opinion became enlivened in the summer of 1986 with discussion of the need for political reform as a prerequisite to further economic reform, triggering a wave of sympathetic student demonstrations, veteran party leaders became so irate that they clamped down hard, suppressing the demonstrations, purging reform-minded party General Secretary Hu Yaobang for failing to do so, and launching a counter-campaign against "bourgeois liberalism."

In the spring of 1989 a similar scenario played itself out with far more tragic consequences. Upon the death of Hu Yaobang on April 15 the students mobilized once again, aiming not to overthrow the regime but to seek common cause with the proreform wing of the leadership. By eschewing vandalism and other forms of indisciplne the demonstrators were able to forestall a crackdown for nearly a month while their own numbers swelled to unprecedented proportions. By mid-May, the issue of how to respond had clearly split the leadership; the hard-line majority faction may have felt it necessary at that point to vigorously suppress the demonstrations in order to intimidate the students and delegitimize the reformist opposition. It seems unlikely that either the extent or the severity of international reaction to the well-publicized bloodbath of June 3–4 had been anticipated by the hardliners.

Thus the years 1986 and 1987 brought a shift from the pattern of Chinese reform initiative and cautious Soviet response to a new pattern of Soviet initiative and Chinese ambivalence or even violent reaction. A common problem giving rise to both patterns may have been the premature exhaustion of economic reform—i.e., its tendency to run aground before achieving its intended results. In the Soviet case, economic reform made very little headway before running up against insuperable bureaucratic roadblocks, necessitating political reform in order to achieve a breakthrough. In the Chinese case economic reform achieved significant progress before political reform became an urgent necessity; yet whenever "liberal" reformers attempted to broach the subject of fundamental political change this tended to provoke a violent elite response. Where Soviet elites generally adopted a low-key (but apparently effective) passive resistance to economic reform while accepting sweeping political reforms (even when these jeopardized their own tenure), Chinese elites seem to have been far more receptive to pragmatic economic reforms—while remaining adamantly opposed to any political reforms that threatened their positions.

In part, these different elite responses to the problem of political reform stem from the fact, noted above, that the European communist systems have had more extensive experience with constitutional engineering and other forms of nonviolent political change than have the Chinese. A second factor has to do with profound differences between the Stalinist and Maoist legacies. Whereas Stalin was an autocrat who ruled through a vertical hierarchy, enhancing his power by playing off one bureaucratic apparatus against another, Mao was a populist who seems to have lost control of the "commanding heights" of the party-state apparatus relatively early and was able to regain control only by mobilizing the "revolutionary masses" to criticize— even to overthrow—alleged "bourgeois powerholders" within the party. Many of the leading party figures who bore the brunt of mass criticism in the Cultural Revolution (e.g., Deng Xiaoping, Peng Zhen, Chen Yun) went on to become leaders in the post-Mao reform movement. The contrast between the Stalinist and Maoist patterns boils down to this: in areas under direct or indirect Stalinist rule, the democratic impulse, including the willingness publicly to disobey bureaucratic authority, was virtually eradicated through the demonstration effects engendered by such measures as forced collectivization, secret police terrorism, show trials, concentration camps, and, most unforgettably, blood purges. In areas under Maoist rule, on the other hand, the boldness in daring to challenge bureaucratic authority (known as "swimming against the tide") was encouraged and even strengthened, notwithstanding Mao's well-known intolerance for ideological deviance. These contrasting historical patterns of Soviet and Chinese social mobilization and control have presented the Soviet Union's post-Stalinist leaders with greater obstacles to overcome in their attempt to stimulate the initiative of the masses than has been the case with China's the post-Mao leaders; and the Soviets have thus had to resort to more dramatic concessions to popular sentiment in the political arena in their effort to generate innovative momentum and public support for economic reform.

Another relevant contrast between the two cases lies in the fact that the leaders of the Soviet and East European reform efforts often suffered personally at the hands of Stalinist autocracy, which under the aegis of the "permanent purge" terrorized the apparatus as well as the masses. Thus Soviet and East European elites are likely to seize upon the occasion of leadership succession as an opportunity to deliver themselves from the Stalinist nightmare. China's reform leaders also have their own *via dolorosa* to look back on; but in their case it was not a matter of having been intimidated by the repressive apparatus of the communist party-state, but of having been terrorized by the unleashed fury of Mao's mobilized masses. Where Stalinist tyranny left a pervasive control apparatus in its wake, Mao's populist form of despotism bequeathed a particularly disruptive pattern of mass participation. This does not imply that post-Mao defenders of Mao's legacy retain this populist impulse; still less does it imply that China's democratic activists are covert Maoists; but it has meant that reform leaders in the PRC continue to adopt a much more cautious—even seemingly paranoid—stance toward the participatory effects of political liberalization than their contemporary counterparts in Eastern Europe or the Soviet Union. While Soviet and East European reformers thus use political reform to generate support for apparently unpopular economic reforms, Chinese reformers use political centralization, even occasional repression, to rein in economic reforms (and their political spillover effects) that threaten to career out of control.

Thus the correlation between economic and political reform is quite different in the two cases. In both systems, political reform appears to be a means to economic reform, rather than an end in itself. The early Chinese success with economic reform in the absence of political reform seems to have encouraged conservative CCP elites to presume that the latter might be dispensed with altogether. Thus they have become somewhat enthusiastic about a notion of "new authoritarianism" borrowed from the postwar history of Asia's newly-industrialized countries (NICs) that would preserve the political authority and prerogatives of central elites while promoting rapid economic development through state-supported entrepreneurship and innovation. If this plan goes awry due to the tendency for reform to generate its own socioeconomic constituency in favor of further political reforms, the post-Tiananmen elite seems prepared to rescind economic reforms as well.

The Soviet case is quite different on the face of it. There the utter failure of economic reforms has perhaps led the elite to overload political reform with aspirations for a comprehensive transformation of the system that in all likelihood cannot be sustained. The role of democratization as an independent variable has not often been studied, but little evidence is at hand to support the view that democracy *per se* leads to enhanced economic efficiency. The risk is that if political democratization and *glasnost* do not give rise to perceptible improvements in Soviet living standards, the masses will look on indifferently while the whole reform experiment is swept into history's dustbin by a reinvigorated authoritarian leadership prepared to smash eggs to make omelettes.

Thus the convergent trajectories of Sino-Soviet reform and the concomitant movement toward diplomatic rapprochement seem to have gotten snagged at precisely their moment of probable consummation. After ten years of patient negotiation and cultural-economic bridge building, the process of party-to-party normalization was crowned by the visit of First Secretary Gorbachev to Beijing on May 15–18, 1989. His visit happened to coincide with (indeed, was interrupted by) the most massive spontaneous popular demonstrations on behalf of reform and democratization since Liberation. Although China's democracy activists greeted him even more enthusiastically than the CCP leadership, Gorbachev shrewdly avoided involvement, making carefully ambiguous statements expressing sympathy both for the Chinese reform effort and for its attendant difficulties. After the Tiananmen massacre he expressed regret, but declined to join the international chorus of condemnation. On the one hand the crackdown may have embarrassed Gorbachev, reinforcing hard-line Soviet critics who have urged a similar solution to Soviet protests—a solution later adopted, with disastrous results, by the Romanian communist leader, Nicolae Ceausescu. On the other hand, Gorbachev appeared determined not to embolden his own protesters by disavowing the "Chinese solution."

Following the crackdown, Sino-Soviet relations continued to improve for a few months, benefiting from the PRC's ostracism from the West.[25] Amid the purge of residual liberals from the CCP regime and an anticipatory succession struggle, a Soviet "connection" became a political litmus test for the selection of trustworthy hard-liners from the younger generation. Thus the so-called Soviet returned students (*liu Su pai*), who were educated in the USSR, have clearly acquired an upper hand over the potentially more numerous (but younger) American returned students (*liu Mei pai*). Most prominent of the former are Premier Li Peng, Zhou Enlai's foster son, who studied at the Moscow Power Institute from 1948 to 1955, and Jiang Zemin, recently appointed CCP general secretary, who was Li's classmate at the same institute. Others in the Soviet-educated group include President Yang Shangkun and Politburo members Li Tieying and Ding Guangen, as well as State Council members Song Jian, Zou Jiahua, Zou Jinmeng, and Ding Henggao. The broad potential constituency that favored improved relations with the USSR included not only the foregoing returned students, but many in the central foreign trade apparatus who have found their monopoly over trade slipping away in the context of economic decentralization; those in the planning apparatus who find it easier to deal with a fraternal planned economy than with the uncertainties of a free market; the interior western areas of China, which find themselves being neglected by capitalist investment preferences and wish to cultivate economic ties with the Soviet Far East; enterprises and ministries which produce goods with no market or stiff market competition in Western markets; and the propaganda apparatus and security organs, who find "open" policies eroding their functions. This coalition could plausibly argue in the aftermath of the new Soviet-American detente that ties to the USSR need not come at the expense of China's ties to the West.[26]

Despite the obvious allure of the Soviet Union as an alternative source of developmental support for China in the aftermath of Tiananmen, the renormalization of Sino-Soviet relations hit a deep snag in the autumn and winter of 1989–90, when a wave of "gentle revolutions" overthrew established communist regimes throughout Eastern Europe—with Gorbachev's tacit consent, if not his blessing. When Romania's hardline leaders sought to impose a "Chinese solution" on demonstrators in December, only to be resisted and quickly overthrown by an enraged citizenry, Chinese leaders reacted defensively, blaming Gorbachev for undermining socialism and stirring up political unrest in Eastern Europe. In the aftermath of this Chinese diatribe, Sino-Soviet relations took a brief turn for the worse.

Conclusion

The long-term developmental perspective adopted here helps to explain why Sino-Soviet cooperation was sustained for a fairly long period in the past and why—despite periodic disruptions—it may be expected to resume again in the future. In our framework, the periodic deterioration or even rupture of Sino-Soviet relations is to be understood primarily in terms of issues of national identity and geostrategic rivalry rather than economic advantage; although the two systems have demonstrated that each could survive the interruption of trade and other forms of exchange and even launch diverging routes to socialist modernization, neither has realized any great material advantage from doing so. Thus developmental convergence may be seen as a *necessary but not sufficient condition* for political cooperation. Once successfully undertaken, however, political cooperation may be reinforced and accelerated by developmental convergence.

The long-term prospects for renewed convergence under the auspices of socialist reform seem reasonably favorable, despite China's hostile reaction to Gorbachev's initiatives in Eastern Europe. Indeed, as we have seen, in many respects the two reform efforts are already complementary. Soviet *perestroika* has clearly benefitted from the Chinese experience in economic reform. This is particularly true in the agricultural sector, but even in industry and commerce Chinese experiments with administrative decentralization, foreign investment, and privatized or quasiprivatized enterprises have proven instructive.

It must be said, however, that at this writing the reform dynamic remains dissynchronous in the two countries. While the Soviets proceed with political reform amid economic gloom, surviving Chinese reformers fight to salvage their achievements in the face of a powerful antireform backlash. Under the circumstances, the CCP finds it necessary not only to jam Voice of America broadcasts, but to quarantine its population from news of Eastern Europe and the Soviet Union. Despite this Chinese antireform backlash, however, in the PRC the advances made under reform auspices over the past ten years have been considerable; and since any substantial retreat from either reform or the "opening" would entail severe social and economic costs, it is not likely that the current retrenchment will long outlive the gerontocrats who have imposed it.

If China does resume its economic reform program, and if socioeconomic convergence does, in the long run, continue to facilitate political reconciliation, this could lead eventually to renewed strategic collaboration between China and Russia—although the Chinese continue emphatically to deny such a possibility. Certainly the advantage of some form of border settlement to a Soviet system apparently bent on massive reassignment of resources from the military to the civilian consumer sector is obvious: if the USSR can shift from a two-and-a-half to a one-and-a-half war strategy, it will vastly improve its prospects for beating swords into plowshares. Chinese leaders have already realized this advantage; over the past decade their own defense budget has sharply declined as a percentage of national GNP.

Any predictions about the future of Sino-Soviet relations must be tempered by a strongly cautionary note. Recent upheavals in Eastern Europe and within the Soviet Union itself present the possibility of a highly paradoxical development, viz., expansive socialist pluralism which threatens to disintegrate internally even as its external appeal increases. Gorbachev's repudiation of the Brezhnev Doctrine, his tolerance of bourgeois liberalization in

Eastern Europe, and his tentative embrace of multiparty pluralism within the Soviet Union all have served to increase the attractiveness of the Soviet reform program to the outside world; at the same time, however, they have also stoked the fires of incipient regional, ethnic, labor, and consumer unrest in virtually every corner of the Soviet empire, leading to dangerous levels of political turbulence and instability. And this most recent development, in turn, points to the possible emergence of yet another paradox—to wit, that the final "victory" of convergence theory may bring with it a violent, implosive disintegration of the socialist world. While many in the West may cheer this prospect, its full implications cannot yet be adequately anticipated or assessed.

Notes and References

1. See Alfred G. Meyer, "Theories of Convergence," in Chalmers Johnson, ed., *Change in Communist Systems* (Stanford, Calif.: Stanford University Press, 1970), pp. 313–42; also Zbigniew Brzezinski and Samuel Huntington, *Political Power USA/USSR* (New York: The Viking Press, 1964); John H. Kautsky, *Communism and the Politics of Development: Persistent Myths and Changing Behavior* (New York: John Wiley, 1968); and Peter C. Ludz, *The Changing Party Elite in East Germany* (Cambridge, Mass.: M.I.T. Press, 1972).

2. The political implications of convergence have been explored in Hisahiko Okazaki, *A Japanese View of Detente* (Lexington, Mass.: D. C. Heath, 1974).

3. This hypothesis was initially advanced by Francis Fukuyama, "The End of History?" *The National Interest* 16 (Summer 1989), pp. 3–18.

4. *Izvestiia*, June 1, 1985, p. 3; *Pravda*, October 25, 1984, p. 5.

5. The brigade contract system was one of the few experiments authorized in the New Agricultural Program of 1982. Based on Zaslavskaia's results in Altai, the May 1982 CC Plenum decided to extend the experiment to all collective farms. But the state farms refused to participate and the bureaucracy was unenthusiastic. See Marshall I. Goldman, *Gorbachev's Challenge: Economic Reform in the Age of High Technology* (New York: W. W. Norton, 1987), p. 59; see also Alec Nove, "Soviet Agriculture: Problems and Prospects," in David Dyker, ed., *The Soviet Union Under Gorbachev: Prospects for Reform* (London: Croom Helm, 1987), pp. 91–106.

6. G. I. Shelev, "Sotsial'no ekonomicheskii potensial semeinogo podiada," *Sotsiologisheskie Issledovniia*, April 1985, pp. 16–20; as quoted in Goldman, note 5, p. 190; see also Marshall Goldman and Merle Goldman, "Soviet and Chinese Economic Reform," in *America and the World, 1987–88* (New York: Pergamon Press, 1988), pp. 557–74.

7. For analysis of the relationship between the two, see the chapters by Baum, Friedman, and Halpern in the present volume.

8. Constitutional amendments to this effect were passed at the Seventh National People's Congress in March 1988: Article 10 legalized introduction of a free market in land-use (lease) rights, Article 11 gave legal protection to private enterprises, and Article 13 gave the right to inherit private property (including lease rights). The situation has become more ambiguous since the Tiananmen massacre, however, as denunciations of "privatization" have repeatedly appeared in the official press. See below, pp. 98–100.

9. Between 1978 and 1985, the private sector grew spectacularly, from 180,000 to 11.64 million units (still representing less than one percent of total industrial output value). *Far Eastern Economic Review*, November 20, 1986, pp. 68–69. For analysis of the urban private sector, see Thomas Gold's chapter in the present volume.

10. Whereas state budgetary allocations had accounted for 90 percent of all capital-construction investment in 1957 and 83 percent in 1978, by 1984 the state budget's share of investment had fallen to 54.4 percent, dropping further (to 40–45 percent) in 1985.

11. *New York Times*, September 6, 1987, p. E2.

12. In a major policy speech in mid-1985 to a private meeting of high-level Eastern European economic planners, Gorbachev pronounced himself opposed to such reforms as had been introduced in Yugoslavia or the PRC. "Many of you see the solution to your problems in resorting to market mechanisms in place of direct planning," he said. "Some of you look at the market as a lifesaver for your economies. But comrades, you should not think about lifesavers but about the ship. And the ship is socialism!"

13. *New York Times*, March 20, 1988, pp. 1, 5.

14. China's total trade with the rest of the world as a percentage of GNP has risen from an average of 2.62 percent per annum in 1950–76 to 5 percent in 1980, to 8.31 percent in 1982–84. Whereas average GNP growth in 1982–84 was 10.6 percent, the rate of growth for total trade was 18.7 percent. He Hinhao, "Exploit the Role of Foreign Trade and Accelerate the Rate of China's Economic Development," *Guoji Maoyi* 5 (1982), trans. in *Chinese Economic Studies* 16, no. 4 (Summer 1983), pp. 37–50.

15. As soon as joint ventures were approved in China, there was immediate response. In 1980 there were two joint ventures and one wholly owned foreign enterprise; by mid-1987 the number had grown to over 7,800 Sino-foreign joint ventures and wholly owned foreign businesses. In addition, by 1987 China had established 277 enterprises outside China. There were also reported to be 130 wholly owned foreign enterprises in China. See *Beijing Review*, July 6, 1987, p. 23, and April 10, 1987, p. 20.

16. See Yang Wenda, "New Trends in the Development of Soviet Economic Relations with the West," *Guangming Ribao*, January 22, 1987, p. 4, in *Foreign Broadcast Information Service—China* (hereafter, *FBIS*), February 3, 1987, pp. C1-C2. Both Poland and Hungary have since applied for full membership in the EC.

17. See David Dyker, "Soviet Industry in the International Context," and Alan H. Smith, "International Trade and Resources," in Dyker, note 5, pp. 75–91 and 106–25, respectively.

18. To alleviate the impact of energy price rises in the mid-and late 1970s (they peaked in 1979–80), the USSR agreed to provide oil and gas to CMEA members at a price that would only gradually catch up with the prices other countries were paying on the world market. Eastern Europe is thus estimated to have received an implicit Soviet subsidy amounting to US $5.8 billion in 1974–78, about $11.6 billion in 1979, $17.8 billion in 1980, and $18.7 billion in 1981. The average subsidy for 1982–84 is however estimated to have dropped to $12.1 billion (as world prices sagged), reaching $10–11 billion in 1984. Michael Marrese and Jan Vanous, *Implicit Subsidies and Non-Market Benefits in Soviet Trade with Eastern Europe* (Berkeley: University of California Press, 1982).

19. *New York Times,* February 19, 1988, p. l.

20. See Stephen White, "The USSR Supreme Soviet: A Developmental Perspective," and William A. Welsh, "The Status of Research on Representative Institutions in Eastern Europe," in Daniel Nelson and Stephen White, eds., *Communist Legislatures in Comparative Perspective* (Albany: State University of New York Press, 1982), pp. 247–74 and 257–308, respectively.

21. Standing committees, not unlike the various committees in the American Congress, typically engage in three activities: (1) periodic investigations of the acts of government ministries; (2) monitoring the implementation of parliamentary acts by the state bureaucracy on a continuous basis; and (3) participating in the drafting of legislation.

22. See Seweryn Bialer, "The Changing Soviet Political System: The Nineteenth Party Conference and After," in Bialer, ed., *Politics, Society, and Nationality Inside Gorbachev's Russia* (Boulder: Westview Press, 1989), pp. 193–243; *Christian Science Monitor,* August 1, 1988, p. 9; *New York Times,* March 9, 1989, p. 1.

23. See Lowell Dittmer, *China's Continuous Revolution* (Berkeley: University of California Press, 1987).

24. See Benedict Stavis, *China's Political Reforms: An Interim Report* (New York: Praeger, 1987).

25. In September the Chinese regime announced a new "half-half" policy, according to which future foreign trade should be equally divided between the West and the Communist bloc. See *Renmin Ribao,* September 24, 1989.

26. See David Michael Lampton, "China's Limited Accommodation with the USSR: Coalition Politics," in *AEI Foreign Policy and Defense Review* 6, no. 3 (August 1986), pp. 26–35.

3

Economic Reform, Social Mobilization, and Democratization in Post-Mao China

Nina P. Halpern

Major reform movements in communist countries typically produce both economic and political change, raising important questions about the precise linkage between the two. Focusing primarily on reforms in the Soviet Union and Eastern Europe, scholars have long debated the nature of the relationship between economic reform and political democratization. To some it seems obvious that economic reform cannot occur without giving rise to substantial social mobilization and thence to increased pressures for democratization.[1] But others argue that the two processes are quite distinct and that economic reform is possible without any significant change in the political system.[2] The dramatic reforms in post-Mao China provide an excellent opportunity to reexamine the merits of these competing arguments.

This article suggests that neither line of argument is wholly adequate, and that the relationship between economic reform and democratization in communist systems is neither linear nor constant, but is rather contingent and variable. Although economic reform in such systems is often followed by increased mass political activity—i.e., social mobilization—the extent, nature, and timing of such mobilization relative to economic reform vary significantly across nations. Likewise, regime responses to social mobilization, and elites' willingness to introduce democratic reforms, vary substantially. The Chinese government's military crackdown on mass demonstrations in June 1989 illustrates the unhappy consequences when social mobilization—produced in part by post-Mao economic reforms—encounters an elite unwilling to countenance democratization.

Linking Economic Reform and Democratization

Exploring the relationship between economic reform and democratization requires a definition of terms. Economic reform is generally defined as decentralization of economic decision making combined with an increased role of

A preliminary version of this article was presented at the Stanford University Seminar on "Liberalization and Democratization in Global Perspective," Stanford, December 6, 1988. I would like to thank the participants in that seminar, as well as Richard Baum, Ramon Myers, and an anonymous Routledge press referee, for helpful comments on earlier drafts.

market forces in resource allocation. The political change which might result from such reform can take several forms. This article distinguishes between *social mobilization,* i.e., increased mass political activity which may involve demands for change in the political system, or may make use of new political forms—for example, demonstrations, formation of organized interest groups, or a petition movement—to pose economic or other nonpolitical demands, on the one hand, and *democratization,* i.e., adoption of reforms to institutionalize a larger citizen role in the selection of leaders and policies, on the other. Social mobilization describes what happens at the mass level; democratization describes institutional changes, requiring elite sanction, that alter, in a permanent fashion, the relationship between elites and masses.

One additional terminological distinction requires elaboration, viz., the distinction between political *liberalization* and political *rationalization.* Liberalization describes a process of depoliticization leading to enhanced political tolerance, wherein elites acknowledge that certain types of social activity (e.g., intellectual discussion, religious worship, or individual pursuit of economic self-interest) should be treated as private activities, not subject to state intervention on political grounds. By contrast, reforms that alter the workings of the political system without significantly depoliticizing social life or increasing mass social mobilization and popular control will be referred to as *rationalization.*

Scholarly arguments link economic reform to social mobilization in several ways, direct and indirect. One such putative linkage is that liberalization is necessary to convince intellectuals and others to participate in the economic reform process; such liberalization then permits expression of various demands, including political ones.[3] A second suggested linkage is one of rising expectations: economic reform creates expectations of a rise in living standards; groups that have not experienced such an increase will become mobilized to demand it.[4] Finally, decentralization of economic decision making and resource allocation is said to produce social mobilization by creating a greater diversity of socioeconomic interests and by simultaneously providing the necessary economic autonomy to permit political expression of the new interests.[5]

These arguments focus attention on various factors that are likely to influence people's calculations about whether or not to become politically active. They focus, first, on the existence of unsatisfied demands (created by rising economic expectations or socioeconomic pluralism), and second, on factors that alter mass calculations about the costs and benefits of political action (liberalization and economic independence increase the perceived benefits and lower the perceived costs of such action).

This article does not dispute the claim that economic reform promotes social mobilization by altering mass calculations about the efficacy of political action; it suggests instead that a full understanding of the relationship between economic reform and mobilization must also take account of other factors. A number of political or attitudinal factors may alter or mitigate the effects of economic reform. The result may be economic reform without significant social mobilization (for example, Hungary during the 1960s and 1970s); social mobilization without economic reform (as occurred in the GDR and Czechoslovakia in 1989); or simultaneous, but only partially inter-related, change of both types. China, I will argue, provides an example of this latter situation.

What kinds of political or attitudinal variables make a difference? In the East European case, international variables have been crucial: the Soviet invasion following the 1956 uprising greatly diminished the incentives for political activism in Hungary, outweighing the effects of later economic reform (other factors were also at work, such as the prevalence of moon-lighting, or holding second jobs),[6] while the Gorbachev reforms, and explicit renunciation of any Soviet intention to intervene in the domestic affairs of neighboring countries, have made mass activity in support of political change seem potentially much more efficacious. In the Chinese case, international variables are less important, but domestic political variables matter greatly. In particular, rising expectations for *political* change generated by limited political reforms and by elite rhetoric in support of democracy, were at least as important as rising economic expectations in producing social mobili-zation.

Underlying attitudes produced by historical events and socialization expe-riences are also vital for explaining the pattern of political mobilization, i.e., the types of groups which become politically active in the new reform environment. In China, students proved initially most active, although their actions eventually triggered a much broader social movement. While eco-nomic and political reform provided new incentives for participation to many social groups, the response of students seems best explained by the experiences of the Cultural Revolution and historical symbolism, not by the economic reforms *per se*. Thus, economic reform provides only a partial explanation of social mobilization—both the general phenomenon and the particular pattern—in post-Mao China.

The arguments summarized above address the likelihood that economic reform will give rise to increased political activity among the general popula-tion. Some scholars suggest that economic reform will also produce democra-tization through its effects on elite thinking. The need to obtain expert input into the policy process, or emergent social pluralism, supposedly persuades elites that economic reform cannot succeed without corresponding political reforms to institutionalize the political expression of diverse interests.[7] Ac-cordingly, if elites are sufficiently committed to economic reform they will introduce measures to make the political system more democratic.[8] These arguments generally rest upon an assumption that reformist elites perceive a clear and necessary connection between economic reform and democratization. However, this assumption may not always be met; as this study of the Chinese case will demonstrate, elite responses to economic reform may vary as widely as those of the general population.

The Chinese Case

Since the death of Mao, and particularly since 1978, China has been engaged in a remarkable reform movement, incorporating both economic and political elements. At the same time, significant social mobilization has been reflected in mass movements of various kinds, including student demonstrations, ethnic protest, and labor unrest. From late April 1989 until the June 4 military crackdown, student-initiated demonstrations and hunger strikes triggered huge demonstrations in Beijing, incorporating over a million people and drawing in almost all segments of the urban population. China thus provides an excellent test case for the arguments set forth above.

The economic reform process began toward the end of 1978. The December 1978 Third Plenum declared the need for such reform and initiated a series of reform experiments in both agriculture and industry (prior economic reform experiments were very small in scale and not publicly announced). During 1979 and 1980, industrial reform experiments (including enterprise profit retention and decentralized decision-making with respect to a small portion of production, marketing, and investment decisions) spread rapidly, to encompass over six thousand state enterprises. At the same time, the initiation of joint ventures and the creation of special economic zones opened the economy to international economic forces. Inflation and budget and trade deficits produced a moratorium on reform and some recentralization of controls at the end of 1980; in 1982, however, the reform process resumed, with the adoption of a "tax for profit" scheme permitting enterprises to keep surplus profits after paying a set of taxes to the state. In 1984, the Party adopted a major document calling for more extensive urban industrial reform, including price and wage reform and an end to mandatory planning for all but the most important products. In subsequent years industrial reform deepened to include preliminary creation of capital and labor markets, as well as changes in the nature of ownership or management of industrial enterprises. Small enterprises were leased out to individuals or groups, and a shareholding system introduced for large state enterprises. In 1988 a five-year plan for price reform was announced, and then quickly abandoned after a surge of panic buying and inflation.

Agricultural reform has moved even more quickly since the late 1970s, with a near-universal shift from communes to the "household responsibility system" (involving contracting of land to individual households) completed by the beginning of 1983. A shift from mandatory government procurement quotas to contracted purchases of agricultural products occurred in 1985. Peasants subsequently acquired the right to buy and sell land contracts. In both industry and agriculture, the reforms actually implemented do not go as far as those proposed, and in many cases old patterns are found to persist in a new guise.[9] In the aftermath of the June 4 crackdown, the future of economic reform appeared quite uncertain. Nevertheless, since 1978 economic decision making has clearly been decentralized, and market forces have come to control a substantially greater share of both industrial and agricultural production and marketing decisions.[10]

The remainder of this article will explore the impact of these economic reforms on political change in China, asking how they have affected both elite and mass behavior. The discussion will make three major points. First, the major impetus behind initial elite moves to liberalize and reform the political system and behind social mobilization came not from economic reform, but rather from a combination of two political factors: the post-Mao succession struggle and the Cultural Revolution. Second, as economic reform has gone forward, it has generally *not* led elites to adopt democratizing reforms. Instead, the process of economic reform has convinced Chinese elites of the need for a more rational and efficient system of governance, characterized by political liberalization but not democracy. Dramatic proof of this was provided by the June 4 crackdown, but substantial evidence was available much earlier as well. Third, although it is true that the social mobilization evident in China in the mid-1980s was partly a response to the economic reforms and their political effects (particularly continued political liberalization), economic reform has not determined the *pattern* of social mobilization. Preform political attitudes provide a better explanation of this pattern; and future social mobilization is thus likely to reflect both prereform experiences and the transforming effects of the events of April–June 1989.

The Initiation of Reform

Economic reform did not emerge in a political vacuum, giving rise to subsequent social mobilization and political reform. Rather, all three emerged out of a common, complex process in which the same set of factors that motivated economic reform also produced political reform and social mobilization. Both economic and political reforms were largely a reaction to the experiences of the Cultural Revolution, although the post-Mao succession struggle also played an important role. These same factors also gave rise to the democracy movement of 1978–79. This movement demonstrated that prior to the initiation of economic reform a segment of the population had already acquired participatory values that inclined them to act politically to achieve their goals.

Elite-Initiated Reform:
The Post-Mao Succession Struggle

The succession struggle that followed Mao's death was an important source of reformist sentiment, both economic and political. Elite cleavages were not new, as the Party had been seriously divided since the early 1960s; during the last years of Mao's life a struggle for succession was already underway. With Mao's death, however, it became possible, as it had not been before, to pursue power by proposing new policy approaches that would have been unacceptable to Mao.

After his rehabilitation in July 1977, Deng Xiaoping gradually wrested power from the man initially chosen as Mao's successor, Hua Guofeng.[11] Deng followed a number of political strategies to undermine Hua,[12] but an important one was his promotion of an ideological campaign—the "practice" campaign (calling for "practice as the sole criterion of truth")—that attacked the notion of blind continuity with the Maoist past. Hua's major basis of legitimacy was his supposed selection by Mao and his commitment to upholding Mao's policies; the "practice" campaign thus simultaneously attacked Hua and laid the groundwork for the adoption of new, reformist policies.[13]

These reformist policies were partly economic. However, political reforms, including calls for "people's democracy," provided a particularly effective succession strategy for Deng Xiaoping. While Hua was still the official leader, calls for collective leadership and diffusion of power helped to diminish his power. Indeed, in 1980 Zhao Ziyang replaced Hua as premier on grounds that party and state power should be separated, and Hua should therefore not hold both top positions.[14] Dorothy Fontana has also suggested that calls for "legal practices" indirectly attacked Hua and his followers because they had assumed office extralegally, i.e., without benefit of formal appointment by the appropriate political bodies.[15] Finally, as I shall argue below, Deng almost certainly supported the democracy movement because of its effectiveness in undermining Hua's leadership.

The Cultural Revolution was the second major source of reformism. Among the victims of the movement, the Cultural Revolution engendered both a belief that excessive concentration of power could be dangerous and a perception of the need to regularize and institutionalize the workings of the political system. At the same time, the economic and political hardships that the Cultural Revolution visited upon most groups within the population, and the consequent delegitimation of the political system, motivated an attempt to reestablish political legitimacy. This attempt incorporated both economic reforms aimed at producing a substantial rise in living standards, which had stagnated for almost two full decades, and political reforms designed to create a more tolerable political order. These concerns—and not just tactical movements of the succession struggle—prompted political liberalization, as well as calls at the Third Plenum to increase "people's democracy" and "socialist legality,"[16] and subsequent electoral and legal reforms in 1979.[17]

Social Mobilization:
The Democracy Movement

Pressures for democratization (and for economic change) also came from below in 1978, caused by much the same factors: the Cultural Revolution and the succession struggle. These pressures appeared in the form of the democracy movement, which began in the last few months of 1978 and continued into the spring of 1979. The movement was a complicated one, consisting of several different types of mass activity. It began with the posting of wall posters expressing political grievances and demands. Subsequently, a number of unofficial journals were published. The movement also became linked with a petitioners' movement composed of individuals who flocked to Beijing to seek redress of grievances suffered during earlier years (including many young people who had been sent to the countryside during the Cultural Revolution). The demands expressed by these various elements were diverse, ranging from solutions to very personal kinds of problems to calls for changes in political personnel and policies. Democracy appeared as both an instrumental and an absolute value: some participants, reminiscent of nineteenth century reformers, saw it as a means to modernize and strengthen the nation;[18] others, calling democracy the "fifth modernization," clearly regarded it as an end in itself.[19]

The succession struggle does not explain why the movement originated, but it helps explain why it was tolerated, and even encouraged, by some within the elite. By criticizing existing policies and supporting Deng Xiaoping and other victims of the Cultural Revolution, the democracy movement facilitated the rise to power of Deng and other reformist leaders. It was undoubtedly at least partly with this in mind that Deng signaled his support of the movement in late November 1978. Deng's support presumably lowered the perceived costs of taking political action, while increasing the perceived likelihood of success. Although Deng withdrew his support for the movement by the spring of 1979,[20] his initial response clearly facilitated its growth.

But Deng Xiaoping's approval affected mainly the growth of the movement, rather than its existence. The movement's origins lay not in participants' calculations about likely success or failure, but rather in a participatory political disposition produced by the experiences of Cultural Revolution. Although the perils of that period, the political twists and turns, and the high costs of committing political errors (all of which added up to a form of political terror not previously experienced in China) induced in some people a withdrawal from politics, this was not the case for all segments of the population. In some people, primarily young and urban, cynicism and a temptation to refrain from political action were more than counterbalanced by a strong belief in the legitimacy of popular participation created by the rhetoric and experiences of the time.[21] Kjeld Erik Brodsgaard[22] has traced the emergence after 1966 of political movements and groups made up of students and/or workers, including the Red Guards, the 1967 Shanghai Commune and Hunan Sheng-wu-lian group, the Li Yizhe group in 1974, and finally the Tiananmen incident of April 1976 (when thousands gathered in Tiananmen square in spontaneous commemoration of Zhou Enlai's death and in protest of existing policies). Brodsgaard regards each of these, although differing in their specific critique of the existing system, as precursors of the democracy movement of 1978–79.[23] They had in common an anti-elitist tone and an emphasis on mass participation that was generally congruent with the Maoist ideology of the Cultural Revolution. The Tiananmen incident, which was spontaneous, large-scale, and anti-regime in its implications, and which came at the end of the Cultural Revolution, was a particularly strong indicator that some segments of the population had been sufficiently resocialized with participatory values to take action even when the costs of political dissent must have appeared extremely high.[24]

In sum, when the economic reforms were introduced at the end of 1978, the experiences of the Cultural Revolution had already convinced Chinese leaders of the need for significant political change, including political liberalization and some form of "socialist democracy and legality." Likewise, a segment of the population had given evidence of its resocialization with participatory values and consequent inclination to take political action to achieve its goals. These attitudes shaped the political response to economic reform, although their effects would subsequently be seen more at the mass than the elite level.

The Political Dynamics of Economic Reform

Economic reform emerged out of a particular political process, but in turn produced its own political dynamics. Particularly from the mid-1980s, a growing number of spontaneous mass protests occurred. Students in particular became increasingly active, but by spring 1989 they were joined by additional segments of urban society: older intellectuals, workers, and others. I will argue below that economic reform helped produce these activities, largely by encouraging elites to maintain a relatively liberal environment, but also by providing new economic grievances. First, however, I will show that elite rhetoric and actions on political reform during the period also served to encourage social mobilization, despite the fact that elites demonstrated little if any interest in democratization. Contrary to the argument examined earlier, neither the process of economic reform nor the social mobilization that accompanied it convinced most Chinese leaders of the need for democratization; if anything, they became more firmly convinced of the opposite: the need for enhanced political stability.

Elite Responses to Economic Reform

Beginning in 1978, elite actions substantially raised mass expectations for political change without simultaneously producing any significant democratization of the political system. Despite ending the democracy movement, Chinese leaders, including Deng Xiaoping, continued to speak of the need for "socialist democracy."[25] Electoral reforms adopted in 1979 provided for multiple candidacies and more open nominating procedures in elections to local-level people's congresses. County-level elections were held in 1980 and 1985, but with few exceptions, even where more than one candidate stood for office, the nomination process and election results remained subject to at least indirect party control.[26] And in any event, the 1980 experiment in grass roots electoral democracy has not been repeated since. In general, the political changes of 1978–85 involved considerable rhetorical support for "socialist democracy" but no significant change in the Leninist nature of the political system.

In mid-1986, political reform rose briefly to the top of the political agenda. During the latter half of the year the media carried numerous articles on political reform, many arguing specifically that continued economic reform required collateral political reforms. These articles provide unusual insight into elite thinking on the connection between economic reform and democratization. They reveal that the economic reform process did not convince the leadership of the need for this type of political change. Although pressures for democracy exist (at least among prominent intellectuals, and perhaps in hidden form within a segment of the elite), such pressures seem to have been inspired by factors other than economic reform.

The media discussions revealed two very divergent views of the necessity of political reform. Most articles argued that political reform was urgently needed in order to facilitate and support the economic reforms. But the types of reform urged by these articles were basically rationalizing or administrative ones, i.e., they were reforms that would alter the structure, operation, and internal relationship of decision making and administrative bodies without significantly increasing popular control over the government or its policies. Most authors called for three specific types of reform: separating party and government; streamlining the government structure; and cadre reform. Socialist democracy and legality were usually also on the list of goals, but were generally mentioned last and were given less attention.[27] Moreover, as was made clear by Deng Xiaoping himself, "socialist democracy" was to be sharply distinguished from the forms of "democracy and freedom" practiced in Western capitalist countries.[28] An article published on September 24, 1986, in the *Economic Daily*[29] made clear the un-(and even anti-) democratic orientation of some economic reformers. Arguing that it was essential to be clear on the priorities of political reform, the article stressed that reforms should rationalize the leadership structure (by separating party and government, decentralizing decisionmaking, streamlining administration, and increasing work efficiency), but not alter the political system itself. In this article, which appeared in an economically oriented newspaper, democracy disappeared entirely as a goal.

Thus, some of those most interested in furthering economic reform did not regard democratization as essential, but rather argued for administrative reform and rationalization. An alternative view of political reform was expressed by a minority of writers with a less direct interest in the economic reforms, particularly researchers at the Institutes of Political Science and Marxism-Leninism-Mao Zedong Thought of the Chinese Academy of Social Sciences (CASS). These individuals argued for treating political reform as a distinctive, high-priority goal, independent of the needs of economic reform. For these authors, whose primary concerns were political, democratization had a much greater urgency; they thus engaged in much more concrete discussion of needed democratic reforms than did those authors who focused on the need to promote economic reform.[30]

In addition to differing on the reasons for and desired components of political reform, the two types of articles also suggested different approaches for carrying out political reform. Those emphasizing the priority of economic reform and stressing administrative rationalization typically argued that the proper method of reform was top-down and controlled; they stressed the need to maintain stability and order. Again, Deng Xiaoping was one of the primary proponents of this view, repeatedly emphasizing the need for caution in political reform and the overriding importance of political stability if economic reform was to proceed.[31] On the other hand, those according democratization higher priority often emphasized the necessity of arousing the people. A September 1986 forum organized by the Institute of Marxism-Leninism-Mao Zedong Thought, for example, argued that the precondition of political restructuring was to open politics to the public and to arouse people's enthusiasm to participate in politics.[32]

The political reform discussions of late 1986, therefore, revealed two significantly different views of the necessary type of political reform. Arguments for democratization generally set forth political goals (such as preventing another Cultural Revolution), while those promoting economic reform sought a rationalization of the political order. The discussions of political reform basically ceased in the aftermath of the student demonstrations of winter 1986–87, which were followed by the resignation of CCP Secretary-General Hu Yaobang and the initiation of a campaign against "bourgeois liberalization."

When the discussions resumed in July 1987 (with the republication of Deng Xiaoping's August 1980 speech calling for reform of the party and state leadership), the reaction to the student protests altered the overall tone of the debate in some interesting ways. First, the balance of expressed opinion had shifted even further in favor of administrative reforms that would facilitate economic reform, and in favor of carrying out reform under party leadership, thus strengthening social stability. Successful economic reform was said to require such stability. Although establishment of socialist democracy remained an eventual goal, it was now clearly established as a secondary one that would come much later than other political reforms and take a very long time to achieve.[33] Second, and even more interesting, when democracy was discussed, its meaning had seemingly been altered. Gone were discussions of institutional change and the incorporation of different interests in the political process; instead, democratization had been redefined in a way very similar to Mao's mass-line approach. Indeed, there were specific references to the mass line, and to the need for cadres to go down to the grass roots.[34] This altered conception of democratization was reflected in Zhao Ziyang's report to the September 1987 Thirteenth Party Congress: the section dealing with socialist democracy stressed the need for "consultation and dialogue" and for publicity of government activities.[35] These notions of democratization—quite different from some of the conceptions expressed prior to the student demonstrations—had in common their noninstitutionalized nature, and the fact that each depended upon elite initiative.

In the aftermath of the 1986–87 student demonstrations, then, intellectual voices arguing for institutionalized democracy were largely stilled, at least within the party-controlled media. The leaders themselves seemingly became even more firmly convinced that democracy and economic reform were inherently separable. By 1989, even Zhao Ziyang—the Chinese leader most strongly committed to "liberal" economic reform—was apparently supporting the political theory of the "new authoritarianism," a theory which explicitly argued that economic reform required not democracy but firm central leadership.[36]

In sum, even prior to the June 1989 decision to use military force to crush mass demonstrations, Chinese leaders had made clear that their desire for economic reform did not incline them to seriously consider democratizing the political system. Instead, they sought to limit political change to rationalizing reforms and to the maintenance of a more liberal intellectual and social environment. Despite these efforts, social mobilization increased, reaching levels that the dominant leadership faction apparently could not tolerate.

The following section examines this increase in social mobilization and its linkage to the economic reforms.

Social Mobilization

Despite the leadership's repression of the various components of the 1978–79 democracy movement, mass demonstrations and other forms of social mobilization continued to occur periodically, particularly after the mid-1980s. Most of these episodes involved students, who held sizable demonstrations in 1985, winter 1986–87, and April–June 1989, in addition to organizing many smaller protests. Nonstudent protests have included large and violent demonstrations in fall 1987 (continuing sporadically after that) on behalf of Tibetan independence, Moslem demonstrations in Xinjiang province, and occasional reports of incidents involving workers or peasants.[37] Although individual intellectuals were particularly outspoken on behalf of political change—notably the physicist Fang Lizhi—intellectuals as a group did not become particularly active until the winter of 1988–89, when two letters calling for amnesty for political prisoners, each carrying the signatures of thirty to forty intellectuals, were circulated to foreign journalists.[38] By the late spring of 1989, however, student demonstrations and hunger strikes following the death of former party chairman Hu Yaobang elicited a response from a much larger set of actors. The demonstrations of 1989 were unprecedented in several ways: the fact that well over a million people took part; the large number of social groups that participated; and the new political forms that emerged, including hunger strikes, organization of an independent workers' union, and a petition drive among NPC delegates.

To what extent can this growing social mobilization be linked to the economic reforms? The fact that mobilization had already begun—in the form of the Tiananmen incident and the democracy movement—prior to the introduction of economic reforms suggests that economic reform alone cannot provide an adequate explanation. Similarly, the *pattern* of mobilization—i.e., the nature and social characteristics of the groups which became politically active—does not correlate particularly well with the direct effects of economic reform. Underlying attitudes produced by differential socialization experiences seem more relevant for explaining this pattern. Nevertheless, economic reform clearly contributed to accelerating social mobilization both by encouraging political liberalization and by spawning new (or intensified) economic grievances—in part by raising economic expectations.

The political liberalization of the late 1970s and early 1980s—marked by a declining emphasis on class struggle and greater tolerance for intellectual and social diversity— contributed to social mobilization in two ways. First, it encouraged political activity by making it appear less likely that the leadership would impose harsh penalties for such activity. Second, it allowed intellectuals to engage in discussions of democracy that encouraged students in particular to take political action in support of the ideas expressed by those intellectuals. In effect, liberalization both lowered the perceived costs and increased the perceived benefits (by creating rising expectations of political change) of taking political action in support of democracy.

As mentioned earlier, political liberalization preceded the introduction of economic reform, and arose to a large extent from an attempt to enhance the legitimacy of the political system. Nevertheless, the maintenance and expansion of liberalization, in the face of social activities distasteful to at least some of the leadership, were motivated largely by an elite desire to promote the development of the economic reforms. Concrete evidence for this is provided by the fact that twice since the Third Plenum China's leaders took action to halt or to strictly limit political campaigns directed against the effects of liberalization because these campaigns threatened to undermine the economic reforms. Whether China's current leaders will act in similar fashion to limit the damage done by the most recent—and most severe—campaign against bourgeois liberalization remains to be seen.

Despite having declared an end to political campaigns, the post-Mao leadership twice before 1989 initiated large-scale movements directed against social and intellectual activities considered unacceptable: the "spiritual pollution" campaign of winter 1983–84, and the first "bourgeois liberalization" campaign of spring 1987. In both cases, the campaigns were relatively short-lived. The spiritual pollution campaign was initially directed against pornography and economic corruption, but soon began to have obvious spillover onto the economic reforms themselves. Reformist ideas began to be labeled by party conservatives as "spiritual pollution," and hostile accusations began to be directed, e.g., at peasants who had grown wealthy by taking advantage of opportunities provided by the production responsibility system. As a result of such spillover, in January 1984 the campaign was terminated.[39] Three years later, a campaign against bourgeois liberalization was initiated in the wake of the winter 1986–87 student demonstrations; the campaign was directed against those intellectuals who had called for "all-out Westernization." Zhao Ziyang's decision to limit the scope of this campaign—by restricting it to CCP members and by limiting its punitive measures to expulsion from the party—apparently was intended to lay to rest growing concerns, both in China and abroad, that the campaign had signaled a general retreat from reform.[40]

The ending of the spiritual pollution campaign appears to have been followed by greater elite tolerance for diverse intellectual discussions and private activities and, equally important, by a stronger popular belief in the elite's commitment to that liberalization. Foreigners visiting China at the time reported unprecedented openness on the part of Chinese with whom they talked, and China's intellectuals subsequently branched out into areas of inquiry, both economic and political, that would have seemed politically impossible even a few years earlier. Among the ideas publicly expressed during this period were the calls for democracy and for mobilizing the public discussed in the previous section. Such indicators of renewed liberalization, though admittedly imprecise, strongly suggest that it was an important factor in the growing mobilization of social protest in the mid-1980s. Likewise, the decision to limit the scope of the 1987 bourgeois liberalization campaign probably explains why the demobilization of the 1986–87 student demonstrations did not bring an end to student activism.

Apart from allowing more freedom of intellectual activity, China's post-Mao leaders have been far more tolerant of spontaneous mass protest than their predecessors—notwithstanding the fact that many mass demonstrations were eventually suppressed. Until the June 4 crackdown, the regime's response to these movements—at least those involving student activism—had not been particularly severe. This is probably the most important reason why such movements continued to recur, and grew into the massive demonstrations of 1989. As students carried on their demonstrations, suffering few obvious consequences, this undoubtedly convinced other segments of the population that they too could take political action to express their dissatisfaction and their demands.

The more liberal social protest environment of the 1980s thus provided signals that political action would be less costly and more potentially effective than in the past. Yet not all groups responded to the new incentives provided by this more tolerant environment. Moreover, the pattern of response seems only partly attributable to the effects of economic reform. Contrary to one scholarly argument noted earlier, growing economic independence apparently played a minimal role in motivating political action. Until the massive social protest of spring 1989, when most urban groups participated in demonstrations, urban entrepreneurs (getihu) were generally politically inert.[41] Similarly, peasants, whose economic independence increased considerably with the adoption of the rural responsibility system in the early 1980s, have generally been relatively (though not entirely) passive.[42] As Thomas Gold suggests, opportunities for economic advancement appear to have served as an alternative to, rather than a motivation for, political activism.[43]

On the other hand, economic grievances and rising economic expectations generated by the reforms did play a role—though not a decisive one—in motivating political action. The secondary role of such grievances is indicated both by the types of groups that first became mobilized, and by the character of their expressed demands. The two groups that became most politically active before 1989 were those with an established prereform history of political activism: students and Tibetan nationalists. Tibetan nationalism produced a major uprising in 1959; the events of 1987 represented a revival of this earlier activity—albeit under liberalized political conditions. Similarly, Chinese students have a long history of political activism, with the Cultural Revolution being only the most recent—and most spectacular— example.

The student demonstrations merit particular attention in our attempt to assess the political effects of economic reform because they have been the most frequently recurrent protests and because they provided the trigger for the broader social movement of 1989. Student demands have been extremely diverse. Suzanne Pepper argues convincingly that student demonstrations in 1985 against Japanese militarism and commercialism actually constituted a critique of the ways in which economic reform fostered corruption and inflation and served the interests of privileged bureaucratic groups[44]— though she is arguably too dismissive of the genuine nationalistic concerns of the students.[45] In the winter of 1986–87 demonstrators raised a number of demands; these included demands for better living and working conditions, but most centered on political change, reflecting raised expectations produced by recently liberalized media discussions of political reform. Students demanded democratization of university administration and of the political system in general; their initial protests were directed at failures to implement the country's electoral laws.[46] Apart from these relatively large-scale demonstrations, students have also carried out numerous smaller protests—for example, over the authorities' unwillingness to close a tobacco factory located on the grounds of the Central Institute of Finance and Banking,[47] over the beating to death of a student by "hooligans,"[48] and over the allegedly flamboyant lifestyles and privileges of African students.[49]

What does such diversity in the objects of protest suggest about the role of economic reform in motivating political action? When a group is already predisposed to act politically, a variety of precipitants may trigger action. Although the adverse effects of economic reform provided one set of grievances, these were not the primary source of student activism. Instead, as suggested earlier, one must look to student attitudes about politics and about their own political role. Earlier, I argued that these attitudes were in large measure a product of the Cultural Revolution, when Mao encouraged students to rebel against political authority, and when official propaganda promoted mass participation in politics. Later, historical symbolism also became significant, as students were reminded of the important role played by their predecessors in anti-Japanese protests in the 1930s.[50]

A similar argument can be made about the broader popular movement of mid-1989. The nature of the movement—massive street marches and resistance, both violent and nonviolent, to the use of the army against student demonstrators—does not lend itself to easy analysis of its causes. Certainly, the manifest political demands of the students (for a free press, an end to corruption, and so on) did not represent the primary concerns of all participants. For workers in particular (who during the course of the movement formed an independent union), concern over inflation and falling living standards in 1988–89 were undoubtedly more central. Public opinion polls from this period reveal widespread dissatisfaction with rampant inflation and inequality of opportunity, among other issues.[51] It thus seems clear that economic reform produced grievances—stemming both from the negative by-products of reform and from the generally heightened expectations of the urban populace—that helped motivate political activism. But the broader mass movement of May and June did not occur spontaneously; it occurred in support of demonstrations and hunger strikes initiated by students, and only after several years of such student activism. Accordingly, it appears that the changed political climate, more than the economic reforms themselves, provides the primary explanation of the growing social mobilization.

In sum, a full explanation of Chinese political mobilization in the mid and late-1980s must take account of pre-existing orientations toward political participation as well as calculations about the diminished political costs of expressing demands produced by the post-Mao liberalization. Economic reform clearly played a role in keeping that liberalization alive, and in generating some of the heightened expectations that then received expression. But economic reform alone cannot explain the current pattern of Chinese political mobilization. Similarly, future Chinese political activism will necessarily reflect both the pattern of incentives and tolerances established by elite policies, both economic and political, and new political attitudes generated by the experience of participating in the remarkable social movement of 1989.

Conclusion

The Chinese case illustrates a number of points about the relationship between economic reform and social mobilization. It demonstrates that economic reform is not the sole source of such mobilization; the earliest mass demonstrations on behalf of democracy and social justice actually preceded the onset of economic reform and appeared to be largely an outgrowth of the Cultural Revolution—though they were also accelerated by elite actions during the post-Mao succession struggle. It also shows that communist elites do not necessarily share the assumption of many scholars that economic reform is impossible without democratization. When Chinese elites have called for "socialist democracy," they generally have not been motivated by economic concerns. Those Chinese elites most committed to promoting economic reform have seemingly concluded that this requires construction of a more rationalized and tolerant—but still undemocratic—

political system. Finally, the Chinese case illustrates that economic reform can help to promote social mobilization—primarily by convincing elites to maintain a politically tolerant environment in which dissent appears less costly; but this does not explain the pattern of mobilization that results. Elucidation of that pattern requires attention to other variables, particularly the nature of political attitudes produced by prereform experiences. When Chinese leaders next attempt to move ahead with economic and political reform, they are likely to find that those social groups which participated actively in the 1989 demonstrations will become mobilized even more readily to demand democratic change the next time around.

Notes and References

1. For example, R. V. Burks, "The Political Implications of Economic Reform," in Morris Bornstein, ed., *Plan and Market* (New Haven: Yale University Press, 1973), pp. 373–402; and Gregory Grossman, "Economic Reforms: The Interplay of Economics and Politics," in R.V. Burks, ed., *The Future of Communism in Europe* (Detroit: Wayne State University Press, 1968), pp. 103–140.

2. Wlodzimierz Brus, "Political Pluralism and Markets in Communist Systems," in Susan Gross Solomon, ed., *Pluralism in the Soviet Union* (New York: St. Martin's Press, 1982), pp. 108–30; Ellen Comisso and Paul Marer, "The Economics and Politics of Reform in Hungary," in Ellen Comisso and Laura D'Andrea Tyson, eds., *Power, Purpose, and Collective Choice* (Ithaca and London: Cornell University Press, 1986), pp. 245–78.

3. R. V. Burks (note 1, p. 383) cites Czech reformers in support of a version of this argument.

4. This linkage was suggested to me by Richard Baum, personal communication.

5. Burks, note 1, p. 382. Brus (note 2, pp. 125–27) discusses these arguments, pointing out that the evidence in their favor—derived from either logic or the East European experience—is mixed and generally rather weak.

6. Laszlo Bruszt, talk at the Stanford University Faculty Seminar on Democratization, Stanford, California, October 31, 1989.

7. Andrzej Korbonski, "Political Aspects of Economic Reforms in Eastern Europe," in Zbigniew M. Fallenbuchl, ed., *Economic Development in the Soviet Union and Eastern Europe*, vol. 1 (New York: Praeger, 1975), pp. 28–29.

8. The more usual form of this argument is the negative one: Communist elites do not adopt marketizing reforms because they recognize that they would have to institute such political changes. See, e.g., Burks, note 1, pp. 381–85.

9. See, for example, Jean C. Oi, "Commercializing China's Rural Cadres," *Problems of Communism* 35, no. 5 (September–October 1986), pp. 1–15; and Dorothy J. Solinger, "Industrial Reform: Decentralization, Differentiation, and

the Difficulties," *Journal of International Affairs* 39, no. 2 (Winter 1986), pp. 105–18. See also Solinger's chapter in the present volume.

10. For an excellent overview of the economic reforms and their results, see Harry Harding, *China's Second Revolution: Reform after Mao* (Washington, D.C.: The Brookings Institution, 1987), chapters 5 and 6.

11. Personnel and policy changes announced at the Third Plenum in December 1978 indicated Hua's declining power and the rise of a more reformist coalition dominated by Deng. Hua finally resigned as party chairman in June 1981.

12. See Dorothy Grouse Fontana, "Background to the Fall of Hua Guofeng," *Asian Survey* 22, no. 3 (March 1982), pp. 237–60; Parris Chang, "Chinese Politics: Deng's Turbulent Quest," *Problems of Communism* 30, no. 1 (January–February 1981), pp. 1–21.

13. Valerie Bunce has suggested that leadership succession usually produces policy innovation (aimed particularly at improving mass welfare), but in the Chinese case Hua's emphasis on policy continuity made reformism a particularly effective succession strategy for Deng. See Valerie Bunce, *Do New Leaders Make a Difference? Executive Succession and Public Policy under Capitalism and Socialism* (Princeton: Princeton University Press, 1981). Bunce's ideas have been applied to the Deng Xiaoping succession by Joseph W. Esherick and Elizabeth J. Perry, "Leadership Succession in the People's Republic of China: 'Crisis' or Opportunity?" *Studies in Comparative Communism* 26, no. 3 (Autumn 1983), pp. 171–77.

14. See Hua Guofeng, "Speech at the Third Session of the Fifth National People's Congress (September 7, 1980)," in *Main Documents of the Third Session of the Fifth National People's Congress of the People's Republic of China* (Beijing: Foreign Languages Press, 1980), p. 196.

15. Fontana, note 12, pp. 245 and 252.

16. "Communiqué of the Third Plenary Session of the 11th Central Committee of the Communist Party of China," *Beijing Review* (hereafter, *BR*) 52 (December 29, 1978), p. 14.

17. These reforms included passage of an electoral law providing for direct, multi-candidate elections to local-level people's congresses, as well as new civil and criminal codes and a new constitution specifying equal rights before the law and other rights. For good discussions of the political reforms of this period see Harding, note 10, chapter 7, and Brantly Womack, "Modernization and Democratic Reform in China," *Journal of Asian Studies* 43, no. 3 (May 1984), pp. 417–39. On the legal reforms see Richard Baum, "Modernization and Legal Reform in Post-Mao China: The Rebirth of Socialist Legality," *Studies in Comparative Communism* 19, no. 2 (Summer 1986), pp. 69–103.

18. Andrew Nathan, *Chinese Democracy* (Berkeley: University of California Press, 1985), pp. 4–6. See also Kjeld Erik Brodsgaard, "The Democracy Movement in China, 1978–79: Opposition Movements, Wall Poster Campaigns, and Underground Journals," *Asian Survey* 21, no. 7 (July 1981), pp. 747–74.

19. Their model of democracy was not necessarily a contemporary Western one, however; some organizers of the movement called for implementing the principles of direct democracy of the 1871 Paris Commune. See Nathan, note 18, p. 10. The Paris Commune (praised by both Marx and Lenin) had been held up as a model at the beginning of the Cultural Revolution and had inspired a brief takeover of the Shanghai government (the "Shanghai Commune") in January 1967.

20. In a speech delivered in March 1979, Deng stated that the democracy movement had "gone too far" and that all discussions must uphold the four cardinal principles, i.e., the socialist road, dictatorship of the proletariat, leadership of the CCP, and Marxism-Leninism-Mao Zedong Thought. Several of the movement's leaders were soon arrested, and over the next year further steps were taken to crush the movement. See Brodsgaard, note 18, pp. 770–73.

21. The emigré respondents in Victor Falkenheim's study of Chinese political participation, although reporting forms of participation involving mostly informal lobbying and personal networking, also felt that the Cultural Revolution was "democratizing" in its effects and had produced a much bolder younger generation of Chinese that was far less likely to tolerate earlier authority patterns. See his "Political Participation in China," *Problems of Communism* 31, no. 3 (May–June 1982), p. 32.

22. Brodsgaard, note 18.

23. Stanley Rosen similarly traces the democracy movement in Guangzhou to the Cultural Revolution period, specifically Cultural Revolution factionalism and the 1974 Campaign to Criticize Lin Biao, Criticize Confucius. See "Guangzhou's Democracy Movement in Cultural Revolution Perspective," *China Quarterly* 101 (March 1985), pp. 3–12.

24. Chinese public opinion surveys of the late 1970s and early 1980s also revealed the changed values of Chinese young people, in particular their greater independence of thinking and unwillingness to blindly follow party leadership. See Stanley Rosen, "Students," in Anthony J. Kane, *China Briefing, 1988* (Boulder and London: Westview Press, 1988), pp. 86–87.

25. See, for example, Deng's August 1980 Speech on "Reform of the System of Party and State Leadership," in *Selected Works of Deng Xiaoping (1975–1982)* (Beijing: Foreign Languages Press, 1984), pp. 302–25.

26. For discussion of the elections see Nathan, note 18, chapter 10; Brantly Womack, "The 1980 County-Level Election in China: Experiment in Democratic Modernization," *Asian Survey* 22, no. 3 (March 1982), pp. 261–77; and Barrett McCormick, "Leninist Implementation: The Election Campaign," in David M. Lampton, ed., *Policy Implementation in Post-Mao China* (Berkeley: University of California Press, 1987), pp. 383–413.

27. For example, Zhang Youyu (a prominent jurist) argued that reform of the political structure must begin by separating party and government, with the second step being restructuring of the government bureaucracy. Perfecting the democratic and legal systems came later on the list and were discussed in much

less detail; they were described as necessary to arouse people's enthusiasm, and to protect those speaking out for economic reform. See *Foreign Broadcast Information Service—China* (hereafter, *FBIS*), October 30, 1986, p. K17.

28. Deng Xiaoping, *Fundamental Issues in Present-Day China* (Beijing: Foreign Languages Press,1987), pp. 113, 152–53.

29. Translated in *FBIS*, October 3, 1986, p. K7.

30. For example, Su Shaozhi (then director of the Institute of Marxism-Leninism-Mao Zedong Thought) argued that although the one-party system should be retained, ways should be found to allow discussion of different interests within the party. He also cited approvingly the proposals made by the third estate during the French Revolution, including a general election system, balance of power, democracy, and human rights. *Ta Kung Pao*, September 17, 1986, p. 2, in *FBIS*, September 29, 1986, pp. K16–17. A report on an April 1986 forum sponsored by the Chinese Academy of Social Sciences argued that democracy required division and balance of power; it then listed a more specific set of requirements: guaranteeing democratic rights; strengthening the role of the people's congresses; judicial independence; strengthening legal supervision of the bureaucracy; and inner-party democracy. *Social Sciences in China* (Beijing) 3 (1986), pp. 9–24.

31. Deng Xiaoping, note 28, pp. 114, 150.

32. *Radio Beijing Domestic Service*, September 15, 1986, in *FBIS*, September 23, 1986, p. K15.

33. For example, a July 27, 1987 article in *Renmin Ribao* (hereafter, *RMRB*), translated in *FBIS*, August 5, 1987, p. K3, argued that high-level democracy would require two or three more generations to build.

34. *Xinhua*, October 27, 1987, in *FBIS*, November 5, 1987, pp. 23–24.

35. Zhao Ziyang, "Advance Along the Road of Socialism with Chinese Characteristics," *BR*, November 9–15, 1987, pp. 41–43.

36. Andrew Nathan, "Politics at the Crossroads," in Anthony J. Kane, ed., *China Briefing, 1989* (Boulder and London: Westview Press, 1989), p. 23.

37. The Kong Kong *Agence France Presse* (in *FBIS*, June 30, 1988, p. 25) reported an incident involving peasants, as well as earlier incidents involving Moslems and Xian taxi drivers. The *Chicago Sun-Times* reported on December 28, 1986, that in at least two cities factory workers joined in the winter 1986–87 student demonstrations, protesting price increases.

38. Dorothy J. Solinger, "Democracy with Chinese Characteristics," *World Policy Journal* 6, no. 4 (Fall 1989), p. 623.

39. For a discussion of the campaign see Tom Gold, " 'Just in Time!' China Battles Spiritual Pollution on the Eve of 1984," *Asian Survey* 24, no. 9 (September 1984), pp. 947–73.

40. *Xinhua*, January 29, 1987, in *FBIS*, January 30, 1987, pp. K4-K8 (see esp. p. K7); Stanley Rosen, "China in 1987: The Year of the Thirteenth Party Congress," *Asian Survey* 28, no. 1 (January 1988), p. 37. *Far Eastern Economic*

Review, June 1987, p. 9, reports that potential foreign investors had been disturbed by the campaign.

41. Significant financial support was supposedly provided to the 1989 student movement by the Stone Company, an independent consulting firm headed by Wan Runnan. Wan was also accused of helping gather signatures of NPC delegates in an attempt, made in late May, to call a special session of the NPC to revoke martial law and dismiss Premier Li Peng. (*RMRB,* August 17, 1989, in *FBIS,* August 18, 1989, pp. 13–18.)

42. David Zweig ("Peasants and Politics," *World Policy Journal* 6, no. 4 [Fall 1989], pp. 633–45) argues that peasants failed to respond to the 1989 urban unrest because the issues of that movement affected them very little; he predicts that rural unrest will likely increase in the future in response to specifically rural grievances.

43. "Social Consequences of Private Business," Paper prepared for the Center for Chinese Studies Fall Regional Seminar, University of California at Berkeley, October 29, 1988, pp. 23–24. A revised version of the paper will appear in Deborah Davis and Ezra Vogel, eds., *Chinese Society on the Eve of Tiananmen: The Impact of Reform* (Cambridge: Harvard University Council on East Asian Studies, 1990). See also Gold's chapter in the present volume.

44. Pepper argues that the demonstrations of winter 1986–87 reflected an elite-manipulated deflection of student attention from their "real" concerns about the economic reforms to less central (for them) political ones; I do not find her argument wholly persuasive, however. See Suzanne Pepper, "Deng Xiaoping's Political and Economic Reforms and the Student Chinese Protests," Universities Field Staff International Reports no. 30, Asia, available from 260 Union Drive, Indianapolis, Indiana, 46202.

45. Allen S. Whiting presents the case for the anti-Japanese and nationalist aspects of these demonstrations. See "The Politics of Sino-Japanese Relations," in June Teufel Dreyer, ed., *Chinese Defense and Foreign Policy* (New York: Paragon House, 1989), pp. 142–48.

46. Student demands for democracy probably responded both to media discussions and to the speeches of prominent intellectuals. At the Science and Technology University in Hefei, where the 1986–87 student demonstrations began, the university vice-president, Fang Lizhi, had been calling for democratization of universities and the political system; students obviously responded to his actions. For excellent discussions of the 1986–87 events, see Suzanne Pepper, note 44, and Ruth Hayhoe, "China's Intellectuals in the World Community," unpublished manuscript, pp. 11–13.

47. *New York Times,* June 15, 1987.

48. *New York Times,* June 9, 1988.

49. *Chicago Sun-Times,* December 28, 1988; *New York Times,* January 4, 1989.

50. The autumn 1985 demonstrations specifically referred back to historical episodes, particularly the December 9, 1935, student protests against Japanese

imperialism and KMT oppression. See Pepper, note 44, p. 4. Edward Friedman argues that a form of reactionary chauvinism was involved in some of the student demonstrations of the mid- and late 1980s. See his chapter in the present volume.

51. For discussion of public opinion polls in the mid- to late 1980s, see Stanley Rosen's chapter in the present volume.

4

The Rise (and Fall) of Public Opinion in Post-Mao China

Stanley Rosen

Throughout the Communist world, party and government decisionmakers have turned to the public for support in their efforts to restructure stagnant economic and political institutions. Recognizing that policies for coping with complex societal problems cannot be effectively formulated—much less implemented—in the absence of feedback that accurately reflects public sentiment, reformist leaders have sought to mobilize popular opinion against a conservative opposition that remains wary of change.

To enable the public to play its designated supportive role in the reform process, authorities have gathered and made available a wealth of new information about socioeconomic conditions and problems and have tolerated—even encouraged—a variety of citizens' groups and "interests" to speak out. Those countries which have gone farthest down this road of political pluralization—such as Poland and Hungary—have already held or scheduled competitive elections.

The process of pluralization has occurred within a highly fluid, unstable political environment wherein Communist parties, increasingly under attack from civil society, have had to struggle to remain relevant. In the midst of epochal societal challenges to traditional communist legitimacy, intellectuals in general—and social scientists in particular—have been granted greater autonomy then ever before, and social research and public opinion polling have increasingly been used as guides to enlightened policy-making.

As the Chinese reform experience shows, however, opinion polling is often a double-edged sword. Initially, China's post-Mao leaders encouraged the employment of sophisticated social science methodologies to gauge popular sentiment; the result was a resounding success for Deng Xiaoping's reform coalition, as public enthusiasm played a positive role in facilitating the introduction of sweeping policy changes. Once legitimized as an important component of the political process, however, the public pulse required constant monitoring, and public demand for the tangible benefits of reform grew faster than the available supply. When popular expectations began to go unfulfilled, survey results turned sour, compelling Chinese leaders to reassess the public's role in the reform process.

The student occupation of Tiananmen Square from April to early June 1989 brought the opinion pollsters out in force.[1] In the aftermath of the military crackdown, however, those most influential in the development of opinion polling either were arrested, forced into hiding, or fled from China. The leadership's sober reassessment of the function of *vox populi* in a socialist society, which had started even before the spring demonstrations, was quickly accelerated, leaving the future of public opinion polling in the PRC in considerable doubt. In this chapter we examine the rise—and recent eclipse—of public opinion as a societal feedback mechanism in post-Mao China.

The Early Development of Chinese Social Research

The Chinese were relative latecomers in recognizing the utility of survey research and public opinion polling. Elsewhere in the Communist world the de-Stalinization movement of the mid-1950s had encouraged a reevaluation of the causes of economic and administrative failures. Particularly in Poland, followed later by the Soviet Union, there was grudging official recognition that the Communist party's claim to possess *a priori* knowledge of society's needs and aspirations was an insufficient basis on which to formulate policy, that a more critical analysis of communist practice was needed, and that empirical sociological research could play an important role.[2]

De-Stalinization had no such impact in China. Social investigation "with Chinese characteristics" had developed independently in the late 1920s and 1930s during the period of guerilla warfare. Using what he called a "panel discussion" method, Mao Zedong would travel to mountain villages in the heartland and interview a variety of local people. Based on such interviews a picture of Chinese social class structure was drawn, which in turn suggested appropriate revolutionary strategies and tactics.

In promoting the panel discussion method (later refined and elaborated as the "model" method), Chinese leaders were not necessarily concerned with scientific sampling or statistical averaging.[3] In Maoist China, social engineering was considered to be independent of and more valuable than a mere depiction of current reality. Advanced or positive models—e.g., Dazhai in agriculture and Daqing in industry—were heavily publicized in order to demonstrate what was possible and desirable. While Western-trained social scientists could reasonably argue that the models were unrepresentative and reflected an obvious subjective bias, supporters countered that social conditions were constantly changing—and improving—and that model research was thus sensitive to emergent trends and potentialities.

With such a strong legacy of support for the classic Maoist approach to analyzing social problems, it is not surprising that survey research was introduced into post-Mao China rather tardily, and largely from the outside—paralleling the revival of the social sciences more generally.[4] It was not until the early 1980s that survey research information became available

in the PRC in the form of invited lectures and translated writings by prominent foreign scholars. The dissemination and legitimation of new sociological
research methods were facilitated by the appearance of signed articles by
leading Chinese social scientists with powerful political connections, such as
economist Yu Guangyuan.

Concurrently, important organizational and personnel changes were occurring. The Chinese Academy of Social Sciences (CASS), founded in 1977,
was undergoing expansion, with many new research institutes established
between 1979 and 1981. At the same time, a crash program was undertaken
to identify and recruit Chinese social scientists; for example, the Shanghai
Academy of Social Sciences located some 150 individuals with some—often
quite rudimentary—social science experience and made them academy researchers. Beginning in 1982, Chinese social scientists were encouraged to
establish direct contacts with their Western and overseas Chinese counterparts. In May of that year, the first large-scale meeting of Chinese sociologists
was held in Wuhan, attended by some 200 researchers, including a group of
overseas Chinese sociologists from North America. While support for the
traditional Maoist methods of social investigation by no means completely
disappeared after this time, Chinese survey research subsequently began to
develop characteristics familiar to students of other "developed" socialist
societies.

Survey Research and Public Opinion in Communist Systems

Opinion surveys in communist systems serve many purposes.[5] *Inter alia,*
they provide practical information for decision makers—particularly about
"negative phenomena"; they also facilitate the identification of citizen preferences regarding future societal development; provide information about the
level of "mass consciousness"; reveal citizen reactions to specific government
policies; expose the mistakes and malfeasances of government officials;
stimulate citizens' sense of civic duty and interest in social affairs; measure
the achievement of societal goals; and provide citizens with a legitimate
channel for expressing grievances and opinions.

Not surprisingly, many Western writers see communist regimes using polls
not so much to measure public opinion as to create and manipulate it; not
so much to gather information as to present "correct" attitudes for emulation
and to overcome mass apathy. Indeed, some writers have questioned whether
Communist leaders really want a complete and objective picture of mass
thinking, noting that "statistically valid results of polling might cast doubts
on—even contradict—the official assertions of monolithic unanimity in support of the party and its policies."[6] Others note that Soviet leaders have
managed to avoid such pitfalls in the past by fostering a group of "ideological

sociologists" who are willing and able to manipulate the design and implementation of survey research in order to generate data that tells leaders what they want to hear—and what they want the population to hear. Among the research techniques favored by such ideological sociologists are closed questions with biased alternatives and questions about abstract topics—such as attitudes toward work or peace.[7]

One may accept that opinion surveys are largely manipulated while still recognizing the party's need to understand the views of the masses. Alex Inkeles put the matter well almost forty years ago, when he noted that for Soviet leaders the main purpose in promoting public opinion research "is not to cater to public opinion but to move it along . . . as rapidly as possible without undermining your popular support. But one cannot determine his own pace, according to this formula, unless he knows the state of mass thinking."[8]

The appeal to public opinion in communist systems has generally been strongest during periods of reform or political change. In the Soviet Georgian Republic, for example, the reformist leader (now foreign minister) Eduard Shevardnadze, after assuming power in 1972, sought to consolidate his support by arguing that the bribe taking and cronyism characteristic of the previous regime were the result of leaders ignoring public opinion. In order to correct this deficiency and to obtain accurate feedback on official policies, a Public Opinion Council was created in 1975, under the auspices of the Central Committee of the Georgian Communist party.[9]

The early years of the Gorbachev era have demonstrated at the highest political levels the new Soviet leader's commitment to the accurate measurement of Soviet social attitudes and opinions.[10] Under the new conditions, collection of trivial or lacquered statistics—an endemic tendency under previous leaders—is strongly discouraged, and professional sociologists are expected to play an important role; by the same token, many ideological sociologists who had been prominent under Brezhnev now find themselves unable to find outlets for their published work.[11]

Survey Research with Chinese Characteristics

Much of what has been suggested for the Soviet Union under Gorbachev applies also to China. While relatively crude and unsophisticated survey research began to appear in the early years of post-Mao reform, the development of more sophisticated, scientific public opinion studies only took place in the mid-1980s, when the reform program faced a series of problems whose solution required a comprehensive understanding of Chinese social reality.

Much of the survey literature generated and disseminated in China in the last half of the 1980s served primarily political or educational aims, e.g., to demonstrate widespread public support for particular policies. Survey results disseminated in this form often were severely truncated, reflecting the didactic "message" the survey was meant to convey to the paper's readership (e.g., general public acceptance of a bankruptcy law; gradual development of a "civilized, healthy, and scientific lifestyle"; or public approval of price reform, to cite some salient examples).[12]

It would be a mistake, however, to focus attention exclusively on the didactic, self-congratulatory function of surveys. Equally interesting is the manner in which a variety of different social and political groups used survey research to pursue their own particular policy agendas.[13] This was possible, in part, because of the unique Chinese system of information dissemination. In the PRC survey results are disseminated in a variety of ways, including specialized newspapers and journals, and, most importantly, through a complicated system of "internal" (neibu) publications, many of which can be found in Chinese libraries and research institutes, though remaining unavailable to the general public and to those abroad.

Surveys appearing in specialized publications have sometimes reflected the views of a particular interest group on an issue still under debate, while those disseminated in internal publications have, in certain instances, actually sought to refute or question an official policy. In this respect, China's system of internal publications appeared to permit greater freedom and contention than was true of other communist systems. The Chinese system also has permitted the posing of questions which might otherwise not be raised at all.[14]

It should be noted that the freedom to employ surveys for partisan policy ends by no means implied that survey results necessarily influenced policy decisions. In part, this was because the meaning of survey results was often far from self-evident; results of this type were subject to interpretative "spin" applied by advocates of different policies. Moreover, those groups which had little influence within the bureaucracy or in the corridors of elite power were sometimes compelled to use surveys as an alternative to more conventional means of exerting influence. Thus, when faced with the likely adoption of an unwanted policy, weak political actors could resort to surveys to demonstrate the putative unpopularity of the policy.

CESRRI and the Rise of Public Opinion as a Tool of National Policy

In the late 1980s the majority of Chinese surveys appeared either in open or in internal specialized journals and newspapers. Primarily local studies carried out on a small budget, such surveys generally appear to have had little impact on national policy. Officially, many of these surveys did not even qualify as "public opinion." The latter term began to be used widely in the Chinese press only after the Thirteenth Party Congress, held in October 1987. At that meeting, then General Secretary Zhao Ziyang emphasized the need for public opinion to play a "supervisory role." This marked the first time the issue had been openly addressed by the top party leadership. Thereafter, the Chinese press began to distinguish earlier surveys and opinion polling from more recent examples, criticizing the early polls, *inter alia,* for "their unscientific framework and method of investigation, limited focus on only one system or one unit, and limited coverage, so that all these polls had little general social significance and did not attract general social attention."[15]

The breakthrough, according to one account, came with the establishment of several public opinion research centers in 1986 and 1987, and the concomitant publication in the official media of the results of large-scale opinion surveys relating to political and economic reform. The origin of these surveys is traceable to key political decisions taken in 1984, to the public response to these decisions, and to the work of the Chinese Economic System Reform Research Institute (CESRRI), under the State Council.

Embarking on a series of complex and controversial urban economic reforms in 1984, party reformers required a more sophisticated understanding of the views of the masses. By the fall of that year, decentralization of decision-making powers had begun to produce big deficits in foreign trade, excessive local investment, high inflation, and other alarming imbalances, all of which created "an uneasy public mood" toward various reform measures.[16] It was in these uncertain conditions that CESRRI, founded by Zhao Ziyang in 1984 as a think tank to provide guidance to government leaders on the strategic planning of economic reform, was authorized to conduct a series of large-scale national surveys. Objectives included ascertaining the actual situation of urban economic reform, public response to price reform, attitudes of youth toward social and economic affairs, and citizens' views on the subject of governmental functions and operations. Conducted between February and November 1985, the project brought together 21 units, including ministries, research institutes, colleges, and universities; a workforce of 447 people was employed, including statisticians, university postgraduates and undergraduates; 14 million items of data were collected; and 156 reports were produced, totaling 1.3 million words. Not surprisingly, the policy conclusions drawn from the CESRRI study constituted a staunch defense of the urban reform program.[17]

Senior reform economists such as Wu Jinglian added prestige to the surveys by contrasting their own, ostensibly "scientific" research results with the results of those employing more traditional techniques, whose research was allegedly filled with "superficial, empty points . . . [often] based on single facts." CESRRI head Chen Yizi suggested that the old techniques were no match for the new methodology of social science:

First of all, we must combine investigation based on "typical examples" with the sampling method . . . Individual cases, no matter how rational, cannot be universally applied. The traditional method of analyzing a typical example is not enough for a scientific survey. Scientific sampling must be employed at the same time. Second, we must combine the investigation at one point in time with investigation over a period of time. Finally, we must promote comprehensive, interdisciplinary research.[18]

Chen's views received political legitimation in a widely publicized speech by then Vice-Premier Wan Li to the National Forum on Research in "Soft Sciences" in July 1986. Wan pointed out that in the past, the use of qualitative analysis based on "typical" cases, particularly as drawn from the personal investigations or experiences of individual leaders, had caused great damage to China. Nor, he argued, could reliance on the "mass line" (i.e., soliciting the raw, unsystematized views of the masses) serve as a rational guide to decision making in a complex, modern society. Rather, policy-making should rely on advanced, scientific quantitative methods, combining insights drawn from such fields as systems engineering, operations research, information theory, and cybernetics. Finally, recognizing that the intelligentsia might be reluctant to challenge powerful interests, Wan called for the adoption of legislative measures to grant legal protection to those engaged in policy-related research and to guarantee their relative independence from political forces.[19]

This and subsequent CESRRI efforts—fourteen large-scale social surveys were conducted through the end of 1986—linked the use of survey research to national policy. The surveys had a major impact on young social science researchers in Beijing, many of whom had been a part of CESRRI efforts. In quick succession, several new centers for public opinion research were set up—several of them privately funded.

The CESRRI surveys demonstrated how the power of social science could be harnessed to serve the reform program. But therein lay a dilemma for the CCP: by legitimating public opinion polling and survey research, party reformers had created conditions under which these powerful tools might some day pose a threat to their own program. For one thing, the decentralized development of polling, including the growth of private opinion research centers, combined with the complicated system of specialized and internal publications described earlier, made it difficult for party leaders to exercise tight control over the content, conclusions, and dissemination of opinion surveys. Second, the widespread media publicity given to the proreform findings of the early CESRRI surveys triggered rising—and often unrealistic—expectations for improved living standards among the urban populace. Rising expectations, in turn, bred rising discontent, thereby eroding popular support for the reforms.

With the *vox populi* having been legitimated as an arbiter on reform issues, it became necessary to seek continued validation from the same source. The difficulties of maintaining strong mass support for the economic reforms come through clearly in the fourteen longitudinal surveys conducted by CESRRI. According to members of the survey team, there were three stages in the evolution of mass attitudes.[20] The first stage followed the October 1984 party plenum at which the urban reforms were adopted, and was marked by nationwide enthusiasm. In this stage the mass media fueled the aspirations of urban dwellers, who embraced reform as a route to enhanced income. Significantly, the media avoided any discussion of possible complications ahead. The second stage—from early 1985 to the last quarter of that year—centered mainly on price reform. Although the primary finding of opinion polls in this stage was an increase in public dissatisfaction, particularly over recent rises in commodity prices, widespread belief that the reforms were yielding positive results convinced many people that their aspirations for higher income were justified, and that an expanding market orientation would further enhance their social mobility.

After the last quarter of 1985, the reform program became stalemated. This third stage witnessed a "pluralism" of both discontent and desire. In addition to public dissatisfaction over rising prices, surveys showed a mounting tide of opposition to such things as cadres abusing power for personal gain, employers giving jobs only to relatives, the inability to choose employment freely, inequalities in pay, an imperfect legislative system, and so forth. Similarly, reform hopes were no longer limited to rising income, but covered a wide variety of political, social, and economic issues. Throughout 1986, inequality of opportunity registered as the public's leading complaint, intensifying with each successive survey. For example, a February 1986 survey revealed that only 29.3 percent of the people felt that the reforms offered equal opportunities to all. At the same time, the surveys revealed a steadily increasing disparity among different social groups with regard to aspirations and attitudes toward the reforms.

Subsequent studies of urban residents by the China Social Survey System—established as an arm of CESRRI in 1987—show a continuation of these trends.[21] For example, in November 1986, 73.8 percent of those surveyed expressed dissatisfaction with inflation, rising to 79.9 percent in May 1987, 83.2 percent in October, and 92.1 percent in May 1988. Moreover, the perception of growing inequality of opportunity exacerbated social contradictions and convinced people that society was unjust. For example, researchers noted a sharp rise in popular complaints concerning price gouging by individual entrepreneurs; government cadres were similarly scored for using their authority to profiteer in the sale of goods and materials, enjoy preferential rights in contracting to run or in leasing enterprises, establish profit-making companies, and so forth. On the other hand, workers—particularly those in state enterprises—and most intellectuals had no such opportunities.[22]

So long as the CESRRI surveys continued to show public support for reform, they played a positive role in pushing the reform agenda forward, blunting the opposition of more conservative elements. As the survey results turned mixed, however, they became more ambiguous and less self-evident, requiring an interpretation which became inseparable from larger political and economic agendas. Although students of public opinion have long argued that the linkage between mass opinion and public policy is indirect at best, it is instructive to examine the reactions of certain key players to the mounting crisis of public confidence in the Chinese reform program.

The Problem of Partial Reform

To CESRRI researchers, the survey results indicated the disadvantages of partial reform. They traced mass dissatisfaction to fundamental structural problems, arguing that public discontent was inevitable and would remain a long-term hazard. While continuing to call for gradual price reform, they saw the more basic obstacle as inequality of opportunity. The solution, they argued, was to strip officials of their power to monopolize resources and factors of production and to encourage privatization, gradually creating a new, more equitable economic order. Noting that the surveys revealed that in those areas where reforms had gone furthest, where controls had been relaxed, where free choice had become possible—for example, the city of Guangzhou—the people were less likely to worry about rising prices, they also called for an acceleration of reforms in the personnel, wage, and social security systems, and for the formation of a labor market. At the same time, they warned in March 1988 that "public opinion polls . . . clearly showed a resurging concern about the price problem among city dwellers," suggesting a number of measures—including close consultation with the public on price reform policies and the establishment of consumer organizations—to eliminate insecurity and prevent "price panic."[23]

Such reasoned arguments, based on a close reading of years of survey results, were subsequently nullified by what appears to have been a reversion to policy-making more typical of the Maoist years. In August 1988, when the annual inflation rate had reached an all-time high of 19 percent, and when some goods had gone up almost 500 percent, the party without warning—and reportedly at the insistence of Deng Xiaoping—announced a five-year plan to decontrol virtually all prices in China. Almost immediately there were nationwide bank runs and panic buying on a scale not seen since the Communists came to power in 1949. By late September the government backtracked, announcing a price freeze and a two-year slowdown in reforms in order to "rectify the economy." Zhao Ziyang, already under attack from conservatives because of rampant inflation, was reportedly forced to make a self-criticism.[24]

CESRRI itself became a partial casualty of the economic turmoil. Because of its strong advocacy of decentralization and a market economy, it could not escape criticism. In fact, CESRRI's influence had started to decline in 1987, when the more cautious Li Peng replaced Zhao Ziyang as premier. Subsequently, Li became the head of CESSRI's parent organization, the State Commission for Restructuring the Economy. The new premier quickly distanced himself from CESSRI, relying instead for advice on an in-house organ, the newly established Research Office of the State Council.[25] With the creation of rival opinion research organizations, the debate over reform policy in effect became a battle of the think tanks.

Because of the decentralization and relative autonomy of the Chinese media, CESRRI remained active in promoting reformist views even after losing the confidence of Li Peng. In January 1989, Shanghai's *World Economic Herald*, the nation's premier outlet for liberal reform ideas, which had come under criticism from central leaders for its dissident editorial line, began a series of high-profile articles based on interviews with leading CESRRI researchers, designed to keep their ideas before the public.[26]

The Rise of Private Polling Institutes

Despite the decline in its influence on national economic policy by late 1988, CESRRI's early success had been responsible for spawning a number of other public opinion institutes, almost all of which remained active until the military crackdown of June 4, 1989. By mid-1988, there were at least fifteen such organizations in Beijing alone, including three well-known private organizations and several that could be called "semiprivate."[27]

The new public opinion institutes had several points in common. First, their staff personnel were predominantly young and well educated. For example, the average age of the members of China Social Survey was below thirty, with the oldest thirty-seven; most were college graduates. Second, a number of those who took the lead in establishing private polling institutes had played a direct role in China's recent, turbulent political history. One institute head, for example, had been the top Red Guard leader of Beijing's high school students during the Cultural Revolution; another, the son of a senior cadre, had become nationally famous as a result of his activities in the 1976 Tiananmen incident. Both had been arrested and imprisoned during the 1970s. Their complex political histories at times hindered the development of smooth working relations between the pollsters and various governmental organs. Third, funding was a problem for all nongovernmental institutes. As one interviewee noted in the summer of 1988: "Two years ago, perhaps the main difficulty was political; now it is financial." Aside from expense money provided by contracted projects, several institutes had raised money by running businesses. The Opinion Research Center of China was in the best position to do so since its parent unit was fully supportive of its efforts and contributed RMB 500,000 a year to its work. All the new institutes were actively seeking joint projects with foreigners, and at least one institute head had been given official permission to establish a public opinion foundation, to be funded by foreign and domestic capital.

To maintain their independence, several institutes rejected funding offers from the government. Following the Thirteenth Party Congress, Zhao Ziyang authorized the social group under the Research Office on Political Structural Reform of the party Central Committee to meet with specialists in public opinion who would conduct polls to help the central authorities better understand Chinese society, provide an outlet for public discontent, and aid in policy decisions. Two nongovernmental organs were chosen to conduct polls for the government, with Zhao suggesting that "when necessary, the government may allocate funds to these organs." Both groups responded that they did not need government subsidies, just protection to ensure their safety in social investigations.[28]

The more rigorous opinion centers steadily improved their methodological techniques. For example, in the course of the fourteen social surveys conducted by CESRRI, a number of sampling techniques were tried. In the beginning, researchers placed advertisements in newspapers, which were to be mailed in. They found this to be least reliable in terms of both rate and quality of response. Since newspapers are generally sent directly to work units, rather than individuals, it was impossible to obtain a representative sample. Respondents were primarily intellectuals or cadres, who felt intensely enough about the issues to mail in their questionnaires. The initial solution to this problem was to distribute questionnaires through mass organizations, such as the trade union, women's association, and youth league. This also produced unrepresentative results, however, since the distribution and collection of forms was handled by organization cadres and survey participants were often hesitant to make their true feelings known to such people. To overcome this difficulty, local university students were employed to canvas door to door. While this method was the most satisfactory, the expense of training, transporting, and maintaining a large staff of student pollsters made this the most costly method. Still, door-to-door surveys became the method of choice for those institutes that could afford to maintain their own national investigation networks, such as the China Social Survey System and the Opinion Research Center of China.

The private centers had a complex relationship with officialdom, one which sheds interesting light upon the partial development of privatization in post-Mao China. Had the opinion institutes been completely independent from governmental sponsorship, they would not have been able to function.

Legally, each private institute had to be "registered" (*guakao*) with a state organization. CESRRI had at times served this purpose, but so had the State Science and Technology Commission, the newspaper *Economic Daily*, and other agencies. Such organizational linkages varied in their benefits and costs. In one case, after CESRRI had severed its affiliation to a private institute over a political matter, it was replaced by another state unit which charged a fee of RMB 10,000 for the privilege.

What the private polling agency received from the *guakao* relationship, of course, was legitimacy. A governmental affiliation made it easier to conduct survey research at the local level; indeed, the official link was indispensable in China's highly bureaucratized society. For example, even to use the term "China" in a unit's name, or to establish branch agencies in other cities, governmental approval was needed. Without such bona fides, it would be difficult to distribute questionnaires, respondents would be reluctant to be surveyed, university graduates would decline to accept job allocations to work there, and few organizations would initiate the all-important projects from which a portion of the operating and administrative expenses derive. When CESRRI broke off its connection in the case mentioned above, the number of projects dropped drastically and staff size quickly declined from over seventy to under twenty.

Even with the *guakao* tie, private institutes faced a series of political and economic problems. First, survey topics either came from a governmental unit—which paid expenses—or, if self-initiated, had to be approved from above. This often created pressure to produce "favorable" results. In one case, a sensitive survey on public reaction to the Thirteenth Party Congress, including questions on the prestige of the party, had been verbally approved by a senior official in the governmental affiliate. However, when the survey was conducted on the streets it drew the attention and ire of a suspicious public security bureau, which complained to the affiliate that the polling agency had "upset public order." The affiliate, under pressure, denied giving its permission and the head of the public opinion institute was disciplined.[29]

Public security personnel in general were uncooperative with the pollsters. Even CESRRI researchers complained that investigators in their national network, armed with official letters of introduction, often confronted public security bureaus that refused to provide the necessary household registration (*hukou*) information needed to select an accurate sample. Such problems were multiplied for nongovernmental public opinion organizations.

In addition to conflicts over public security, private institutes had difficulty gaining the access necessary to do "political" surveys. For example, several organizations planned to do a survey of the attitudes of the delegates to the National People's Congress in 1988, but could not gain entrance to the meeting hall. One agency appeared to find an imaginative solution. Relying on friends who had secured press passes issued by news agencies, they sought to obtain help in distributing the questionnaires. The day before the meeting, however, an official directive was enacted specifically prohibiting such access. Finally, again using personal connections (*guanxi*), they obtained the addresses of the delegates and mailed out the questionnaires.

Dissemination of the results of polling was generally beyond the control of the public opinion institutes. On projects contracted with government agencies, the results were simply turned over to the contracting agency; researchers noted that these official organs were generally only interested in "satisfactory" results. One survey, for example, examined the attitudes of outsiders toward Beijing. Jointly funded by the Propaganda Department of the Beijing Municipal Party Committee, Beijing Television (which was filming a documentary on the subject), and *Beijing Daily*, all negative findings were excised from the published accounts. Thus, while newspapers frequently reported survey results from private polling institutes, they were highly selective and often misleading.

For those conducting political surveys, there were both spoken and unspoken guidelines. Only rarely would an intrepid pollster proceed in the face of official opposition. The first session of the Seventh National People's Congress (NPC) held in March–April 1988 provides a good example of acceptable and unacceptable survey topics. Several agencies conducted officially approved surveys of the views of NPC delegates. The joint survey by the Institute of Journalism under CASS and the Capital Press Society on attitudes toward China's much-discussed press law was given broad media coverage, particularly within their own specialized journals. The results—along with a similar poll of delegates to the Seventh Chinese People's Political Consultative Conference—showed that an overwhelming majority of the delegates supported an expansion of socialist press freedom, open publication of a draft press law to allow free popular discussion, and so forth. These findings supported the position of working journalists and liberal reformers alike.[30]

Even more widely reported was a survey of the aspirations and views of 1,172 NPC delegates by the Opinion Research Center of China. Although some potentially interesting issues were addressed in the survey, when truncated official press reports mentioned them at all there was little discussion or commentary on the implications of the findings. Rather, the reports emphasized that the delegates, as the headline in the overseas edition of *People's Daily* put it, "affirm the achievements of reform, and are optimistic about the future."[31]

The surveys discussed above presented relatively few problems for authorities. However, a number of private polling agencies were more interested in the reaction of the masses to the new leaders chosen at the NPC. Since public criticism of individual leadership performance has always been a forbidden subject prior to official evaluation, they were warned that this topic was unacceptable. One agency which had already prepared its questionnaire backed down under pressure.[32] Another pollster ignored official warnings and conducted a local, nonsystematic survey of public reaction in Beijing to a televised press conference given by Premier Li Peng in April 1988, to which foreign reporters had been invited. Asked to rate the premier's performance, 30.4 percent of the ninety respondents in this survey (most of whom were relatively young, urban, and well educated) rated the premier's press conference as "dull and insipid" or "disappointing." Fully 40 percent evaluated Li Peng's theoretical understanding as only "average," while almost two-thirds (64.8 percent) rated his ability to respond to questions as "average" or "poor." Finally, a whopping 72.2 percent of the respondents viewed the premier's personal charisma as "average" or "poor."[33] Judged by traditional Chinese standards of ritualized public obeisance to higher authority, these results—however unsystematic—suggest that more than a full year before he declared martial law in Beijing, China's premier already had a very poor public image.

Interestingly, despite the strong negative findings of this survey, its sponsors put the best possible face on their results for the benefit of readers at higher levels. They thus argued that a mathematical analysis of the data showed that Premier Li's performance had been given "relatively high marks" by the public. They then suggested that this first open evaluation of a leader's performance by the public had been intended as a contribution to the democratization of political life. Not surprisingly, when results of the survey were sent to the State Council, as required by government regulations, no official response was forthcoming.[34]

Public Opinion as a Double-Edged Sword

In the course of engaging in social, economic, and political reforms, communist leaders have found it necessary to understand the public mood in order to mobilize the masses in support of the reform agenda. At the Thirteenth Party Congress Zhao Ziyang went further, calling for public supervision of party and government work. However, when the reforms encountered problems, and public reaction became mixed, even unfavorable, party leaders recognized the inherent dangers of such an open reliance on the public's mood. One party journal referred to the "double-edged nature" of public opinion, which has a "power [that] can be . . . enormous or dreadful." Retreating to the standard Chinese definition of democracy—one that posits a fundamental harmony of interests between the people and their rulers— the journal noted that when public opinion operates "with one heart and one mind, [the public] can build a town; they can also confuse right and wrong."[35] The journal went on to note that complaints about inflation (estimated by Western economists at more than 30 percent in China's cities in 1988) and unequal social distribution, as well as public unrest over party corruption and unhealthy social practices, had produced "anger and helplessness" among the masses, some of whom "expect too much of reform." To prevent widespread demoralization, the article suggested that a distinction must be made between "popular opinion" and "mass opinion." The former was said to involve a common will rooted in perceptions of the public interest (roughly analogous to Rousseau's "general will"), while the latter ostensibly stood for the accumulated wills of various different societal interests and interest groups (roughly analogous to the Western concept of group pluralism). The former type was officially judged to be "fair and correct," and thus worthy of support, while the latter allegedly contained certain "negative and unhealthy" components that required higher-level guidance.[36]

With group interests thus officially stigmatized, reformers had a difficult time explaining and justifying policies that impacted differentially on specific groups and strata. Illustrating the difficulty of legitimizing interest group competition and conflict in a society where stress has perennially been placed on the unitary nature of the public good, one article presented a somewhat confusing account of China's shifting social structure in the initial period of reform. Noting that the group structure of Chinese society was subject to "continuous reorganization" in this "turbulent new period," the article argued for the necessity—while conceding the extreme difficulty—of "creating a climate of public opinion which is appropriate to different social interest groups."[37] Elaborating on this theme, a commentary in *People's Daily* noted that what is good for some is not necessarily good for others, and that the development of reform had thus "encroached on the actual interests of quite a few people." Warning against the danger of paying undue attention to partial or one-sided interests, the commentary retreated to the traditional litany of the mass line, concluding that "without the masses' understanding and support, any reformer will fail."

Zhao Ziyang, in a 1989 interview with the American economist Milton Friedman, justified the decision to put off price reform on the grounds that the Chinese people were still "psychologically . . . unable to endure such changes" in an inflationary environment.[38] China's official media, acknowledging the existence of a crisis over economic reforms, admitted that "it is understandable that the government's plan for price and wage reforms over five years . . . led to some misunderstanding among most citizens." At the same time, the crisis was viewed as "a necessary test for Chinese who must change their way of thinking to adopt to the conditions of a market economy."[39]

As socioeconomic discontent mounted, the party talked less of supervision by the public and more of educating and molding public opinion. The contradiction became particularly sharp on the issue of press reform. "Liberal" newspapers and journals had given wide publicity to Premier Li Peng's reaffirmation, under questioning at the 1988 NPC press conference, that "the government welcomes criticism and supervision by public opinion." Thereafter, the liberal media had published a wide range of unorthodox views on reform, calling attention, *inter alia*, to official corruption and other shortcomings.[40] However, under new guidelines introduced in late 1988, the media were admonished to concentrate less on shortcomings. Several newspapers, including *China Youth News*, the *Economic Daily*, and the *World Economic Herald*, were criticized for "singing an opposite tune" to that of the party central leadership. In a similar vein, Politburo standing committee member Hu Qili, quoting Zhao Ziyang, warned that "if the mass media do not change their behavior, the reforms will get nowhere." Several offending newspapers were subsequently targeted for "rectification."[41] These were significant developments because liberal newspapers had been strong supporters of the democratizing tendencies which had contributed to the rise of nongovernmental public opinion institutes. Informants at these newspapers and at the opinion institutes have cited the rejuvenation of leadership groups in the media and government as a key factor in allowing surveys to be conducted and published on sensitive political issues.

The party faced an additional problem in its open stress on the mobilizational function of public opinion. With the legitimation of public opinion surveys, a stage of "polling mania" often appears. Surveys are conducted by anyone wishing to show his sophistication and modernity. This tends to cheapen the value of the polls and gradually leads to declining interest—and eventually to alienation—on the part of the populace.[42] Indeed, this began to occur in China. On one occasion, a poll of scientific and technical personnel in Jilin province was given a "cold reception." One-third of the intended respondents refused to fill in the questionnaires, some drew "a tiger's head and a snake's tail" on the form, and many simply expressed anger that the repeated loud calls to improve the situation of intellectuals had been empty promises.[43] In a few extreme cases, polls were apparently used for more chilling forms of social control. In 1988 the office of the Dalai Lama in India wrote to Chinese authorities to complain that twenty Tibetan monks had been arrested after being entrapped by filling in a questionnaire asking if Chinese officials should be removed from Tibet.[44]

In the party's attempt to contain the "mass opinion" of interest groups while mobilizing "popular opinion" in support of regime goals, it faced an uphill battle. The imperatives of economic reform created an increasingly heterogeneous society, marked by decentralization, rampant commercialism, privatization, even internationalization—all contributing to the erosion of social control by the state. Not only were some groups better placed to benefit from the reforms than others, but it was also no longer possible to treat any social or occupational group as an undifferentiated whole. The emerging social structure presented an opportunity for new alliances among previously isolated social groups; thus, for example, dissident democracy activists began to be funded by newly affluent private entrepreneurs.[45] In effect, the party was seeking to unify public opinion and harmonize political interests at a time when economic and social forces were pulling society *away* from the state.

By the winter of 1988–89, China's economic stresses and uncertainties had contributed to an ideological atmosphere in which various "leftist" and "rightist" forces were given access to the open press. Some well-known personalities of Cultural Revolution vintage—e.g., Wang Li, a theorist who once enjoyed the patronage of Jiang Qing—were interviewed, and there were signs of emerging nostalgia for the "certainties" of the Maoist era. From the other extreme, some young theorists in Beijing, disillusioned by the failures of the pro-democracy movement in recent years, forcefully argued in the official press that the crisis called for strong central leadership in the hands of committed reformers like Zhao Ziyang; otherwise, they averred, conservative political forces could use the current economic difficulties as a pretext to abandon market reforms and return to extreme central planning and political repression. Dubbed the "new authoritarians," these theorists pointed to South Korea and Taiwan to support their argument that authoritarian regimes with vibrant market economies would eventually evolve toward democracy.[46]

By late 1988 there was a widespread public perception that China's leaders lacked answers to the country's most pressing economic problems, with some opinion polls registering dramatic drops in public confidence. One survey of Shanghai residents found that whereas in May 1988, 58.8 percent of the people felt the reforms had a "clear purpose," by October the number had dropped to 20.4 percent.[47] Another poll showed that 58.3 percent of respondents had "very little confidence" in the success of the government's plan to lower inflation. The party had discovered that linking the forward progress of the reform agenda to a diverse—and at times mercurial—public plebiscite had placed them on the back of a tiger; once aboard, there could be no gentle dismounting.

The Tiananmen Crackdown and the
Future of Public Opinion

The regime's loss of social control in the fifty days of "turmoil" from April 15 to June 3, 1989, was, in the very short term, a boon to pollsters. Both official and private agencies were active in taking the public pulse. The limited survey results which have been made available reveal a public very sympathetic to student demands, particularly by the latter half of May.[48] In fact, one day before the declaration of martial law on May 20 an official newspaper ran the results of its own highly unscientific survey as the lead story, coupling its findings of widespread public support for the demonstrations to a plea for the leadership to meet the student demands.[49]

After the military crackdown began on June 3–4, public opinion institutes were quickly targeted by the hardliners in command. At CESRRI, the leaders of the survey research section, who had enthusiastically engaged in polling activities during the fifty days, were among the first to be arrested. After Chen Yizi, the institute's director, escaped to Paris, additional personnel were detained. By late November 1989, eleven members of the institute were under arrest. While CESRRI had not been shut down, its members were engaged in self-criticism under the supervision of a work team.[50] Chen Ziming, head of the private Beijing Social and Economic Research Center—parent organization of the Opinion Research Center of China—was arrested along with another key member of the center, Wang Juntao, after four months on the run. As of this writing the center continues to operate but has temporarily limited its activities to market research. Leading members of the center either were arrested, went underground, or escaped the country.

Despite the hardliners' repressive measures, some pollsters remained cautiously optimistic. For one thing, it seemed reasonably clear that only those individuals with close personal ties to fallen political leaders like Zhao Ziyang (e.g., Chen Yizi) or who actively promoted the "turmoil" through their links with dissident student leaders (e.g., Chen Ziming and Wang Juntao) had been singled out for serious punishment by the government. Lower-ranking members of CESRRI's survey arm were not generally subject to detention; some wrote to colleagues abroad stating that they wanted to continue working on international collaborative projects already initiated, and suggesting that their superiors might soon be released from detention.[51]

Some polling activity actually continued in the aftermath of the June 4 crackdown. In one remarkable case, *Beijing Youth Daily* in October reported on a poll conducted among 1,225 Beijing workers in which "many people" complained that some individuals had been wrongly arrested and beaten during the immediate aftermath of the "rebellion," and that detainees faced unfair trials and excessive sentences.[52] Ironically, the government itself has used the results of earlier surveys among university students to explain why the "rebellion" occurred and to justify the need for a stepped-up program of political and ideological education in the schools.[53]

While it appears that opinion polling will continue, it is likely to be subjected to much tighter political and ideological scrutiny in the future. Articles published in the Chinese press in the latter half of 1989 suggested new guidelines for polling, in effect redefining and circumscribing its role. The official post-Tiananmen assessment of the proper role of public opinion was most clearly articulated in an August article published in *China Youth Daily*.[54] The authors first noted that many Beijing citizens were refusing to accept the party's line that "a small handful" of bad elements could have mobilized so many people to take to the streets. Indeed, the authors reported, the demonstrations were commonly viewed as reflecting the "popular will." This alleged "misunderstanding" of public opinion was said to have stemmed from Zhao Ziyang's mistakes, which prevented the population from differentiating between "those who represent the popular will [*minxin*] and those who defile public opinion [*minyi*]." In Rousseauian fashion, the authors distinguished between these two concepts so that "those who in the past muddleheadedly took part in false or even counterrevolutionary public opinion" might be enabled to correct their misconceptions. The "popular will" was said to have four essential characteristics: it must have majority support; it must be in the public interest; it is subject to restrictions from leaders who have the public trust; and it is susceptible to being misled as well as being guided onto the correct path. Thus, although the use of public opinion polling was said to have "definite value," it could nevertheless, if not subject to proper orientational constraints, easily "cause people to be taken in." And in a rather chilling conclusion reminiscent of the Cultural Revolution, the authors warned that class struggle continued to exist in China and that in such a situation enemies hiding among the people would often claim to represent "public opinion" as a cover to deceive honest citizens.

In the final analysis, the future of opinion polling in China will depend on the regime's response to more fundamental problems, e.g., on the political steps taken to deal with the crisis over reform. The economic and ideological problems identified in surveys conducted prior to the 1989 demonstrations were, if anything, exacerbated in the months following the June crackdown. Thus, for example, factory managers told foreign visitors in the fall of 1989 that the new economic retrenchment program had cut severely into bonus payments, leading to heightened worker apathy and lower productivity; scattered reports of labor unrest and sabotage continued throughout the winter of 1989–90.

More worrisome still was the fact that China's hardline leaders confronted an urban populace that was at best indifferent, and at worst openly hostile. Faced with a clear lack of public credibility—at least in Beijing—the government openly acknowledged its inability to persuade citizens that the military crackdown had been necessary; the government also encountered great difficulty in attempting to assuage widespread public contempt for official corruption, an issue that had proven crucial in bringing large crowds to the streets in May of 1989. Given these lingering problems of public delegitimation, it is hardly surprising that the December 1989 popular uprising in Bucharest, which overthrew the Romanian communist regime and executed its leader, Nicolae Ceausescu, was greeted with signs of alarm by Chinese government and party leaders.[55]

Ironically, the capacity of China's leaders to rebuild an effective, supportive constituency among a skeptical citizenry will ultimately depend, in considerable measure, on their ability to obtain—and respond appropriately to—an accurate, objective reading of the public pulse. In view of the gross official distortions of reality that occurred in the aftermath of the June crackdown, however, it is by no means clear that such unvarnished feedback will soon be feasible in China.

Notes and References

1. Polls concerning attitudes of Beijing citizens toward student demonstrations are reported in *Beijing Qingnian Bao* (hereafter, *BJQNB*), May 19, 1989, p. 1; and *China Information* (Leiden) 4, no. 1 (Summer 1989), pp. 94–124.

2. Emilia Wilder, "Opinion Polls," *Survey* (July 1963), pp. 118–129; Jerry Pankhurst, "Factors in the Post-Stalin Emergence of Soviet Sociology," *Sociological Inquiry* 52, no. 3 (Summer 1982), pp. 165–183.

3. Siu-lun Wong, *Sociology and Socialism in Contemporary China* (London: Routledge and Kegan Paul, 1979), pp. 63–74.

4. See Stanley Rosen and David Chu, *Survey Research in the People's Republic of China* (Washington, D.C.: United States Information Agency, 1987).

5. The following discussion draws upon Zvi Gitelman, "Public Opinion in Communist Political Systems," in Walter D. Connor and Zvi Y. Gitelman, *Public Opinion in European Socialist Systems* (New York: Praeger, 1977), pp. 1–40; also William A. Welsh, ed., *Survey Research and Public Attitudes in Eastern Europe and the Soviet Union* (Elmsford, N.Y.: Pergamon Press, 1981), pp. 8–9.

6. Ronald Hill, *Soviet Politics, Political Science and Reform* (White Plains, N.Y.: M. E. Sharpe, 1980), p. 9, cited in Darrell Slider, "Party-Sponsored Public Opinion Research in the Soviet Union," *Journal of Politics* 47 (February 1985), p. 212.

7. Vladimir E. Shlapentokh, "Two Levels of Public Opinion: The Soviet Case," *The Public Opinion Quarterly* 49, no. 4 (Winter 1985), pp. 443–59. See also his *Soviet Public Opinion and Ideology: Mythology and Pragmatism in Interaction* (New York: Praeger, 1986); and *The Politics of Sociology in the Soviet Union* (Boulder: Westview Press, 1987). Citing Mikhail Gorbachev's outburst against the editor of the popular *Argumenty i Fakty* for publishing unflattering poll results, Shlapentokh recently reiterated the susceptibility of Soviet sociology "to the caprice of the general secretary." See "Glasnost and Polling," *Christian Science Monitor*, November 2, 1989.

8. Alex Inkeles, *Public Opinion in Soviet Russia* (Cambridge: Harvard University Press, 1950), p. 24, cited in Gitelman, note 5, p. 1.

9. Slider, note 6, pp. 219–25. Interestingly, Shlapentokh offers a highly negative account of the Georgian Center based on personal experience, claiming that

Slider uncritically published information he was given by the Georgians. See his *Politics of Sociology,* note 7, pp. 187–88.

10. This section draws on Shlapentokh, *Politics of Sociology,* note 7, pp. 251–67; Gail W. Lapidus, "State and Society: Toward the Emergence of Civil Society in the Soviet Union," in Seweryn Bialer, *Politics, Society, and Nationality Inside Gorbachev's Russia* (Boulder: Westview Press, 1989), pp. 121–47; Richard B. Dobson, "Perestroika and Soviet Public Opinion Research: A New Frontier?", *USIA Research Memorandum,* February 6, 1989; and Murray Yanowich, ed., *A Voice of Reform: Essays by Tat'iana I. Zaslavskaia* (Armonk, N.Y.: M. E. Sharpe, 1989).

11. The top officials at the two most important opinion centers—Tat'iana Zaslavskaia, Boris Grushin, and Aleksandr Yadov—have all been critical in the past of overt political interference in the social sciences and favor the open publication of research findings.

12. See *Liaowang* (hereafter, *LW*) 30 (July 28, 1986), in *Joint Publication Research Service* (hereafter, *JPRS*) CEA–86–121, December 1, 1986, pp. 7–10; *Jingji Ribao,* September 12, 1986, in *JPRS* CEA–86–116, November 4, 1986, pp. 1–8; *LW* 22 (June 2, 1986), in *JPRS* CPS–86–065, August 27, 1986, pp. 78–80; and *Renmin Ribao* (hereafter, *RMRB*), Overseas Edition, March 28, 1986, in *JPRS* CEA–86–109, October 10, 1986, pp. 32–34.

13. For an extended discussion, with examples, see Rosen and Chu, note 4.

14. The existence of a system of internal reporting of results is not unusual in itself. The Chinese model has several distinguishing characteristics. First, there is a gradation of internal levels, ranging from the minimally restricted all the way up to publications prepared only for top officials. Second, the system is decentralized, allowing virtually any organization, sometimes even a single individual, to carry out and print up a survey. Third, the system is used by specialists and officials seeking to influence the policy debate. A contrasting model, that of Czechoslovakia, is elaborated in Jiri Otava, "Public Opinion Research in Czechoslovakia," *Social Research* 55, nos. 1–2, part 2 (Spring-Summer 1988), pp. 247–60.

15. *LW,* December 7, 1987; *Foreign Broadcast Information Service—China* (hereafter *FBIS*), February 26, 1988, pp. 8–11.

16. Chen Yizi, "Social Scientific Research Serves Reform," in Bruce L. Reynolds, ed., *Reform in China: Challenges and Choices* (Armonk, N.Y.: M. E. Sharpe, 1987), pp. xxii-xxiv.

17. The major surveys are translated in Reynolds, note 16.

18. *Ibid.,* p. xxiv.

19. *New China News Agency* August 14, 1986; *FBIS,* August 19, 1986, pp. K22-K33. Soft science is the term the Chinese use to describe policy-making research that is based on the input of experts operating through established institutional channels.

20. *Jingji Yanjiu* 12 (1987), in *JPRS CAR*–88–004, February 12, 1988, pp. 18–
     25; *Zhongguo: Fazhan yu Gaige* 4 (1988), pp. 48–56; *LW* 33 (1986), pp. 15–
     16.

21. *Shijie Jingji Daobao* (hereafter, *SJJJDB*), August 15, 1988, in *JPRS CAR*–88–
     078, December 8, 1988, pp. 15–17; *SJJJD,* March 7, 1988, *JPRS CAR*–88–
     024, May 23, 1988, pp. 18–20.

22. For further analysis of these issues, see the chapters by Connie Squires Meaney
     and Jean C. Oi in the present volume.

23. *SJJJDB,* March 7 and August 15, 1988; *FBIS,* October 6, 1988, pp. 17–19.

24. *Agence France Press* (Hong Kong) (hereafter, *AFP*), November 14, 1988, in
     FBIS, November 14, 1988, p. 22.

25. *Hong Kong Standard,* December 16, 1988, in *FBIS,* December 16, 1988, p. 48;
     South China Morning Post (hereafter, *SCMP*), March 4, 1989, in *FBIS,* March
     6, 1989, pp. 28–29.

26. *SJJJDB,* January 23, 1989, in *FBIS,* February 2, 1989, pp. 32–33; also *SJJJDB,*
     January 30, 1989, p. 10; February 6, 1989, p. 7; February 27, 1989, p. 7. This
     newspaper all along had been one of the main publishing outlets for CESRRI
     researchers and was defended on several occasions by Zhao Ziyang. After
     publishing comments openly supporting student demonstrators, the newspaper
     was banned and its editor-in-chief, Qin Benli, was dismissed on April 24,
     1989. The newspaper's staff continued to operate an information service and
     campaigned actively for greater press freedom until the June 4 crackdown.
     Subsequently, the paper was vilified for its role in "stirring up public opinion"
     prior to the "counterrevolutionary rebellion." See *Xinhua,* August 18, 1989,
     in *FBIS,* August 21, 1989, pp. 22–27; *SCMP,* July 11, 1989, in *FBIS,* July 12,
     1989, pp. 14–15; and *New York Times,* April 25, 1989.

27. The distinction between governmental, private, and semi-private is not always
     clear. Some public opinion centers attached to university departments consid-
     ered themselves as "private" because they had to independently raise much of
     their operating budget, but the university affiliation provided them office space,
     students as staff and researchers, and, most important, legitimacy. This section
     relies heavily on interviews and documentary materials provided by leaders and
     staff members from the three major private institutes, as well as the public
     opinion research institute of Chinese People's University, and the China Social
     Survey System, primarily in the summer of 1988.

28. *Ching Bao* (Hong Kong), January 1988, in *FBIS,* January 14, 1988, pp. 8–13.

29. The problem was reportedly compounded because the institute head had re-
     leased unauthorized information to a foreign correspondent. An innocuous
     story on the survey and the institute head in a popular American news magazine
     was likewise cited as an example of "foreign connections." For a more "official"
     survey on the Thirteenth Party Congress and reform, see *LW* 10 (March 7,
     1988), in *JPRS CAR*–88–019, April 20, 1988, pp. 9–12.

30. *Xinwen Zhanxian* 8 (August 1988), in *JPRS CAR*–88–079, pp. 1–3; *China
     Daily,* December 30, 1988.

31. *RMRB*, Overseas Edition, June 27, 1988.

32. Another agency had listed the names of Politburo members on a questionnaire, seeking to measure their popular support. Party officials, however, excised this question before allowing the survey to go forward.

33. The survey results are reported in *Minyi Jianbao* 9 (May 4, 1988), pp. 3–4.

34. For more positive surveys on mass reactions to Li Peng and the new State Council, see *Guangming Ribao*, April 6, 1988, in *FBIS*, April 26, 1988, p. 29; *Xinhua*, May 9, 1988; and *FBIS*, May 9, 1988, pp. 26–27.

35. *Dang Jian* 9 (September 15, 1988), in *FBIS*, November 9, 1988, pp. 48–49; also Andrew J. Nathan, *Chinese Democracy* (New York: Alfred A. Knopf, 1985).

36. *Dang Jian*, note 35.

37. *Guangming Ribao*, February 29, 1988, in *FBIS*, March 23, 1988, pp. 19–22.

38. *Ching Chi Jih Pao* (Hong Kong), January 26, 1989, in *FBIS*, February 2, 1989, pp. 23–28.

39. *AFP*, September 21, 1988, citing China News Service, *FBIS*, September 21, 1988, p. 24. One recent survey, however, found only 2 percent of respondents in favor of lifting all restrictions on prices. *Zhongguo Xinwen She*, February 20, 1989, in *FBIS*, February 23, 1989, pp. 34–35.

40. *Xinwen Zhanxian* 1–6 (1988); *Minzhu yu Fazhi* 5–6 (1988).

41. *Cheng Ming*, February 1989, in *FBIS*, February 8, 1989, pp. 10–12; *Cheng Ming*, August 1988, in *FBIS*, August 2, 1988, pp. 8–14; *RMRB*, January 2, 1988, in *FBIS*, January 6, 1988, p. 15; *Zhongguo Jizhe*, August 1988, in *FBIS*, September 14, 1988, pp. 29–30.

42. This problem had appeared earlier in several Eastern bloc countries. See Gitelman, note 5.

43. *Keji Ribao*, April 4, 1988.

44. *Los Angeles Times*, November 13, 1988. This is still a far cry from alleged Soviet KGB tactics of the 1960s, which included secretly coding questionnaires to identify respondents and pressuring sociologists to identify the localities where the least acceptable questionnaire results were obtained. See Gitelman, note 5, p. 8.

45. *New York Times*, February 21, 1989.

46. *SCMP*, March 10, 1989, in *FBIS*, March 13, 1989, pp. 28–29; *Christian Science Monitor*, February 22, 1989.

47. *Shanghai Gaige* 2 (February 1989), pp. 43–45.

48. *BJQNB*, note 1; *China Information*, note 1. There is some survey evidence that the citizenry was less supportive of the students in April, but had gone over to the students' side by May. Originally, the government had commissioned private agencies to conduct surveys on public support for the students but, realizing the depth of the problems the regime faced and the sensitivity of survey research, quickly called off the projects.

49. *BJQNB*, note 1.

50. Information on the post-Tiananmen activities of public opinion institutes relies in part on interviews with members of these institutes in China and abroad, including Chen Yizi.

51. The first significant release of political prisoners arrested in the aftermath of the June crackdown occurred in mid-January 1990, when 573 detainees were freed. A second group of 211 dissidents was released in early May. Prominent among the latter group was Cao Siyuan, head of the Stone Company's Social Development Research Institute.

52. *AFP*, October 10, 1989, in *FBIS*, October 10, 1989, p. 22.

53. *RMRB*, Overseas Edition, September 12, 1989.

54. *Zhongguo Qingnian Bao*, August 3, 1989.

55. *New York Times*, December 29, 1989, p. A10.

5

Urban Private Business and China's Reforms

Thomas B. Gold

The Chinese Communist Party (CCP) created an urban private business class virtually from scratch as an integral part of the post-Mao reforms. Some leaders believed that closely restricted urban private business could be functional for solving a number of pressing economic, social, and political problems, and that the CCP could prevent any dysfunctional spread effects which private business might induce. Although its growth was not smooth, the urban private sector mushroomed from a base of 140,000 registered urban enterprises in 1978 to nearly 3.4 million units by the end of 1987, officially employing slightly fewer than 5 million people.

With the reimposition of restrictive policies in June 1989, urban private businesses faced an uncertain future, standing accused of a number of sins in one way or another related to the events of the Beijing Spring. Conservative political figures also attacked theorists who had supported more general privatization of the economy for trying to undermine socialism and reintroduce capitalism.

In this paper, I locate urban private business within the post-Mao structural reforms, showing what its advocates hoped it could do, and examining various problems associated with it. I argue that the inherently contradictory position of urban private business in a socialist economy is symptomatic of deeper contradictions within the reform program itself.

An Expanding Birdcage

In contrast to most of the world's socialist countries, the PRC succeeded in virtually wiping out its urban private business sector and preventing its revival during the Maoist era. To be sure, China suffered from the same endemic shortages and bottlenecks which had stimulated gap-filling entrepreneurial activity elsewhere in the socialist world; yet constant Maoist campaigns against "tails of capitalism," a pervasive formal and informal system to monitor urban citizens, and the state's monopoly over urban employment had spared China the type of "second economy" commonly encountered in other centrally planned systems.[1]

Notwithstanding such success, in March 1978, more than half a year before the watershed Third Plenum of the Eleventh Central Committee, the National People's Congress reaffirmed the legality of private individual enterprise. Over the next several years the party and state went on to create a business climate conducive to the expansion and institutionalization of private business.[2] To understand why the CCP made such a drastic volte-face, we first must analyze the decision to permit and then encourage private business within the context of systemwide structural reforms.

By 1978, many members of the CCP believed the party was in a life-and-death struggle for survival and control of China. Facing a profound legitimacy crisis, economic decline, administrative paralysis, severe unemployment and underemployment, the Third Plenum of the Eleventh Central Committee, held in December 1978, formally shifted the focus of the CCP's work away from the Maoist emphasis on class struggle to the goal of building socialism through the Four Modernizations.[3] It redefined the "major contradiction" of the era as being between socialist relations of production and backward productive forces. It paved the way for reforms in law, institutions, ideology and society aimed at stabilizing the political system and preventing the arbitrary exercise of power characteristic of the Maoist era, stimulating the economy, and improving people's lives to reduce discontent and restore the party's tarnished image.

Deng Xiaoping and other leaders asserted that "socialism means eliminating poverty. Pauperism is not socialism, still less communism. The superiority of the socialist system lies above all in its ability to improve the people's material and cultural life."[4] The success of socialism would be determined by how well it developed the productive forces and how much it raised the standard of living. In a later formulation, Zhao Ziyang claimed that China was only in the "primary stage of socialism." In that stage, so long as the state sector dominated the private one and the plan regulated the market; so long as distribution was based on work (and not exploitation); and so long as the "four cardinal principles"[5] held sway, then China could experiment with mixed ownership and a variety of other heretofore unthinkable reforms.[6] Some theorists began to advocate increased privatization of ownership of the means of production.[7] In a further departure from Maoist egalitarian principles, Deng proclaimed that, "some people in rural areas and cities should be allowed to get rich before others. It is only fair that people become prosperous through their own hard work. It is good for some people and some regions to be prosperous first, a development supported by everyone."[8]

Without commenting on the veracity of the last phrase, we can agree that the reformers did undertake to dismantle many of the economic institutions characteristic of socialist systems,[9] and shift economic responsibility away from the state and collective onto individual enterprises and entrepreneurs. This began with the Production Responsibility System (PRS) in agriculture. It utilized contracts between the state and individuals, groups, or families to sell grain at a fixed price; then, after fulfilling their contract, farmers were free to engage in a broad range of money-making endeavors. These included nonagricultural pursuits such as sideline production, commerce, services, manufacturing, and temporary labor in the cities. As the program evolved, many rural people abandoned agriculture altogether, becoming "specialized households" in one line or another.[10] Despite two decades of collectivism, the foundation for private agriculture had never fully disappeared. The family had remained a basic unit of accounting and distribution. It had retained use of a plot of land to produce whatever it wished and, during more liberal times, it could sell some of its output on free markets. The PRS built on this remaining foundation of family production, strengthening and expanding it.

Rapid and undeniable achievements in the countryside gave the reformers the confidence to shift their emphasis to the urban areas, which they did at the Third Plenum of the Twelfth Central Committee in October 1984. This plenum pushed forward with decentralization of decisionmaking and control. It also called for enterprise autonomy, where state enterprises would be responsible for their own profit and loss, with bankruptcy the price for failure. Enterprises signed contracts with each other and paid taxes to the state in lieu of complete dependence on ministries for funds, plans, and resources. To enhance enterprise flexibility, reformers tried to separate ownership from management. In a further development, smaller state enterprises and many collective enterprises were subcontracted out to their managers or other successful bidders, who ran them as virtual private enterprises. Enterprises began to offer shares of stock to the public and stock exchanges tentatively appeared in some cities. The state promulgated a body of economic laws to regulate the new system.

The scope of the plan shrank as that of the market expanded, and prices of a wide range of commodities were freed or loosened. Workers' wages were more closely tied to effort as the state endeavored to "smash the iron rice bowl" of expensive welfare benefits and guaranteed lifetime employment. A labor market began to replace the often arbitrary job assignment system for all but university graduates, and job mobility became possible for some. With the opening of special economic zones and the arrival of foreign investors, new opportunities opened to many Chinese workers.

It is doubtful that the reformers had a clear plan. They put together their reforms in an *ad hoc,* reactive manner. Obstruction by conservative or recalcitrant officials at all levels meant that many programs became distorted or were never implemented at all. Newly decentralized power over finances, tax revenues, foreign trade, investment and exchange, capital construction, and so on opened the door for local authorities to usurp much of the center's control. In the rural areas in particular, economic actors aggressively took the reform initiative and the authorities had little to do but formalize activities already underway.

One political adjunct of economic liberalization was the idea of separating and clearly delineating party and government functions. Deng Xiaoping had called for such a separation in 1980, but it was not seriously acted on until 1986, and then against great obstruction.[11] The party also granted intellectuals more scope for autonomous research and international exchange, aimed in the first instance at improving the level of productive forces. Scientific and technical personnel benefited the most from this loosening up, but intellectuals in the arts and social sciences also enjoyed unprecedented freedom of expression, inquiry, and participation in a global community.

To sum up the preceding discussion, the affirmation and encouragement of urban private business occurred within a milieu of general systemic liberalization. This refers to increased scope for autonomous action by units and individuals, but not to the point of total independence from party leadership. It is what party elder Chen Yun, in discussing the economy, called the relation between a bird and a cage: giving people a roomier birdcage but not removing the cage altogether.[12] To use the popular Russian terms, the Chinese were permitting both *perestroika* (structural reform) and *glasnost* (openness), with the emphasis overwhelmingly on the former. The reform agenda placed economic development above all else, demonstrating a willingness to experiment with a broad range of techniques aimed at stimulating production and improving the material standard of living. Reformers believed they could control spread effects from economic liberalization to other spheres, and they did not oppose conservative-led campaigns against "spiritual pollution" and "bourgeois liberalism" in the cultural and political realms until these threatened the economic agenda.

The preceding has described those reforms relevant to urban private business, emphasizing the economic liberalization that lay at their core. But we have not yet addressed the question of why the reformers decided to encourage urban private business in the first place.

The Functions of Urban Private Business

China's post-Mao leaders believed that private business could perform several positive functions within the reform program, and that the party and state could regulate its growth and activities. What were these positive contributions?[13] First, private business could absorb many of the tens of millions of unemployed and underemployed urban workers.[14] The majority of unemployed were so-called youths waiting for employment (*daiye qingnian*). Because China did not have a labor market or legitimate way for urbanites to make their own living, school graduates had no choice but to wait for the state to assign work to them. By 1978, the state and collective sectors were suffering from too many employees with little or nothing to do, especially as the economy was stagnant. They balked at accepting more people.

Unemployed young people were a drain on their parents' limited financial resources. An alarming number of them turned to crime, having little else to do and desiring to acquire the consumer goods then hitting the market. The ranks of unemployed recent school graduates were further swelled by the return to the cities of hundreds of thousands of former Red Guards and other urban youths who had been compelled to settle in the countryside during the Cultural Revolution. Most of these newly returned youths now refused to leave the cities.[15] As the reformers began to criticize the Cultural Revolution, they could find little justification for shipping back these people, who viewed themselves as victims of what were now officially called incorrect policies. Yet they had no urban jobs or other visible means of support. By permitting these Cultural Revolution returnees and recent school graduates to set up their own businesses and then declaring that they had jobs, the state could avoid further responsibility for their livelihood.

Second, private businesses would not drain state resources. Loans could be made available, but most of the start-up capital would come from private sources, meaning that the state could channel its own scarce resources to higher priority projects.

Third, through taxation these private enterprises could provide a new source of state revenue.

Fourth, private businesses could fill many of the gaps in the economy, in particular in the service sector. Urban dwellers had long complained of inconveniences in shopping, eating, obtaining needed repairs, and other services. Letting private entrepreneurs supply this demand could have an additional benefit of mitigating discontent among the broader populace.

Fifth, permitting private businesses in a limited number of sectors to compete directly with state and collective enterprises, now responsible for their own profit and loss and facing the threat of potential bankruptcy, would serve to compel the latter to improve efficiency, productivity, and customer service. This would also save the state money, generate more tax revenue from state and collective firms, and improve the general level of urban consumer services, which had become infamous for extreme rudeness and poor quality. Overall, it could contribute to the reform goal of "enlivening the domestic economy" (duinei gaohuo jingji).

Sixth, analyzing the experience of the Confucian "miracle" economies of neighboring Japan, South Korea, Hong Kong, Taiwan, and Singapore, communist reformers saw that small-scale family enterprises were a force for stability and political quiescence. Channeling their energies into business and having a claim to their own personal property gave people in those societies a stake in stability, predictability, and continuity. In all of these economies but Hong Kong's, the state played a major direct role in the economy, so to China's reformers it seemed quite feasible to allow small-scale private business to flourish within a state-dominated economy, for the ultimate benefit of all.

Seventh and last, by tolerating individual enterprise and continuously fine-tuning the investment climate to permit private business to grow, the CCP could demonstrate to Hong Kong, Macao, and Taiwan that it was sincere in its offer to reincorporate them into the PRC through the strategy of "one country, two systems." According to this blueprint, the capitalist economies would continue to maintain their economic and social systems and enjoy great autonomy within the socialist PRC.[16] Permitting private business and promulgating laws to guarantee private property would go a long way to allay the fears of skeptical residents of those other Chinese societies. This would preempt the flight of capital and talent as well as prevent economic instability as the day of reunification drew near. Tolerance and encouragement of private business would also reassure foreign businessmen as to China's dependability and suitability as a partner for investment and trade.

Putting this all together, the reformers believed that legitimizing urban private business could contribute positively to China's overall economic development program. It would not challenge the state's hegemony over the economy, which was being redefined in any case, and, in fact, might help create a fresh social group with a visible stake in the new economic system. The reformers reassured those who feared that this would wreck socialist dominance by insisting that the private sector would always remain supplemental to the state and collective sectors. It had to rely on them for raw materials; individual entrepreneurs had to come to the state for licenses; and through taxation, regulation, and supervision, the private sector would be kept within bounds.[17]

Growth of the Urban Individual Economy

The growth and expansion of urban private business has dramatically altered many aspects of life in China's cities. In addition to designated markets where individual household enterprises (*getihu*) occupy fixed stalls, throughout urban areas private restaurants, barber shops, stores, and other undertakings exist side by side with state and collective firms. Private repairers of shoes, bicycles, glasses, and other goods as well as purveyors of sunglasses, snacks, and trinkets and drivers of taxis, pedicabs, and other vehicles dot city streets and float up and down alleys. Over the last decade, private enterprises have made life immeasurably more convenient for China's urban dwellers. The number of retail outlets and the amount and variety of goods and services have increased exponentially; for instance, free markets (*jishi*) in the urban areas increased from 2,919 in 1980 to 10,908 in 1987, and trade volume in these urban markets soared from RMB 2.4 billion in 1980 to 34.7 billion in 1987.[18] It must be stressed that there is much regional variety in the strength and scope of private business, with southern and coastal areas generally having the liveliest and most freewheeling private sectors.

As table 1 indicates, the growth of the urban private sector (about one-fourth of the total number of individual households in private business) did not take off immediately upon the National People's Congress's reaffirmation of its legality in March 1978. From the late 1970s through the first few years of the 1980s, urban private enterprises were still quite rare, limited often to old women selling hot water, tea or ice lollies, and tiny mom-and-pop sundry stores.

The most rapid expansion occurred between 1982 and 1986–87. In the middle of 1981, the government passed "Some Policy Regulations by the State Council on the Urban Nonagricultural Individual Economy." Then, Article 11 of the revised state constitution, promulgated in December 1982, proclaimed that "the state protects the lawful rights and interests of the individual economy." The revised constitution eliminated an ominous phrase in the 1978 constitution which held that the state guides the individual economy toward collectivization. The new charter additionally protects the

Table 1:
Individual Enterprises and Employees
(in millions)

Year	Number of enterprises		Number employed	
	Total	Urban	Total	Urban
1949—1950	4.14	n.a.	8.26	n.a.
1956	0.43	n.a.	0.51	n.a.
1957	n.a.	n.a.	1.04	n.a.
1978	0.30	0.14	0.33	0.15
1979	0.56	0.25	0.68	0.32
1980	0.89	0.45	1.56	0.81
1981	1.83	0.87	2.27	1.06
1982	2.64	1.13	3.19	1.36
1983	5.90	1.71	7.47	2.09
1984	9.30	2.22	13.03	2.91
1985	11.71	2.79	17.66	3.85
1986	12.11	2.91	18.46	4.08
1987	13.73	3.38	21.58	4.92
1988	14.50	n.a.	23.05	n.a.
1989 (Oct.)	12.30	n.a.	19.43	n.a.

Sources: Zhongguo Shehui Kexueyuan Jingji Yanjiusuo, *Zhongguo Zibenzhuyi Gongshangye di Shehuizhuyi Gaizao;* Willy Kraus, "Private Enterprise in the People's Republic of China" (note 2); *China Daily; Beijing Review.*

right to own and inherit property. Documents from the Third Plenum of the Twelfth Central Committee in the fall of 1984 gave further assurances that the CCP positively supported private business and would not attempt to socialize it in the foreseeable future. At that point, members of various groups and strata embarked on the road of private business, including youths waiting for employment, former Red Guards, ex-prisoners, workers let go from other enterprises, disabled people, pensioners wishing to supplement their income, and other senior citizens—primarily women—who never worked in a state enterprise (and so did not qualify for a pension).[19] From virtually no base, the urban private sector grew rapidly, due to a combination of official encouragement and the demonstration effect of entrepreneurs who got rich quickly with minimal negative consequences. Three decades of socialist remolding had extinguished neither the spirit of entrepreneurship nor the ability to perceive and capitalize on opportunities among urban Chinese, even among young people with no prior experience in a non-socialist economy.

As the individual economy's expansion rate slowed toward the end of the 1980s, a qualitative shift became apparent in the types of people participating in private business. Many state workers quit their jobs to start private enterprises. University students established private businesses during their school days, and many started or joined private firms upon graduation.[20] The most famous example was Wan Runnan, who left his job at the Chinese Academy of Sciences in 1984 to start up the Stone Company, specializing in computer hardware and software. Stone's phenomenal success (with help from contacts high in the party and state leadership) stimulated the growth of Beijing's "Silicon Valley" in the Haidian district in the vicinity of Beijing and Qinghua universities.[21] In addition to these formally registered private entrepreneurs, numerous intellectuals, performers, and ordinary workers caught "moonlighting fever" and began to engage in legal but unregistered and untaxed economic activity.[22] China's entrepreneurial explosion came to a sudden halt, however, in the aftermath of the June 4 assault on Tiananmen; and by the fall of the year a crackdown on illegal business dealings and an overall economic retrenchment had brought about a substantial shrinkage of the private economy to 12.3 million units.[23]

Originally, individual enterprises had been permitted to hire at most two assistants and five apprentices. This was later expanded to seven employees. But formal employment figures greatly understate the actual extent of participation in the private sector. Most enterprises were family businesses, with one member registering as the *getihu* (or actual "individual household"), while others maintained their regular jobs, helping out as time permitted. Government regulators generally did not interfere in this. In addition to the moonlighters referred to above, many legally registered *getihu* were not completely separated from their previous jobs in state enterprises. I have interviewed several who took advantage of a policy called "stop salary, retain place" (tingxin liuzhi), meaning they stop receiving their wage and bonus but pay in a certain amount monthly to maintain their benefits and seniority in the enterprise in case they decide to return. This practice has not been universally permitted, however.

A major watershed in the evolution of the private sector occurred in April 1988, when the National People's Congress amended the 1982 constitution to allow private companies to hire more than seven nonfamily employees. In July of that year, the NPC promulgated a set of regulations for these larger private enterprises, which officially numbered 225,000 and employed 3.68 million people. In Chinese they were called siying qiye, which literally means "privately managed enterprises." Given the fact that there were also a growing number of state-owned and collective-owned enterprises being subcontracted out to private managers, this terminology made for a rather confusing picture of the actual situation. To further complicate the picture, many private enterprises registered as collectives to enjoy a lower tax rate, preferential incentives, and higher political status.

Urban private entrepreneurs tend to be concentrated in a limited number of sectors. According to nationwide statistics, more than one-half were in retail trade late in 1987.[24] About 10 percent each were in light industry and catering, 8 percent in transportation, 7 percent each in repairs and services, and the rest in sideline industries and construction. In absolute terms, they actually came to dominate certain trades. In 1986, for instance, 82.6 percent of the enterprises involved in retail trade were either private or some type of joint operation. Private units alone accounted for 49.7 percent of the employees in these sectors and 16.3 percent of retail turnover. Their presence in industry, by comparison, was considerably smaller—accounting for only 0.3 percent of output value (RMB 2.9 billion).[25] Yet, by 1989 the state sector's percentage of total industrial enterprises, workers, and output value had all declined relative to collective and private enterprises. The state also privatized some types of enterprises, such as many theatrical troupes,[26] and let it be known that further expansion would come from outside the state sector. In a sign of the times, the watchword for Hainan province, established in April 1988, was "small government, big society," with Chinese leaders promising that the state sector in Hainan would be restricted.[27] Such promises were placed in doubt, however, in the aftermath of the June crackdown.

Ambivalence toward the Private Sector

In spite of periodic ebb and flows, the official media prior to June 1989 evidenced a generally positive attitude toward the urban private sector. This tended to confirm that the urban private sector had made positive contributions to the reforms, as its advocates had intended. From 1983 to

1987, 4.22 million newly employed urbanites found their first jobs in the private economy,[28] while 20 percent of the 4.9 million youths entering the labor force in 1988 took the private road.[29] In 1988 individual household enterprises paid more than RMB 9 billion in taxes to the state—almost one-third as much as the sector had paid over the previous eight years[30] combined. Managers of state enterprises frequently called themselves "entrepreneurs" and demanded further reforms to facilitate doing their jobs successfully in the new environment.[31]

The authorities went out of their way to reassure individual entrepreneurs that the private economy was not an expedient tactic but a crucial long-term player in China's economy.[32] Party and state leaders received entrepreneurs and checked up on their situations, listening solicitously to their problems. Then-Premier Zhao Ziyang received delegates to the first National Congress of the Self-Employed Laborers Association in December, 1986 at the Great Hall of the People. Zhao also toured some private hostelries at the Beidaihe resort during his 1984 August sojourn there.[33] Individual businessmen enjoyed official status as "laborers" (laodongzhe), rather than capitalists, exploiters, or other derogatory labels. Some were recruited into the Communist party[34] and others held political office. An example of the latter is private entrepreneur (i.e., not an individual household) Zhang Baoning, who served as a delegate to the Beijing Municipal People's Congress.[35] Party organs that blocked the membership applications of private businessmen received a public chastising.[36] The fact that state organs, with party backing, passed legislation permitting individual households to evolve into private businesses and introduced a raft of other laws and regulations testified to the sincere desire of the reformers to protect the status and rights of private business.

Numerous literary works explored the contradictions of being a private businessperson in a socialist society—invariably from a sympathetic perspective. Media reports illustrated how former convicts or juvenile delinquents had straightened out their lives after becoming private businessmen and how they had made philanthropic gifts to society in order to help other young people avoid the missteps they themselves had taken. Other reports explored the values and aspirations of entrepreneurs to show that they were not merely consumed with greed and hedonism.

Over the course of the decade, the media also exposed the darker side of getihu life, thereby also revealing much of the ambivalence within the party establishment and population at large toward this new social force.[37] Some cadres, especially in the rural areas, took advantage of the 1983–84 drive to clean up "spiritual pollution" to accuse wealthy entrepreneurs of "unhealthy" activities. The crime and divorce rates among private business people were said to be high, and they were charged with being at the root of the increased amount of pornography circulating in China. In August 1987, at the tail end of the campaign against "bourgeois liberalization," officials attacked entrepreneurs who engaged in a wide range of illegal activities, including speculation, operating without a license, earning exorbitant profits, smuggling, and manufacturing and selling counterfeit and fake goods. Media reports were always careful to distinguish these bad types (*daoye*) from the law-abiding majority of private businessmen. The latter also came forth to criticize evildoers for harming the reputation of the entire group,[38] and to show how the law protected those who obeyed it. While some reports praised the loftier ambitions of entrepreneurs, others dwelt on their decadence and obsession with money. The title of a 1988 book, *Money, the Mad Cornered Beast*, gives the flavor of this latter genre.[39] Based on interviews, I would argue that most entrepreneurs had little confidence in the life expectancy of the policy that spawned them. They therefore earned as much money as they could, consuming it aggressively in the expectation that their halcyon days were numbered.

A 1988 survey conducted by the State Administration of Industry and Commerce revealed that "the overwhelming majority of self-employed industrial and commercial workers across China receive an average annual income of 3,000–4,000 yuan, or about twice the 1,400 yuan average for workers in state-owned enterprises."[40] Adding the value of fringe benefits to the state workers' cash salaries still brought the average only up to 2,000–3,000. About one-tenth of the private businessmen reportedly earned more than 10,000 RMB, and one percent of that group earned much more.[41] *Getihu* who flaunted their wealth set a bad example for impressionable young people. In order to start earning money as soon as possible, many youths began to drop out of school or canceled plans to go on for advanced education.[42]

As their iron rice bowls were smashed, many talented state workers came to believe that the potential for wealth as a private businessman outweighed whatever benefits still remained in the state sector. Consequently they quit their jobs, or took leaves of absence, to embark on the private road.[43] If allowed to go unchecked, these worrisome trends could have seriously reduced the ranks of skilled workers and technicians needed to achieve the Four Modernizations.

Urban Private Business and the Events of 1989

Both the massive demonstrations that spread throughout China in the spring of 1989 and the military crackdown that terminated them grew out of contradictions that had been heightening for some time. Urban private business people did not cause the problems by any means, but many of their activities were symptomatic of the deeper dilemmas that came to a head early in 1989. Their inherently delicate position in a self-styled socialist society made them easy scapegoats, and in the post-June crackdown they were dealt a heavy blow.

Reforms Derailed

By late 1988, the reform program had clearly reached an impasse. Partial reforms had brought about notable achievements in many areas. But in the difficult and unprecedented transition from a Stalinist command economy to the vaguely conceived "socialist commodity economy," a number of problems had arisen that both demanded and defied solution. Although detailed analysis is beyond the scope of this paper, some of these problems were highly relevant to the fate of the urban private sector. They included runaway inflation, huge budget deficits, rampant corruption, rising income inequality, and macroeconomic chaos.[44]

Serious inflation

For the first half of 1988, the consumer price index rose 19.2 percent, but in some cities retail prices rose 20 to 30 percent or higher. The rise in the price index for the first half of 1989 topped 25 percent, partly a carryover from the rapid rise of 1988. Consequently, the standard of living of approximately 20 percent of China's urban dwellers declined. From May to August 1988, party and state leaders talked of stepping up the pace of price reform, and in May the prices of many agricultural commodities were decontrolled, and efforts were made to eliminate the double-track system where the same goods had two prices—one for the amount produced under the plan, the other for that above quota. Rumors that all prices would be freed starting September 1 set off a wave of panic buying and hoarding in mid-August. In response, banks raised interest rates on deposits, and the State Council hastily declared that there would be no further price reform for 1988 and that reforms for 1989 would be very limited. With each successive round of price decontrol, the government increased its subsidies to disadvantaged urban residents and also printed more money, predictably fueling an inflationary spiral. Private entrepreneurs could not escape blame for wanton price hikes. They sold many goods also available in state stores, but usually of better quality—and at a much higher price.

Budget deficits

Revenues from state enterprises and taxes could not cover Beijing's expenditures. Money-losing state enterprises and extrabudgetary investment, especially at the local levels, exacerbated the problem. Mushrooming rural and township enterprises claimed raw materials, energy, and transportation at the expense of state enterprises, further stymying their growth. Tax evasion was rampant across the board, including the private sector. Continuing payout of subsidies to urban residents drained the budget. In the fall of 1988, the state lacked the cash to pay peasants for the harvest, issuing IOUs instead, causing widespread rural dissatisfaction. In 1989, cash-short government authorities announced compulsory purchase of government bonds by state workers.

Corruption run riot

At the bottom level, there were private businessmen paying off tax officials as well as a host of others in position to extort "fees." Entrepreneurs also paid off salesmen and other key employees of enterprises who were in position to funnel scarce goods to them for resale in private markets. But this was relatively minor corruption compared to the large-scale profiteering, bribery, and extortion activities of high-level cadres and their relatives—all the way up to the sacrosanct official residential compound at Zhongnanhai. These people set themselves up as middlemen between Chinese corporations and foreign businessmen, demanding bribes from the latter in the form of cash, goods, foreign bank accounts, trips abroad, tuition in foreign universities, and so on, in exchange for arranging deals. They set up state "companies" but ran them for private gain. They demanded to be taken as partners in profitable private and collective enterprises. They profiteered off the dual-track price system, buying goods at the fixed state price and reselling them at a market price. These activities were widespread, well known, and almost universally resented by ordinary Chinese. From the point of view of individual households and other private entrepreneurs, the system was terribly unfair; how could they ever hope to compete on a playing field tilted heavily in favor of the children of high-level officials? How could they even conceive of doing business without paying off a long chain of cadres with the power to shut them down or deny them resources?

Unequal income distribution

Top officials and their families enjoyed high salaries plus perquisites money could not buy. Below them, the ostentatious lifestyle of many private businesspeople—in particular young men, some with jail records and little formal education—irked law-abiding citizens trying to get by on fixed wages. This included many students who felt that the returns to education did not justify the effort. For those without official connections or the wherewithal to bribe cadres in charge of job assignments, the system seemed totally inequitable. Hard work, obeying the rules, personal achievement got one nowhere. Why go to college when one's top salary could never match that of a junior high school dropout fresh from a labor reform camp who was selling blue jeans on the street?

Macroeconomic chaos

The government had plainly lost control over the macroeconomy, and had no clear vision or solutions. This eroded public confidence. Elite paralysis was obviously tied into the power struggle underway at the top over the succession to Deng Xiaoping. In spite of repeated calls for austerity, especially after the Third Plenum of the Thirteenth Central Committee in September 1988, ordinary Chinese believed that their squabbling leaders were unwilling or unable to solve the problems of corruption which benefited themselves and their families.

In the latter part of 1988, some theorists associated with the increasingly embattled Zhao Ziyang faction floated ideas to push the reforms forward. One was to expand the realm of privatization. The other called for political "neo-authoritarianism." That meant a strong leader sweeping aside all obstacles to reform until the economy could get back on track and political democracy could proceed.[45] It drew legitimacy from the successful modernization of neo-authoritarian societies such as Taiwan, Singapore, and South Korea.

Private Entrepreneurs: Spring 1989

It is difficult to gauge the activities of private entrepreneurs during the tumultuous days of April and May 1989. According to some reports, many of them supplied food, blankets, and other provisions to demonstrators.[46] One group used its motorcycles to run messages around Beijing on behalf of the students; ironically, other reports describe *getihu* providing the same type of services to soldiers stationed in and around the capital.

The activities of China's best-known private businessman were exposed after June 4. It turned out that Wan Runnan, chief of the Stone Company, had provided $25,000 to support the Tiananmen demonstrators, as well as donating electronic broadcasting equipment. In addition, the Social Development Research Institute under Stone had done theoretical work on democratization, and its head, Cao Siyuan, became actively involved in the NPC delegates' May petition drive opposing martial law. Cao was subsequently arrested and held in detention for ten months; Wan, under threat of arrest, fled and resurfaced in Paris, where he became general secretary of the Front for a Democratic China.[47]

Urban Private Businesses since June 1989

While claiming to have suppressed a counter-revolutionary rebellion, the hardline CCP elite has also acknowledged the legitimacy of many of the complaints voiced by demonstrators in April and May. It has taken steps to address the most flagrant violations. Measures taken will affect the overall business climate and touch on private urban business more or less directly.

On July 29, the Politburo declared its determination to solve "seven things the masses are concerned about."[48] These included: (1) proceed further in cleaning up companies; (2) resolutely restrict the sons and daughters of high officials from doing business; (3) eliminate the "special supply" of a small number of food items for leading comrades; (4) strictly assign cars by the rules and strictly prohibit the import of sedans; (5) strictly prohibit feasting and gift-giving; (6) strictly control leading officials going abroad; and (7) earnestly and conscientiously investigate corruption, bribery, speculation, and other criminal cases, especially big, important cases.

A resolution on cleaning up companies, promulgated by the CCP Central Committee and State Council on August 17, included efforts to deal with private companies registering as state or collective enterprises.[49] The state went after companies involving illegal cadre participation; by early November more than one million rural collectives had been shut down, and 2.2 million private enterprises had been forced out of business.[50]

The most concerted cleanup effort focused on tax collection. On August 1, 1989, the director of the State Taxation Bureau announced that during August and September his agency would undertake a nationwide inspection of *getihu* taxes. Although the 14.5 million rural and urban individual businesses had paid RMB 9.2 billion in taxes for 1988, the director claimed that they had evaded another 70 to 80 percent. He set a goal of RMB 12 billion in tax payments for 1989. Through September, payments reached 8.8 billion, with August and September remittances running 92 and 93.5 percent ahead of the same period a year earlier. Previously, assessments had been made orally through bargaining; henceforth, entrepreneurs were required to keep written accounts.[51] Required profit disbursements were broken down as follows: 52 percent as tax, 30 percent as reinvestment, and 18 percent as profit for the owner.[52]

Authorities also targeted other activities for cleanup: engaging in business without a license; black marketeering; pornography; unlawful networks; engaging in activities outside the specifications of their licenses; and illicit hiring practices, including employment of child labor.[53]

Private entrepreneurs also took a large share of the official blame for problems of unfair income distribution. In a June article published in the party's new theoretical journal *Qiushi* (Seeking Truth) prior to his ascension to the post of CCP general secretary, Jiang Zemin analyzed the problem of income inequality and the public outcry it provoked. While criticizing egalitarianism, he nonetheless emphasized that big income gaps, especially under conditions of inequitable access to money-making opportunities, needed to be resolved. Of six major problems related to income distribution, Jiang emphasized that "what is particularly important is that we must strengthen our control over business operations of individual traders, and supervise their incomes."[54]

Since June 1989 the private sector has sustained the most focused attack since its revival in the early post-Mao period. Though it was not held to be a prime source of the many socioeconomic problems mentioned above, it certainly exacerbated and embodied them. Private businessmen already in the CCP would now be required to undergo strict supervision, and no new entrepreneurial applicants would be approved.[55] The practices of individual business people had allegedly contributed to the atmosphere of lawlessness, free-wheeling, and economic chaos so rampant in 1988–89. Some people stood accused of using private business as a front for promoting broader privatization of the economy and bourgeois liberalization. The authorities clearly hoped that a crackdown on tax evasion and other economic crimes would have beneficial spread effects for improving general social order.

Nevertheless, party and government leaders continued to reaffirm the legality of the private sector and the positive contributions it had made. In the months following the assault on Tiananmen, the Fourth Plenum of the Thirteenth Party Central Committee, Jiang Zemin's speech for the fortieth anniversary of the PRC, as well as subsequent speeches and articles by Li Peng and others, all reassured individual businessmen that their lawful practices and "reasonable profits" enjoyed protection under the constitution as well as other statutes.[56]

Conclusion

The contradictory signals sent to the private sector in the wake of the June crackdown reflected the leadership's ambivalent attitude toward liberalization in general. While acknowledging the pressing necessity of party-state relaxation of traditional restrictive controls over the economy and social life, and while defending the achievements made so far, CCP leaders had no sense of how far to go in loosening up or how to channel and control the forces unleashed by liberalization. The party could not cope with the speed with which private business grew and evolved or the stepped-up demands for more social and political freedom elsewhere in society. The private sector had made positive contributions but also exhibited its own pathologies, highlighting problems inherent in the effort to partially reform a rigid Leninist system.

In the fall of 1988 the Politburo had already announced its intention to retrench and readjust the economic reforms for two years. The disturbances of spring 1989 provided an opportunity to extend and deepen control over social, cultural, and political life as well. For urban private business it augured a spell of closer supervision and intensified demands by officials. At the same time, however, lingering intra-elite disagreement over the direction of reforms, coupled with the regime's apparent inability to push a genuine cleanup, meant that exploitable opportunities to make money continued to exist.

Notes and References

1. I discuss the role of the private economy under socialism in greater detail in "Urban Private Business in China," *Studies in Comparative Communism* 22, nos. 2–3 (Summer-Autumn 1989), pp. 187–90.

2. Two articles which review policies concerning the private sector are: Willy Kraus, "Private Enterprise in the People's Republic of China: Official Statement, Implementations and Future Prospects," in Joseph C. H. Chai and Chi-kuang Leung, eds., *China's Economic Reforms* (Hong Kong: University of Hong Kong Centre of Asian Studies, 1987), pp. 64–97; and Susan Young, "Policy, Practice and the Private Sector in China," *The Australian Journal of Chinese Affairs* 21 (January 1989), pp. 57–80.

3. For an overview of the reforms, see Harry Harding, *China's Second Revolution: Reform after Mao* (Washington: The Brookings Institution, 1987). On the economic aspects of the crisis, see Carl Riskin, *China's Political Economy* (New York: Oxford University Press, 1987), chapter 11.

4. Deng Xiaoping, *Build Socialism with Chinese Characteristics* (Beijing: Foreign Languages Press, 1985), p.37.

5. These are: keeping to the socialist road; upholding the dictatorship of the proletariat (relabeled the "people's democratic dictatorship"); upholding the leadership of the CCP; and upholding Marxism-Leninism-Mao Zedong Thought as the guiding ideology. The *locus classicus* is Deng Xiaoping's speech "Uphold the Four Cardinal Principles," in Deng Xiaoping, *Selected Works of Deng Xiaoping* (Beijing: Foreign Languages Press, 1984), pp. 166–91.

6. Zhao Ziyang, "Advance along the Road of Socialism with Chinese Characteristics," *Beijing Review* (hereafter, *BR*) 45 (November 9–15, 1987), pp. 23–49.

7. Two key articles providing a summary of arguments on privatization appear in *Foreign Broadcast Information Service—China* (hereafter, *FBIS*), August 31, 1989, pp. 29–34, and October 27, 1989, pp. 25–28.

8. Deng Xiaoping, "Our Work in All Fields Should Contribute to the Building of Socialism with Chinese Characteristics," in Deng, note 4, p. 12.

9. Reforms are discussed in a comparative framework in Victor Nee and David Stark, eds., *Remaking the Economic Institutions of Socialism: China and Eastern Europe* (Stanford: Stanford University Press, 1989).

10. See William L. Parish, ed., *Chinese Rural Development: The Great Transformation* (Armonk, N.Y.: M. E. Sharpe, 1985).

11. Deng Xiaoping, "On the Reform of the System of Party and State Leadership", in Deng, note 5, pp. 302–325.

12. David M. Bachman, *Chen Yun and the Chinese Political System.* (Berkeley: Institute of East Asian Studies, Center for Chinese Studies, 1985). Also, Jan S. Prybyla, *Market and Plan under Socialism* (Stanford: Hoover Institution Press, 1987).

13. Some of these functions are discussed in *Geti Laodongzhe Shouce* (Beijing: Beijing Ribao Chubanshe, Gongshang Chubanshe, 1984), pp. 73–76.

14. In 1981, 26 million urbanites were reportedly unemployed. See Wotjek Zafanolli, "A Brief Outline of China's Second Economy," *Asian Survey* 25, no.7 (July 1985), p. 726, note 35. In 1988, a survey of 11 provinces revealed that 8 to 15 percent of the labor force in state enterprises was surplus. See *BR* 51 (December 19–25, 1988), p. 22.

15. Thomas B. Gold, "Back to the City: The Return of Shanghai's Educated Youth," *China Quarterly* 84 (December 1980), pp. 755–70.

16. See Deng, note 4, pp. 30–34 and 41–42.

17. Many of these fears are dealt with in *Geti Laodongzhe Shouce,* especially section 2. See also *Chinese Economic Studies* 21, no. 1 (Fall 1987), pp. 84–92.

18. State Statistical Bureau, *A Statistical Survey of China* (Beijing: Zhongguo Tongji Chubanshe, 1988), p. 82.

19. Many examples can be found in Marcia Yudkin, *Making Good: Private Business in Socialist China* (Beijing: Foreign Languages Press, 1986).

20. I discuss this in "The Private Sector as an Alternative for China's University Graduates," paper presented at the Annual Meeting of the Association for Asian Studies, Washington, D.C., March 17–19, 1989.

21. The company collected articles about itself and published them in January 1989 as "Stone in Worldwide Press." See *Wall Street Journal,* June 3, 1988.

22. *Shehui* 11 (1988), pp. 16–8; also *BR* 45 (November 6–12, 1989), p. 25–27.

23. *China Daily* (hereafter, *CD*), November 7, 1989, p. 1.

24. *BR* 18 (May 4, 1987), p. 8; Ellen Salem, "Peddling the Private Road," *Far Eastern Economic Review* (hereafter, *FEER*), October 8, 1987, p. 106. These percentages held into 1989. See *CD,* November 7, 1989, p. 1.

25. *BR* 40 (October 5, 1987), pp. 26–27. In 1987, household retail sales increased to 17.4 percent of the total, just slightly behind collective retail sales, which accounted for 19.5 percent. See *BR* 52 (December 26–January 1, 1988/1989), p. 21. In March 1989, the percentage was 13.84 although the volume grew 37.6 percent to RMB 102.4 billion (*Shichang Bao,* March 30, 1989, p. 1.). The

industrial percentage grew as well, to 4.3 percent in 1988. See *BR* 40 (October 2–8, 1989), p. 20.

26. *CD*, May 14, 1988, p. 1. This does not extend to some traditional forms, such as Peking Opera, which require state support due to dwindling audiences.

27. *Renmin Ribao* (hereafter, *RMRB*), Overseas Edition, May 7, 1988, p. 1; *FEER*, September 8, 1988, pp. 130–31; *New York Times*, March 20, 1989, p. C10.

28. *BR* 9 (February 27–March 5, 1989), p. 27. In one Beijing market, over 80 percent of the male entrepreneurs had served time in jail. See *BR* 5 (January 30–February 5, 1989), p. 34.

29. *FEER*, August 24, 1989, p. 52. See also *Chinese Economic Studies*, note 17, pp. 43–71.

30. *Shichang Bao*, note 25.

31. BBC *Survey of World Broadcasts*, FE/8449 BII/9 (December 23, 1986).

32. *Geti Laodongzhe Shouce*, note 13, pp. 84–86.

33. *Asian Wall Street Journal*, September 3, 1987, p. 1.

34. In April 1989, there were 200,000 private businessmen among the CCP's 47 million members—a ratio of roughly 1:235 (*Wenhui Bao* [Shanghai], April 9, 1989).

35. *BR* 9 (February 27–March 5, 1989), pp. 23–26.

36. *Jingji Ribao*, November 23, 1987, p. 1; *FBIS*, January 2, 1984, p. K19.

37. This is well discussed in Linda Hershkovitz, "The Fruits of Ambivalence: China's Urban Individual Economy," *Pacific Affairs* 58, no. 3 (Fall 1985), pp. 427–50.

38. For instance *RMRB*, Overseas Edition, August 30, 1989, p. 4.

39. Xie Peihui, *Qian, Fengkuang di Kunshou* (Changsha: Hunan Wenyi Chubanshe, 1988).

40. *BR* 33 (August 15–21, 1988), p. 7. *CD* claimed on July 31, 1989 (Business Weekly Supplement, p. 1), that "the average income of private entrepreneurs is about 7,500 yuan, 3.7 times that of employees in state-owned enterprises."

41. *BR*, note 40.

42. See, e.g., *RMRB*, Overseas Edition, February 25, 1989, p. 4.

43. *Chinese Economic Studies* 21, no. 2 (Winter 1987–1988), pp. 65–66.

44. For overviews on the economic aspects, see *Asia Yearbook, 1989* (Hong Kong: Far Eastern Economic Review, 1988), pp. 102–12; also *BR* 36 (September 4–10, 1989), pp. 19–22 and 22–28.

45. Many of the ideas appeared in Shanghai's *Shijie Jingji Daobao* (World Economic Herald). On privatization, see note 7, above, and *New York Times*, January 10, 1989, p. 1. A summary of neo-authoritarianism can be found in *FBIS*, March 24, 1989, pp. 40–43.

46. *South China Morning Post,* October 23, 1989, Business p. 9.
47. *RMRB,* Domestic, August 17, 1989, p. 1; *Wall Street Journal,* August 22, 1989, p. A12; *Financial Review,* October 4, 1989, p. 15; *FBIS,* July 5, 1989, pp. 27–28. Cao Siyuan was released from detention in May 1990; see *New York Times,* May 11, 1990, p. A1.
48. *RMRB,* Domestic, July 29, 1989, p. 1.
49. *RMRB,* Domestic, August 28, 1989, p. 1.
50. *San Francisco Chronicle,* November 8, 1989, p. 21. On August 29, Ren Zhonglin, director of the State Administration of Industry and Commerce, reported to the Ninth Meeting of the Seventh NPC Standing Committee on progress in cleaning up companies. See *FBIS,* August 30, 1989, pp. 7–8.
51. *Jingji Ribao,* August 2, 1989, p. 1; *RMRB,* Domestic, August 2, 1989; *RMRB,* Overseas Edition, October 25, 1989, p. 1.
52. *CD,* August 2, 1989, p. 1.
53. *CD,* November 6, 1989, p. 3; *FBIS,* October 3, 1989, p. 61.
54. *FBIS,* July 12, 1989, pp. 15–20.
55. *South China Morning Post,* October 2, 1989, p. 1.
56. *CD,* November 7, 1989, p. 4; *BR* 45 (November 6–12, 1989), pp. 11–12; *FBIS,* October 27, 1989, pp. 15–18.

6

Urban Reform and Relational Contracting in Post-Mao China: An Interpretation of the Transition from Plan to Market

Dorothy J. Solinger

Urban economic reform in China has been geared toward effecting a transition from a centrally planned economy to one significantly driven by market relations. In fashioning this transition, China's reformist leaders have sought to create an economic system that matches, in many essential respects, the ideal-typical model of market exchange presented in neoclassical economics. They believe that through market reform it will be possible to overcome a host of structural weaknesses that have led to recurrent inefficiencies and stagnation in the operation of China's socialist planned economy.[1]

In its bare outlines, the reformist argument neatly counterposes the administrative logic of state-determined prices and state-mandated coordination of exchange to the market logic of supply-and-demand-responsive prices and voluntary contracting. Thus framed, the issue of systemic reform appears to be one of dichotomous choice, i.e., a clear and simple either/or proposition. This chapter takes as its main theme the idea that such a dichotomous conception, though elegant and parsimonious in theory, is profoundly misleading in practice. Specifically, I shall argue that the actual line between plan and market in China is not nearly so sharply drawn as neoclassical Western economists and Chinese reformers have averred. I shall further argue that certain operational features of China's prereform economy have clearly survived the demise of mandatory central planning, taking the form of hybridized, informal relations of exchange. One such residual hybrid feature—"relational contracting"—provides the main empirical focus of this paper.

In seeking to account for the actual economic behavior of Chinese enterprises in the period since comprehensive urban economic reform was first introduced in 1984, I have found that the most important operational distinctions do not concern the familiar conceptual dichotomy of plan vs. market, but rather focus on the presence or absence of certain infrastructural/develop-

The comments of Bernard Grofman were very helpful in the final revision of this chapter. Earlier versions benefited from comments by Richard Baum, Peter Gourevitch, William Parish, and Susan Shirk.

mental constraints that exist independently of both plan and market. Three such constraints are of particular relevance to the present study: (1) a *high degree of shortage* of vital productive inputs and capital goods; (2) a *lack of design standardization* (and/or uniform quality control) in the manufacture of productive inputs/capital goods; and (3) a *weakness in existing channels of supply information* (and consequent high managerial uncertainty) concerning the availability and reliability of these inputs/goods. I shall demonstrate that, depending on the degree to which these three constraints are both present and salient, "relational contracting"—a highly-patterned, repetitive form of economic exchange—will tend to occur; and I shall further show that this will hold true regardless of whether the local economy is nominally driven by the plan or by the market.

I begin with a brief sketch of the concept of relational contracting. I then explain how in several crucial ways the planned economy in China before 1979 not only satisfied but also advanced the conditions for this type of exchange, leaving deep imprints on the system—imprints that are very much in evidence today. Next, I offer a brief overview of the main components of the urban economic reform program proposed in late 1984, followed by presentation of empirical data pertaining to the points mentioned above. This data has been drawn from the large central China city of Wuhan, designated in 1984 as one of China's key experimental centers of comprehensive urban reform. Sources include newspaper and journal articles for the three-year period 1984–87, plus thirty-five hours of interviews I conducted in Wuhan. The conclusion brings out explicitly the relevant interconnections between the Chinese data and the various analytical observations and hypotheses presented in the body of the paper.

The Concept of Relational Contracting

Following I. R. Macneil, Williamson identifies relational contracting as one of three generic transaction modes, the other two being classical and neoclassical contracting.[2] The three modes are distinguished by their relative specificity, frequency, duration, and complexity. While classical contracting is generally recurrent and standardized, neoclassical contracting is sporadic and idiosyncratic; both, however, involve contracts of relatively short duration and low complexity. By contrast, relational contracting entails contracts of relatively long duration and enhanced complexity. This third form of contracting also requires "adjustment processes of a more thoroughly transaction-specific, ongoing administrative kind,"[3] as opposed to the more standardized contracts that typically accompany impersonal marketized exchange. Williamson thus argues that relational contracting is the form that develops for transactions of a *recurring* and *nonstandardized* kind.[4]

Other authors stress the point that relational contracting tends to remove many economic transactions from the "invisible hand" of market discipline. Goldberg, for example, notes that much economic activity in the West "takes place within long-term, complex, perhaps multiparty contractual (or contract-like) relationships," and that such relationships are often "shielded in varying degrees from market forces."[5] He also notes that the relational exchange approach "recognizes that [such] sheltering is inevitable and, moreover, that it can be functional."[6] Dore makes a similar point in observing that

> All economies in practice, notwithstanding Adam Smith, contain a fair proportion of . . . trust relationships, as opposed to arm's-length contractual relationships . . . "Relational contracting versus spot contracting" [is one way of putting it].[7]

While Goldberg's conclusions derive from his observation of Western economies, Dore believes that relational contracting is even more pronounced in Japan, where "established customer relations ramify throughout the economy."

The propensity to build trading relationships that offer a premium in trust, predictability, and security of supply, and which cut down on information-search costs, is very likely universal; and the need for such values drives parties to exchanges in many contexts to adopt what Dore terms the "intermediate alternative" of relational contracting, whereby a user combines with a tied supplier in stably patterned "networks of preferential trading relations."[8] Stated differently, relational contracting builds upon the social dimension of marketing. That is, all markets are embedded in a *social context*, so that to varying degrees in different economies such personal, cultural, and political factors as trust, reputation, past dealings, habits, and institutions always have a bearing on the choice of trading partners.[9]

In addition, all transactions take place within a certain *technological environment*. The key technological factor is the stage of development, which affects the infrastructure for trade, e.g., in transport and communications. The developmental stage also influences the amount of supply (shortage vs. plenty) and the degree of standardization of products within an industrial sector, with greater technological sophistication permitting higher levels of quality control. Through its impact on marketing framework and on quantity and quality of output, then, developmental stage determines, from a technological standpoint, the degree of certainty and predictability that pertain in a given market.

Growing out of the social and technological contextual factors is another crucial element affecting the nature of exchange: the richness or impoverishment of information networks.[10] Where information is hardest to come by for social, political, or cultural reasons, and where shortage, nonstandardization, and hence uncertainty and unpredictability are greatest, one would expect relational contracting, with its reassuring recurrence and its catering to idiosyncrasy, to be the solution of choice.[11] Thus, in economies where shortage, nonstandardization, and weak information channels are pronounced, we would expect to find a prevalence of relational contracting. Such "mutually obligated trading relationships," as Dore calls them, sometimes involve the use of nonmarket prices that cause at least short-term economic loss to one or the other party.[12] And Goldberg's "sheltering" means, of course, that deals are not struck with "all comers without restriction." So in those cases where relational contracting is occurring, one could argue that administrative adjustment of some sort will act to disrupt the pure play of neoclassical market forces.

Relevant Properties of The Planned Economy

As a dominant force in the trading environment of the prereform Chinese economy, the state plan itself served to promote relational contracting. In order to appreciate the role played in China today by our three structural constraints—shortage, nonstandardization, and weak information channels—we need to consider how the Stalinist-style command system fed their growth for nearly three decades, embedding these properties deeply into the Chinese political economy. It should be noted at the outset that this was an economy generally characterized by oft-mandated, initially idiosyncratic—but, with time, habitually recurrent—exchanges. And these exchanges were structurally similar to those in other economic systems wherein sunk costs lock buyer and seller into a relationship of bilateral monopoly.[13]

Kornai's famous study of the socialist planned economy explains the prominent role played by shortage.[14] According to Kornai, shortage occurs in the socialist economy's "atmosphere of growth at a forced rate," which leads to an "insatiable demand" for inputs on the part of firms, especially those in the heavy industrial sector, and to an "expansion drive" coupled with "investment hunger," as each firm is instructed by its superior planning authority that it "must grow." As total claims for funding always surpass prescribed investment quotas, competition for investment along with the accompanying tensions serve to exacerbate the general state of shortage.[15] Thus, for example, despite the massive amount of funds invested in the heavy industrial sector—mainly for metals and producer goods—over decades of Communist party rule in China and other socialist systems, shortage inevitably prevailed.

Hanson, writing principally about consumer goods, finds another reason for perennial shortage in these economies. He speaks of sellers' markets, whose presence he blames on controlled prices, which lead in turn to repressed inflation. Thus, at low, fixed prices there is excess demand and a consequent shortage of almost everything consumers want.[16] And, of course, the consumer goods sector generally suffers from an imbalanced pattern of investment in socialist systems, which regularly slight consumption in favor of investment in producer goods.

Kornai also has an explanation for the low level of standardization in centralized command economies. He describes how state-owned firms, charged with meeting specific output targets, engage in "forced substitution." That is, they are compelled to alter the input combination of their products as a result of shortage. If a necessary input is unavailable, firms often end up with a nonstandard product as they attempt to adjust to the shortage.[17]

Kornai also discusses information problems in command economies. He refers to the "imperfect information of the participants in the allocation process"; and he stresses the value of information in reducing costly searches and alleviating the need to make forced substitutions.[18] One structural reason for the existence of deficiencies in the information networks of command economies is the long-term relative neglect of sectors other than heavy industry. Because of the skewed investment patterns in these systems, the infrastructure of transportation and communications, so vital to the establishment of information channels, has long been ignored in all socialist systems, including the Chinese.[19]

Perhaps the most intractable problem in information networks in these systems, however, is the fact that state organs dominate the allocation of goods at each administrative level. The personnel of such organs—particularly, in the industrial sector, workers in the materials supply departments and the planning commissions—are the agents best placed to receive and disseminate market information. There are, of course, other, informal channels of information that grow out of—but exist independently of—the formal state-operated supply channels. But even here, the purchasing agents of the factories who scout for extra economic intelligence must depend upon state-sponsored meetings and "deals" made with other state-run units to locate and procure their required inputs.[20] As a result, state design severely circumscribes the scope and boundaries of economic behavior, and thus limits as well the flow of vital information.

Shortage, nonstandardization, and weak information channels, then, are endemic features of the command economy. Where these features are especially pronounced, relational contracting—recurrent exchanges with known partners—often becomes the most reliable form of exchange. Under the command economy the majority of recurrent exchanges are compulsory, i.e., they result from couplings mandated by the state planning bureaucracy. Thus, in China under the regime of the state plan, with the exception of the largest and most important enterprises, whose managers could at times negotiate and conclude their own supply and sales contracts, most legitimate transactions were arranged by administrative departments.[21] Recent interviews have confirmed that planners recurrently paired the same partners over many years.[22]

Failure properly to match input specifications to need was not uncommon under the reign of the plan. Indeed, such mismatches have attained great notoriety in critiques of the command economy. But the larger picture was one in which, most of the time, most firms got what they needed to produce what they were ordered to turn out, even if quality was wanting. This laid the foundation for a relatively satisfactory recurrent allocation of materials among enterprises, so that firms came to count on supplies from particular plants with which they were conjoined by the plan. When maldistribution did occur, firms tended to engage in illicit or quasilegal activities that made up what is known as the "second economy" or gray market. They did this in order to overcome breakdowns in the formal supply system that threatened to prevent fulfillment of planned targets.[23]

In China in prereform days, gray-market dealings usually took one of two forms, both of which probably led to recurrent exchanges between the same enterprises. These were, first, transactions in which raw materials were supplied by one enterprise to another which made goods for it; and second, barter arrangements—sometimes of inappropriate for appropriate parts, sometimes of such disparate items as chemicals traded for equipment or trucks for steel.[24] Once a procurement agent had identified his source, he was likely to continue to build upon personal connections fostered by previous transactions, thereby saving himself additional, unnecessary search costs.

It is certainly true that relational contracting occurs in commodity transactions in all sorts of economies, especially where a relatively low developmental level renders such behavior optimal.[25] But structural properties peculiar to the socialist command economy clearly reinforce the state plan's forced pairing of enterprises. The result is to make this sort of transaction the overwhelmingly dominant one in economies that are both less developed and centrally planned. The continuing strength of known connections built up over time in these systems, along with the persistence of several conducive features in the technological environment—viz., shortage, nonstandardization, and inadequate information—have led many enterprises to continue doing business with their original, prereform partners long after the advent of the "market." The upshot is that the transition from command to commerce has been smoother (i.e., involving less disruption or dislocation) than would have been predicted by a model that presumes a bold leap from pure planning to open markets.[26]

The Chinese Urban Reform Program

In China a process of economic reform has been underway since the much publicized Third Plenum of the Eleventh Central Committee, held in

December 1978. At first, rural reform commanded center-stage. Despite scattered experiments, urban/industrial reform did not really go forward in an energetic way until October 1984, when the party issued a major document on urban reform at the Twelfth Central Committee's Third Plenum.[27] A new definition of the Chinese economic system emerged from the latter meeting, a definition which, at the rhetorical level, subtly shifted the balance of regulatory forces away from the old, primarily planned framework. It was decreed that China was now "practicing a planned commodity economy on the basis of public ownership," a characterization that legitimized commodity production and exchange, placing them at the heart of the system's operation. Such activities, with all they implied in terms of reliance on market forces, had for decades been viewed in China as lacking in socialist legitimacy.

The 1984 document, which was more a statement of intent than a plan of immediate action, contained four major points, coinciding with the four main arenas of reform—the planning system, management, prices, and wage policy. In planning, central commands (the equivalent of what are called "imperative plans" in developed economies) were to give way to "guidance"-type directives (similar to what is known as "indicative" planning in Japan and the West) and to market forces, with obligatory norms applying only to major products having a significant bearing on the national economy. In management, state control over enterprises was to be relaxed, with firms thenceforth to be responsible for organizing more and more of their own supply procurement and sales. Enterprise managers, taking on new authority, were to be responsible for their own profits and losses. "Irrational" prices, set according to political objectives and largely unchanged since the 1950s, were to be readjusted with the proviso that real incomes should not be disturbed. Finally, wages were to be linked to an individual's actual work output, with differentials between wage grades correspondingly widened.

Since 1984 an effort has been made to implement these general principles. Enterprises have been granted the power to trade materials not procured by the central government; and lower-level administrations have been given the authority to allocate and manage significant proportions of key supplies. The number of commodities handled by the state's distribution system has also declined precipitously in recent years, from 256 in 1978 to only 20 in 1986. By the summer of 1987, a new mode of management had been introduced in 75 percent of China's 12,398 larger state-owned industrial enterprises. Known as the "contract responsibility system," it was designed to give enterprise managers added control over local operations. A new profit retention scheme was also pioneered, under which profits retained by enterprises rose to 39 percent of total profits, a three-fold increase over what they had been permitted to keep at the outset of the reform era in 1979. With respect to the reform of prices, the proportion of items with prices fixed by the state decreased dramatically, from 98 percent in 1978 to only 20 percent in 1986.[28] Based on the above statistics, it would appear that a number of nontrivial alterations have taken place in the form of inter-enterprise trade in China since 1978. Yet, data from the city of Wuhan suggests that despite such alterations there are definite continuities in firms' choices of trading partners—continuities that belie any assumption of radical, market-oriented change. Below we examine this data.

Relational Contracting and Reform in Wuhan

In June 1984, four and a half months before the seminal October urban reform document was issued, the central Chinese city of Wuhan, whose gross value of industrial output then ranked fourth nationwide, was chosen as the second city to be granted separate line-item status in the central plan. Through this move, Wuhan secured economic management powers equal to those of a province; and the city was expected to lead an experiment in comprehensive urban reform for provincial capitals.[29]

Both historically and under the People's Republic, Wuhan has occupied a place of special importance as a transport hub and transshipment center. Sitting astride both the Yangtze River and the Guangzhou-Beijing Railway, almost equidistant from Chongqing, Shanghai, Guangzhou, and the national capital, Wuhan has traditionally served as the "thoroughfare of nine provinces." But this role was to a large extent thwarted under the rule of vertical (that is, central and provincial-level) bureaucracies, with their planned, compulsorily conducted commerce and their transport coordinated by separate, enclosed political authorities along administratively demarcated boundaries.[30] With the advent of urban reform, it was hoped that Wuhan, with its newly-enhanced economic powers, would be able to reenact its historical role as a center of foreign trade, finance, banking, and information, even as it reinforced its post-1949 position as a base of industry, higher education, and research.[31] In short, Wuhan's enhanced status would underline the overall national economic reform's dramatic shift toward market-oriented commerce and economically based, decentralized decision making. It was undoubtedly for this reason that Wuhan was selected as a reform model.

In the remainder of this chapter I will examine in detail one particular aspect of the "model" urban reforms undertaken in Wuhan—the way in which enterprises select their transaction partners. As the material below will illustrate, firms often elect to trade via relational contracting. That is, they frequently pick tested associates, in most cases, the very same supply sources and sales outlets that were once written into their plans. The outcome has been to replace prescriptive relational contracting with relational contracting by preference, thereby preserving the essence, if not the form, of the old state plan. The persistence of the three traditional infrastructural properties mentioned earlier—namely, shortage, nonstandardization, and inadequate information channels—can be shown to have played a significant role in shaping this outcome.

Persistence of Structural Properties

Shortage

Kornai's "insatiable demand" has not disappeared with the diminution of demands from central planners. Indeed, the urge of urban officials and enterprise managers to expand their operations has if anything increased in recent years. Beginning in 1980, financial reforms permitted firms and localities to retain a portion of the profits they generated, instead of having to turn over all receipts to higher-level offices.[32]

Under the new economic regime, not only do firms compete among themselves for a share of centrally allocated supplies and investment as they once did under the old planned economy,[33] but they strive—with considerable success, it would seem—to obtain and hold onto resources that nominally belong to the central government. One measure of this loss of central control over resource allocation is the 1987 nationwide estimate that 47 percent of rolled steel, 48 percent of coal, and 84 percent of cement were at that point no longer distributed by the state.[34] Another effect of the reforms has been to permit the free trading of materials left over after delivery quotas to the state have been met. This has created a dual price structure, with market prices of goods on the second (supply-and-demand-governed) track often at least twice as high as those set by the state. The high market prices clearly indicate continuing materials shortages.[35] Further evidence for the persistence of shortage is the central government's frequent issuance of bulletins bemoaning its inability to carry through with national construction projects. The crux of the problem reportedly lies in the state's loss of control over raw materials.[36]

Yet another indication of shortage is contained in a 1985 report which describes the operation of new wholesale materials "trade centers." The report claims that these markets, authorized in 1984 to sell supplies flowing outside the plan's networks, operate in what are essentially sellers' markets:

When motor vehicles and steel products are in unusually short supply, if the materials departments sponsor some trade centers, they simply go through the form of a "center" in order to concentrate all extra-plan trade in one place, thereby preventing speculation and stopping improprieties. Strictly speaking, this isn't what was originally meant by a trade center, [so] calling it a sales center is probably more appropriate.[37]

Continuing materials shortage is further revealed in a decision made by the Wuhan Heavy Machinery Plant. This huge plant was supposedly placed under Wuhan's municipal control under the 1984 urban reform program. However, at a meeting at the Ministry of Machine Building in Beijing in 1985, plant managers were given a choice: thenceforth, they could either depend upon the central ministry, the province (which previously had controlled the plant), or the city in order to procure their basic allotment of material supplies guaranteed under the state plan. Because plant officials believed that there was a greater certainty of supplies coming from the central level, they picked the Ministry of Metallurgy as their supplier of choice. Even so, the amount of materials they were able to obtain from the ministry decreased each year after this arrangement was instituted. Where 40 percent of the plant's total input needs had been met through the state plan in 1983, successively lesser amounts were delivered to it thereafter, varying in accordance with the amount of supplies the ministry had on hand at any given time.[38] This example shows the continued presence of shortages in two critical respects: first, in the firm's perception of a shortage of supplies at the local government level—this despite the grant of increased managerial autonomy at that level; and second, in the steady decline of inputs provided by central authorities—thus reducing the state's capacity to direct resources in accordance with national objectives and priorities.

Nonstandardization and Shoddy Goods

The widespread presence—indeed, the apparent prevalence—of inferior goods and nonstandardized products further predisposes economic agents to opt for relational contracting. One telling piece of evidence for the continued salience of this problem is the curious saga of an exhibit of "shoddy products" that was scheduled to be held by the Ministry of Light Industry in Beijing in August 1987. The show was designed to shame (and then to fine) factories into improving the quality standards of their products. Substandard goods were to be collected from dissatisfied consumers, who were to be compensated or given replacements, while the negligent producers were required to buy back their products. For about a week following the announcement of the show, the ministry was "bombarded with telephone complaints from [angry] consumers."[39] Ultimately, pressure from the offending factories led to cancellation of the exhibit.

A related problem is that of nonstandardized design specifications and quality controls, leading to serious problems of product incompatibility. A 1987 report in the Chinese press acknowledged the severity of this problem and blamed it on poor management decisions:

> There were cases where different types of equipment bought by a single factory were not compatible with each other . . . In one chemical fibre company, for

example, five production lines were imported from five different countries, leading to poor quality products and small production capacity because of the different characteristics of the equipment.[40]

Reports of uneven quality also appear frequently in my Wuhan data. One incident involved a large department store which invested a sum of RMB 100,000 yuan in a bicycle plant in a distant eastern Chinese city (one with which they had had dealings in prereform days) because the store's buyers trusted this particular plant to produce high-quality bikes.[41] Another case concerned the aforementioned Wuhan Heavy Machinery Plant, which signed a contract pledging the plant to invest three million yuan in a factory in Hunan in exhange for a three-year supply of iron at the low, state-controlled price. The supply relationship between the two plants had its foundation in the prereform days of the plan, when their respective staffs made frequent mutual visits (lailaiwangwangde guanxi). Those earlier shared experiences taught the plant's buyers that only the iron from this particular firm in Hunan could meet their specific quality requirements.[42]

Inadequate Information

Problems of quality and uncertainty are found in markets of many kinds.[43] But where quality is particularly variable and thus questionable, such as in the still rather undeveloped Chinese industrial system (and thus in the incipient domestic market), its link with uncertainty is closest. In such a situation, the need for reliable information is most crucial—the more so if shortage is present as well. And yet Chinese industrial information networks today remain state-dominated and relatively impoverished—despite the government's commitment to developing markets.[44] One press account makes the extreme claim that Chinese information and consulting services are still so weak that firms cannot even locate partners for exchange.[45] A somewhat less dramatic appraisal held that "due to the absence of a regular feedback system, enterprises normally obtain information through personal connections or just by chance. Thus, many of them have reached cooperation agreements with others without being guided."[46] This latter appraisal of the Chinese market system today is wholly consistent with the analysis in this paper.

Because of the glaring weakness of Chinese market intelligence, the state has recently made a heavy investment in information management and control. This effort is most apparent in the section "Information and Consulting" in the 1986 *Wuhan Yearbook*.[47] That section describes the functions of a dozen networks, committees, and centers created in recent years to disseminate internal bulletins to and promote economic intelligence exchanges among Wuhan and similar official, state-managed agencies at city and provincial levels across the country; the new agencies are also expected to engage in economic forecasting. The dozen networks and bodies mentioned in the yearbook include the Wuhan City Economic Information Forecasting Center, the Wuhan City Industrial Economic Information Center, and the Wuhan Commercial Information Network. That all of these are state-sponsored and -managed underlines the persisting dominance of the public sector in this field, and suggests a generalized poverty of market avenues outside its control.

Perhaps the most efficacious information channels of all are those run by state organs and carried over from the days of state planning. One such organ is the local materials supply bureau, which for decades allocated supplies for industrial production in accord with the plan's directives. The bureau now plays a strong role in managing market information in the new reform environment. Its cadres have longstanding ties with factory managers across the country, many of whom have been on the job for years. Another set of key actors is composed of the old factory purchasing agents (*caigouyuan*) who have served their firms over decades whenever the plan proved inadequate. All industrial enterprises have a half dozen to a dozen such personnel. Each agent specializes in one or more materials about which he has built up a stock of knowledge over the years with respect to what can be obtained, where, and how. Most of these people are still in place. They operate by linking into the pervasive enterprise information networks (*qiye xinxi wangluo*) that have long stretched across China, of which there are two main types. The major network, or *da wang*, tells what can be found in particular cities; the minor one, the *xiao wang*, is more specific and pertains to the materials held by individual factories. By continuing to communicate through these networks, factories are able to locate much of what they ostensibly purchase "on the market."[48] In an environment of weak intelligence sources, old connections—those built up under the old state planning system—thus continue to structure exchange.

In sum, abiding shortages, problems of standardization and quality control, and limited information channels all incline firms to continue to rely on those enterprises with which they have longstanding, well-tested, and trusted trading ties. Transaction cost efficiencies of such relational contracting certainly facilitate the smooth implementation of the "market" reforms currently being pushed in China. This type of commerce obviates the need to spend precious time and resources locating new partners, and consequently, more business can be contracted more expeditiously than could be done through a sudden leap to spot markets. It is ironic that such exchanges, which serve to reduce transaction costs, stand in the way of what many critics have presumed to be the most economically rational marketing arrangements in the purest neoclassical sense. A few examples drawn from my Wuhan interviews will demonstrate this general point.

Relational Contracting in Action: The Case of Wuhan

Several of the new reforms are explicitly geared toward encouraging cities and firms to break out of the boundaries previously imposed by the bureaucratic strictures of the state plan, and to link up for what are presumed to be more economically rational purposes. One example is the program of "lateral exchange," *hengxiang lianxi*, which has been advocated as a means of connecting supply sources directly with consumer demand, and to demolish the "blockades" between districts imposed by administrative orders. In conception, lateral exchange entails several enterprises coordinating the flow of capital, technology, materials, and sometimes even personnel across administrative and geographical boundaries. Other recently created forms of lateral exchange include trade centers, markets for the means of production, capital markets, and "enterprise groups" (also called "socialist trusts").[49]

In apparent violation of the spirit underlying these schemes, many relational contracting configurations remain exclusively within local boundaries, maintaining intact linkages initially forged under the old state plan. The 1986 *Wuhan Yearbook,* for instance, reveals a total of 255 external commercial offices registered in the city for the purpose of facilitating exchange with Wuhan. These bodies, representing administrative units from other counties, townships, municipalities, and provinces, were staffed by a total of 4,994 personnel. Yet, less than 5 percent of these commercial agencies—employing only 2.5 percent of the total working personnel—represented higher-level government bodies at the municipal and provincial levels.[50] What this suggests is that the overwhelming bulk of the business being brokered by such agencies was being conducted with small, local units very near Wuhan. It also suggests a continuing reliance on known partners. The remarks of a local economist back up this inference of an unbroken relationship between localism and the state plan:

> In the past we were sealed up (*fengbi*), so we managed work according to administrative [planned] relations. As a result, relations with Hubei province [of which Wuhan is the capital city] and within Wuhan are the main part of our present exchanges.[51]

Indeed, localism shows up in much of the implementation of reform in Wuhan. When the municipal government designated the Wuhan Bazaar (a major department store) as a "keypoint" for reform, extending it permission to draw up a share group (*gufen jituan*) in late 1986, the store picked seven investors.[52] All were city-based firms, including the mammoth Wuhan Iron and Steel Works, an insurance company, and the Wuhan branches of the People's and Agricultural banks. Since, as its managers explained, the risk would be smaller with local partners whose business acumen was well known to the store, these managers intentionally invited only units from Wuhan to join. This strategy was also meant to contribute to the growth of the local economy, thus boosting consumer purchasing power in the city.

Another case in point was a capital market centered in Hubei province. This particular market was one of five interbank networks of which Wuhan constituted the hub. But a researcher from the local branch of the People's Bank admitted that of the five networks, it was the intraprovincial market was the most active. Within the province, he said, communications were easiest (no doubt for both social and technological reasons) and transactions were frequent, if not in large denominations. This was true despite the fact that one of the other capital networks was composed of cities that, like Wuhan, had special status in the state plan, plus several of the special economic zone cities; one might have expected such a network to have comparatively great autonomy—and thus the clout to form a lively market for funds.[53]

The story was not substantially different for Wuhan's department stores. Much of their stock came from factories whose staff the stores' managers had met over the years at state-run semiannual national supply meets. These meets, which each represent a particular type of commodity, were formerly run by the relevant wholesale companies within the state commercial system. In the past, under the regime of the plan, factories, whose total output was automatically purchased and allocated to retailers, participated merely to learn about the stores' demands; now they come to do business. Today, the *guanxi* (personal connections) built up over years of attending the same meets stands these stores in good stead. At the Central-South Commercial Mansions, a sizable department store that opened in Wuchang (one of Wuhan's three component towns) in early 1985, almost all of the staff had previously worked in one of Wuhan's two other large stores. Spokesmen estimated that as much as 40 percent of the store's stock came from factories known to their coworkers from the past. Though this figure may not seem high at first glance, one might well have expected the percentage of old suppliers to be much smaller, given the institution of several new modes of locating stock, such as via advertisements, or by becoming a sales outlet for new industrial enterprise groups.[54]

In lateral exchanges, previous connections have similarly smoothed the transition from the mandatory plan to the market. For instance, of the eighteen units in the Wuhan Cement Machinery Complete-Set Company, a new firm organized around the Wuhan General Machinery Factory, eleven are from Hubei province and five others are from Wuhan. The other two, a design institute in Anhui and a factory in Jiangsu, are units with which this machinery plant had previous business ties (*yewu guanxi*) based on meetings, "exchange of experience," and mutual visits under the plan.[55]

Examples of this type figured prominently in my interviews.[56] The picture suggested by the data is this: in implementing the new reforms, firms have employed a number of specific practices, many of which share certain common features. Most outstanding among these is the general principle of relational contracting, which often works because the plan and its patterns have paved the way. That is, a significant portion of the trading of today takes place through the reinstitution on a voluntary basis of relational contracting, which makes use of previously established channels and ties, and which relies on personnel with inside knowledge of the availability and whereabouts of goods.

Conclusion

Once the argument is laid out, its gist appears commonsensical. We have seen that trading in any context tends to depend upon trust and so is socially embedded; we have also seen that the technological and informational environments of socialist economies such as the Chinese may reinforce existing social propensities for engaging in patterns of recurring, idiosyncratic exchange. Transaction cost analysis suggests that such behavior is economically rational; indeed, it is arguably more rational at this stage of the Chinese reform process than would be the installation of a neoclassical textbook model of a free market, wherein firms search out the optimal partner for each new exchange *de novo* on a nationwide scale. All in all, it seems clear that once the state plan's formal commands were lifted—commands which in the past joined firms by fiat in relational, bilaterally-monopolistic contracts—the pathways they left behind would in many instances persist, at least for a time. And so the networks composed of those pathways continue to bring the old partners together—this time, however, as a matter of *choice*. The overall effect of such a "sticky" pattern of behavior on the reform process is here judged to be positive. This is because relational contracting forms a secure platform for the expansion of market-based economic activity, facilitating an increase in the sheer volume of market transactions. This it does by lowering transaction costs, at least in the short run.

Since China's socialist planned economy in its heyday contributed to the growth of relational contracting, our findings should hold, in principle, for any environment where socialist planning systems institute market reforms. There are a few caveats, however. These would include the possibility that: (1) the historically less tightly planned Chinese economy may have better preserved its traditional marketing networks in the prereform period than was the case in other prereform socialist systems;[57] (2) the relatively greater degree of technological backwardness of the Chinese economy may mean that information channels are less well developed there than elsewhere; and (3) the state and economic system are so much larger in China than in most other socialist countries that localized marketing—where partners know each other well—would be expected to be more prevalent there. Despite the clarity of the evidence presented here, the considerable overlap and reciprocal impact of plan and market—the one shading into, and providing a platform for, the other—has heretofore been completely ignored by theorists of the reform of socialist systems. Instead, commentators have tended to focus their commentaries on widespread bureaucratic obstruction of enterprise autonomy, or on the ways in which pricing-system rigidities have stymied the institution of perfect neoclassical markets. From the opposite vantage point, other observers have seen in the gradual elimination of compulsory targets over the past decade, and in the flourishing of urban produce markets, the birth of a totally new free market phenomenon in the People's Republic. This too is overly facile. In this essay I have deconstructed both of these models. In their place, I have presented an analysis grounded in the empirical observation that in practice the operational distinction between plan and market is much more blurred than neoclassical theory would suggest. The concept of relational contracting has helped to highlight the fact that in the world of social experience there is no clear, unambiguous dividing line distinguishing the pattern of enterprise transactions under the plan from that under a certain type of market.

Notes and References

1. See, for example, *Jingji Guanli* (hereafter, *JJGL*) 8 (1987), in *Foreign Broadcast Information Service— China* (hereafter, *FBIS*), October 6, 1987, pp. 16–20. This article states that "the final goal of a market for the means of production is that through competition on terms of freedom and equality a renewed combination of important factors of production is realized" (p. 17).

2. Oliver E. Williamson, "Transaction-Cost Economics: The Governance of Contractual Relations," *Journal of Law and Economics* 22 (October 1979), p. 248.

3. *Ibid.*, p. 238.

4. *Ibid.*, pp. 248, 250.

5. Victor P. Goldberg, "Relational Exchange: Economics and Complex Contracts," *American Behavioral Scientist* 23, no. 3 (1980), p. 338.

6. *Ibid.*, p. 342.

7. Ronald Dore, *Flexible Rigidities: Industrial Policy and Structural Adjustment in the Japanese Economy, 1970–80* (Stanford: Stanford University Press, 1986), p. 2.

8. See Goldberg, note 5, p. 351; and Dore, note 7, pp. 2, 3, 77, 80.

9. On this point see the seminal article by Mark Granovetter, "Economic Action and Social Structure: The Problem of Embeddedness," *American Journal of Sociology* 91, no. 3 (November 1985), p. 481–510.

10. This idea draws and expands upon Oliver E. Williamson, *Economic Organization: Firms, Markets and Policy Control* (Brighton: Wheatsheaf, 1986), p. 55.

11. Dore (note 7, p. 162) notes that the Japanese system of relational contracting was "created out of shortage." Williamson (note 2, p. 260) points out that "as generic demand grows and the number of supply sources increases, exchange that was once transaction-specific loses this characteristic and greater reliance on market-mediated governance is feasible."

12. Dore, note 7, pp. 70, 162.

13. Williamson (note 2, p. 241) identifies idiosyncrasy of investments as the crucial factor distinguishing relational from other types of contracting: "Idiosyncratic goods and services are ones . . . where investments of transaction-specific human and physical capital are made . . . [T]he relationship between buyer and supplier is quickly thereafter transformed into one of bilateral monopoly—on account of the transaction-specific costs."

14. Janos Kornai, *The Economics of Shortage* (Amsterdam: North Holland Publishing Co., 1980), 2 vols.

15. *Ibid.*, pp. 27, 29, 193, 200, 201.

16. Philip Hanson, *Advertising and Socialism: The Nature and Extent of Consumer Advertising in the Soviet Union, Poland, Hungary and Yugoslavia* (White Plains, N.Y.: International Arts and Sciences Press, 1974), pp. 10-13, 20.

17. Kornai, note 14, pp. 37, 39.

18. *Ibid.*, pp. 171–72.

19. On this point, see Ma Hong, *New Strategy for China's Economy* (Beijing: New World Press, 1983), p. 38.

20. Barry Richman, *Industrial Society in Communist China* (New York: Random House, 1969), p. 714, speaks of the large ordering conferences which disseminate information in the industrial sector; Jean C. Oi makes a similar point for the agricultural sector. See "Commercializing China's Rural Cadres," *Problems of Communism* 35, no. 5 (September–October 1986), p. 10.

21. Richman, note 20, pp. 710–20.

22. I shall elaborate on this point below.

23. For example, see Hedrick Smith, *The Russians* (New York: Ballantine Books, 1977), p. 132; Benjamin N. Ward, *The Socialist Economy* (New York: Random House, 1967), p. 179; Gregory Grossman, "The 'Second Economy' of the USSR," *Problems of Communism* 26, no. 5 (September–October 1977), p. 29; Marshall I. Goldman, *Soviet Marketing: Distribution in a Controlled Economy* (New York: Free Press of Glencoe, 1963), p. 62; and Charles Lindblom, *Politics and Markets* (New York: Basic Books, 1977), chapter 5.

24. See Richman, note 20, pp. 389–90; also Audrey Donnithorne, *China's Economic System* (New York: Praeger, 1967), pp. 175, 290, 291.

25. To bolster this point, one external reviewer has called my attention to the fact that shortages, together with shoddy, low-quality work, are endemic in virtually

all underdeveloped economies—socialist and non-socialist alike. See also note 43 below.

26. An important problem not addressed in this paper is the marked increase in the incidence of corrupt behavior as strict, state-imposed controls and prices have diminished and a two-track pricing system has evolved. On the subject of the new sources and forms of corruption in a partially reformed market environment, see the chapters by Connie Squires Meaney and Jean C. Oi in the present volume.

27. This document and the politics surrounding its issuance are analyzed in Dorothy J. Solinger, "Economic Reform," in Steven M. Goldstein, ed., *China Briefing, 1984.* (Boulder: Westview Press, 1985), pp. 87–107. The reform document is in *Renmin Ribao* (hereafter, *RMRB*), October 21, 1984, in *China Daily* (hereafter, *CD*), October 22, 1984.

28. *Far Eastern Economic Review* (hereafter, *FEER*), July 16, 1987, pp. 69–71; *Beijing Review* (hereafter, *BR*) 34 (August 24, 1987), p. 4; *FBIS*, September 11, 1987, p. 25; and *BR* 37 (September 14, 1987), p. 15.

29. Within a year, five additional cities were granted this status in the central plan (Chongqing had already been so designated in early 1983): Guangzhou, Xi'an, Shenyang, Harbin, and Dalian. *RMRB* (July 18, 1987, p. 1) lists two additional cities in this category, Ningbo and Qingdao.

30. *FBIS*, July 3, 1984, p. Pl.

31. *Jianghan Luntan* (Wuhan) (hereafter, *JHLT*) 3 (1986), p. 8.

32. See Christine Wong, "Material Allocation and Decentralization: Impact of the Local Sector on Industrial Reform," and Barry Naughton, "False Starts and Second Wind: Financial Reforms in China's Industrial System," in Elizabeth J. Perry and Christine Wong, eds., *The Political Economy of Reform in Post-Mao China* (Cambridge: Harvard University Council on East Asian Studies, 1985), pp. 253–78 and 223–52, respectively.

33. Kornai, note 14, chapter 9, outlines this competition among what he terms "claimants."

34. *FEER*, June 18, 1987, p. 76. See also *BR* 9 (March 2, 1987), p. 24.

35. As one analyst put it succinctly, "Many production materials are in short supply; and their prices keep rising" (*FBIS*, December 18, 1987, p. 24). Also, an article in *People's Daily* explained that "the formation of a normal means of production market requires that supply and demand are basically balanced. But at present, the phenomenon that the supply of some major means of production falls short of demand is still a serious one in our country" (*RMRB*, February 20, 1987, p. 5).

36. For example, as early as 1983 the central media began decrying the "scattering" of resources that has accompanied the decentralizing reforms. *FBIS* (July 7, 1983, p. K19) carries a translated *Xinhua* report which stated that "from 1965 to 1982 the amount of rolled steel distributed by the state under the unified plan dropped from 95 to 53 percent; of cement, from 71 to 25 percent; and of timber, from 63 to 57 percent."

37. *JHLT* 11 (1985), p. 14.

38. Information from interview at the plant on June 29, 1987.

39. *FBIS*, August 20, 1987, p. 7.

40. *CD*, December 18, 1987, p. 2.

41. Interview at this store, June 23, 1987.

42. Interview, note 38.

43. On this issue see George A. Akerlof, "The Market For 'Lemons': Quality Uncertainty and the Market Mechanism," in George A. Akerlof, *An Economic Theorist's Book of Tales* (Cambridge: Cambridge University Press, 1984), pp. 7–22.

44. Oi (note 20, p. 10) stresses that Chinese peasants are experiencing difficulties in the new rural markets because of their lack of information about demand and prices; thus, they remain heavily dependent on their local cadres.

45. *JJGL* 6 (1987), p.13.

46. *RMRB*, April 10, 1987, p. 5, in *FBIS*, April 22, 1987, p. K14.

47. *Wuhan Nianjian 1986* (Hankow: Wuhan Nianjian Bianzuan Weiyuanhui Bianji, 1986), pp. 356–59, outlines and describes the functions of the massive local information network created by government organs in recent years in Wuhan and nationally.

48. Interview at the Wuhan Chemical Machinery Factory, June 25, 1987.

49. The new enterprise groups (*qiye jituan*) are discussed in *RMRB*, July 21, 1987, p. 2, in *FBIS*, July 29, 1987, p. K14. According to *RMRB* (August 10, 1987, p. 2), there were then over 1,000 such groups registered nationwide.

50. *Wuhan Nianjian*, note 47, p. 359.

51. Interview with a local economist, July l, 1987.

52. Interview, note 41. The group offered a 15 percent dividend on shares (twice the rate of bank interest) and had already collected RMB 10 million in shares by mid-1987, all drawn from partners picked by the store.

53. Interview with representative of the Financial Research Institute of the Wuhan branch of the People's Bank, June 24, 1987.

54. Information obtained from interview at the Central-South Commercial Mansions, June 29, 1987.

55. Interview at the factory, June 24, 1987.

56. I was unable to obtain the sort of data that would indicate the prevalence of such exchanges or the proportion of the total of voluntarily selected transactions that they represent; and available published statistics also fail to provide a clear answer. In early 1985 *Xinhua* reported that 20,000 inter-provincial economic and technical cooperation contracts had been signed in 1984, an amount that was double the figure in 1983 (*Xinhua*, March 11, 1985, in *Joint Publications Research Service* CEA–85–034 [April 5, 1985], p. 72). By the end of 1986, over 32,000 organizations formed via lateral economic ties had formed into 24

lateral economic liaison networks (*RMRB,* May 8, 1987, p. 5, in *FBIS,* May 20, 1987, p. K14). No information about the nature of these unions is available, however.

Nor is there any indication of the degree to which combinations form *within* provinces and more local areas—thus continuing to respect the old administrative boundaries—as opposed to those of a cross-provincial nature. Wuhan reported in 1985 that enterprises there had built up 517 economic associations and cooperative organs with partners in the city's suburban counties, and had signed over 300 cooperation projects with more than 20 counties and cities of Hubei—but without telling how many ties it had established outside the area (*FBIS,* February 5, 1986, p. K7). Yet another source states that in 1986, l,140 enterprises in the city engaged in such cooperation (termed *lianhe xiezuo,* or "united cooperation") with a total of 2,593 firms and units in 28 provinces and municipalities, signing 3,324 cooperative projects involving RMB 251 million yuan, but this time without giving the number of local projects in that year (*Wuhan Jingji Yanjiu* 3 [1987], p. 8).

57.   On the less thorough planning in China as compared with Eastern Europe, see David Granick, "The Industrial Environment in China and the CMEA Countries," in Gene Tidrick and Chen Jiyuan, eds., *China's Industrial Reform* (New York: Oxford University Press, 1987), pp. 103–31.

7

Market Reform and Disintegrative Corruption in Urban China

Connie Squires Meaney

By the spring of 1989, China had gone farther down the path of market reform than any other Leninist system. Reforms begun in the agricultural sector in 1979 were officially extended to the urban industrial sector in October 1984, when the Central Committee issued a major policy document on reform of the urban economic structure.[1] Urban reform allowed enterprises and managers within the state-owned sector to contract with other enterprises, handle their own sales and supplies, diversify operations, and engage in profit-making activities. The new, expanded roles for enterprises and their cadres were linked both to reform of the planning system, which reduced the number of items subject to mandatory planning, and to a reduction in the scope of prices set by the state. The 1984 document also reaffirmed the policy of "opening" to foreign trade and investment.

The party leadership clearly intended market reforms not only to "enliven" the economy but also to bolster the party's flagging prestige, badly damaged by the chaos of the Cultural Revolution, overcome the alienation of the professional classes, and put an end to years of economic inefficiency and cadre corruption. The Asian NICs—Taiwan, South Korea, and Singapore—seemed to provide relevant models of rapid economic development sponsored by authoritarian regimes that could be applied to the PRC (the "new authoritarianism"). In the event, however, China's hopes for pursuing rapid economic development without political upheaval were shattered by the events of April–June 1989.

Many factors combined to prevent a stable authoritarian outcome in China. The legacy of the Cultural Revolution figures prominently in any explanation. The stigmatizing and exclusion from career opportunities of the professional classes and their children alienated a group that otherwise might have formed a foundation for a stable technocratic but authoritarian regime; Deng's expedient courting of this stratum after 1979 could not entirely erase their mistrust.[2] Meanwhile, an entire generation of youth had acquired an experience of political activism, enhancing traditions of student mobilization and predisposing them toward political action.[3] More immediately, a kind of double demonstration effect was created by political liberalization in the Soviet Union and Eastern Europe and in Taiwan and South Korea. These provided models of political change and flexible policy that reflected poorly on the PRC's elderly authoritarians. Finally, as Gold points out, China's rulers appeared to be unaware that East Asia's "Four Dragons" are states in which "political repression was traded off for genuine opportunities for mobility through education and business"—a situation unlike that in China, where such opportunities were widely perceived as blocked by corruption and privilege.[4]

The issue of cadre corruption and privilege was probably the single most prominent issue uniting student demonstrators and the hundreds of thousands of Beijing residents who showed support for them. The students' demand that top leaders publish the incomes of themselves and their families is emblematic of this theme. In the period following the launching of reforms the PRC media had been full of reports denouncing new forms of corruption, both urban and rural.[5] The demonstrations of spring 1989, in which the issue of corruption provided a major focus, were overwhelmingly urban phenomena. Why did corruption become such a heated issue in the cities at this juncture? Had the market reforms begun in 1984 really produced a quantum leap in the incidence of corruption? Or had it perhaps only assumed forms that were more explosive politically?

To address this question we need to discriminate among various types of corruption and hypothesize about the political effects of each. Michael Johnston makes a useful distinction between "integrative" and "disintegrative" forms of corruption. The main variables in his typology are the number of parties involved and the degree to which the stakes of exchange in corrupt transactions are routine (e.g., small favors dispensed by a political machine) or extraordinary (e.g., windfall profits during a boom, huge construction contracts, etc.).[6] The more integrative forms of corruption "link people and groups into lasting networks of exchange and shared interest," while disintegrative corruption, by definition, does not do so, and may "produce divisions and conflict, both among those involved in a corrupt enterprise and between those who are included and those who are left out."[7] Integrative and disintegrative in the typology refer to the effects of corruption on its participants *within* political systems; that is, they do not translate automatically into integration or disintegration of an entire political system. The degree to which the integrative or disintegrative effects of corruption extend beyond the participants to the system as a whole depends on a number of other factors, such as the degree of public knowledge of corruption, the populace's beliefs about right and wrong, and the degree to which the divisiveness produced by corruption overlaps with other cleavages in a society.[8]

This essay will make the case that the postreform environment in China was, by 1989, one in which disintegrative forms of corruption had increased relative to other varieties.[9] Corruption will be defined here as any cadre behavior that violates laws, rules, or official norms against the pursuit of "private" benefit (oneself, family, friends). A convergence of political-cultural and structural factors acted to reinforce the disintegrative effects of corruption and extend them to the political system as a whole. Disintegrative corruption engendered increasing disaffection among the populace with the system and at the same time rendered the regime incapable of timely, effective response.

The situation that pertained in urban China after the onset of reforms in many ways came to resemble what Johnston terms "crisis corruption." This is the most disintegrative form, involving numerous participants in a scramble for extraordinary stakes. This was largely a novel phenomenon in the PRC and was an unintended consequence of the reforms. In addition, nepotism appeared with increasing frequency and magnitude (although it certainly was not new as such). Nepotism in Johnston's model represents the next most disintegrative form of corruption, involving few suppliers (thus many excluded parties) and high stakes. Since crisis corruption presupposes many participants and nepotism relatively few, it may seem paradoxical to propose that both were on the increase. The answer to this paradox is that the reforms unleashed a scramble for extraordinary stakes among a large segment of the urban populace which in turn enhanced the value of nepotistic relationships as a resource in the scramble.

The 1984 reforms supplied some new, structurally determined opportunities for certain forms of corruption and motives to take advantage of them. In particular, the dual economy of plan and market that emerged after the reforms greatly expanded opportunities for profiteering and speculation. Market reform left critical areas, notably prices, under state control. This created a kind of hybrid, two-track economy of plan and market, in which those with official connections could benefit from disparities in prices, inside information, and access to goods. Thus what emerged in the wake of market reform was, in the words of one observer, not a true market, but rather "a plethora of networks protected by cadres and bureaucrats, acting in secret."[10] Regardless of whether the notion of a true market open to all comers is appropriate,[11] these developments meant that many state organizations (and the party cadres serving in them) came to be dominated by cadre networks devoted entirely to money making; much of this activity inhabited a gray area between legal and illegal. Confusion about rules and fear of a change in political winds that would call a halt to the new policies predisposed people in general to think in terms of quick, windfall-type profits even in the absence of criminal intent. Meanwhile, the monetary stakes involved had been greatly raised by the reforms' encouragement of "getting rich" and by the opening to foreign investment and trade. The appropriation of official organizations by private cadre interests and the rush for quick financial killings in turn nurtured the nepotistic practice of cadres placing their offspring or other family members in financially advantageous positions.

Prevalence of crisis corruption and nepotism represents a different pattern from that of the prereform period, in which market corruption (regular exchanges of favors to grease the wheels of production or secure desired benefits for individuals)[12] and clientelism were most pervasive. Johnston proposes that these are less disintegrative because of the more routine character of the stakes involved (routine in both the sense of monetary amounts and the sense of regularized). Calling these patterns integrative does not imply that they lend legitimacy to the system, but rather that they can link a large number of people together in a reasonably stable *modus vivendi*.

We do not want to attribute various forms of corrupt behavior that occurred after 1984 exclusively to the reforms. To distinguish between pre- and postreform patterns of corruption and make a case for an increase in "disintegrative" corruption as a product of the reforms, I begin with a brief sketch of the prereform pattern, which tended toward clientelism and market corruption, as well as nepotism. These all involved relatively small monetary stakes (though often high political stakes). Next I present evidence for an increase in the disintegrative forms of corruption after 1984. In the concluding section I discuss why corruption in any form tends to have generalized political effects in the PRC and why the post-1984 mix may have been especially destabilizing.

Pre-Reform Patterns of Corruption

Prior to the introduction of reform, corrupt and/or particularistic behavior on the part of cadres and populace in the PRC generally arose from structural sources found in other Leninist systems.[13] The Leninist party's monopoly over opportunities for career mobility and material reward provided a firm basis for clientelist patterns.[14] In China the party controlled promotions and assignments, for technical and professional as well as political cadres, for nonparty as well as party cadres. Control over appointments and promotions made the party a vehicle for distributing patronage and exchanging favors. Patronage allowed officals such as party secretaries and cadres in charge of personnel work to form power bases and networks of personal ties.

The cadre appointment system in China corresponded to the *nomenklatura* system in the Soviet Union. It created the foundation for a build-up of clientelist relationships. As characterized by Burns, the Chinese *nomenklatura* system, like its Soviet counterpart, is

[well] suited to patronage politics . . . It centralizes authority over the national personnel system in the party. Although the party is not monolithic, its dominant role in personnel matters confines the search for patrons to those within the party . . . The Chinese system endorses personal recommendation as the best method for filling organizational positions. Abuses like factionalism, nepotism, and localism can be easily accommodated in such a practice.[15]

In such a system, local party officials emerge as patrons, with whom individuals (lesser cadres and ordinary individuals) cultivate relationships in order to pursue their interests. There is a tendency for the privilege and status connected with cadre rank to be made hereditary, which encourages nepotism in personnel appointments. In China, this tendency has been reinforced by a cultural pattern of passing office on from father to offspring. That the family ties of officeholders are a source of considerable criticism and speculation in Taiwan as well as the PRC suggests the strength of the this pattern.

Alongside clientelism and nepotism related to officeholding, the centrally controlled economy and chronic shortages found in Leninist systems help to create a broader social context in which the exchange of favors and cultivation of personal connections are the means to obtain scarce goods, substituting for impersonal market transactions.[16] In the Soviet Union and China these reciprocal exchange relationships and personal ties are denoted by the terms *blat* and *guanxi*, respectively.

A 1986 journalistic account of official abuses in a Chinese municipal grain bureau, coauthored by the well-known investigative reporter Liu Binyan, provides a sense of the various kinds of corrupt activities that flourished at the local level before the urban reforms;[17] it is a picture supported by interview material on the period in question. The case of Liu Shaoshan, a driver in the grain bureau, illustrates the ways in which patronage and nepotism intertwined with corrupt money making schemes on a relatively small scale. Liu was a person who had already engaged in nefarious economic practices at his former job in a market cooperative. After arriving at the grain bureau, he began to hire out a vehicle from the car pool for private use, pocketing the money. He also reportedly engaged in various profiteering and embezzlement schemes. When he was confronted and criticized by the car-pool chief, Liu simply stayed away from the job.

The reason Liu was given this cozy post at the grain bureau was that he was the brother of a deputy secretary of the municipal party committee, who had also appointed several section chiefs in the grain bureau by means of his relationship with a cousin, who was in charge of personnel administration in the municipal finance and trade committee. People working under his supervision who wished to secure promotions reportedly fawned on the latter official; in return, he allegedly "offered official posts and made lavish promises wherever he went."[18]

On weekends and holidays, the jeeps in the streets of Shuangya would shuttle to and fro, and in some of them were cadres of all levels attending dinner parties at the homes of "their own men." Now do not take this for a demonstration of the unhealthy tendencies of "going in for eating and drinking extravagantly." Many personnel questions concerning promotion and demotion, appointment to, removal from, and transference between offices were the subject of bargains finally struck at the banquet tables.[19]

Liu Binyan's journalistic account of the municipal grain bureau also relates the activities of two cadres in the bureau, the party secretary and the chief of the organizational section, who had advanced their careers during the Cultural Revolution and acquired a group of followers based on their control over promotions. They reportedly specialized in "bustling about to establish connections." The *modus operandi* of the two was described in the phrase, "grasp power, grasp personnel, grasp money and materials."[20]

Interviews with emigrés who worked in urban units in the PRC in the 1970s suggest a mixed pattern of routine market corruption, clientelism, and nepotism. One example involved a supply company under a municipal bureau, in which my informant had been employed because his father was a cadre. To get an allocation of materials, factory representatives in the city had to give the bureau and company cadres food, factory products, or other items. One could overcome problems with the bureau and company-level officials only if one had *guanxi* with someone at a higher level in the municipal government. Meanwhile, the materials bureau made a practice of recruiting workers from the countryside who were children of friends.

These kinds of behaviors in Johnston's model represent relatively integrative forms of corruption. As suggested by the publication of investigative reports on corruption and calls for reform, such behavior was a source of widespread popular disaffection with the party and provided part of the original impetus for undertaking economic reforms. However, one effect of market reforms was to transform these patterns into more disintegrative forms.

After the Reforms: Crisis Corruption on the Rise

Johnston defines crisis corruption as a form marked by many participants and very high stakes. He notes two likely causes for the emergence of this kind of activity. The first of these (following Huntington's analysis)[21] may occur in a system undergoing a crisis of institutionalization, in which "private parties may have so thoroughly penetrated the public realm that most public goods and services are up for sale." A second cause would be "an extraordinary influx of illicit resources from without." Crisis corruption might involve new networks of exchange and influence or the transformation of old ones.[22] "Crisis" does not necessarily imply a crisis in the whole system but rather denotes the quality of a frantic scramble for high stakes and the inherently unstable character of such a pattern.

The post-1984 reform climate in the PRC in a number of ways resembles this model of crisis corruption. The reforms created a crisis of institutionalization by turning existing official norms upside down (getting rich was now "glorious," etc.) and changing the rules to permit new economic activities. In this context it was frequently unclear just which activities were legal and which illegal. On top of this, the effects of an influx of money into the system were also felt—most commonly simply by allowing money to be made and spent after decades of prohibitions. Moreover, a substantial influx came in the form of investment from abroad, particularly from overseas Chinese. Unlike drug money in Latin America (an example given by Johnston), the increase in money in circulation in the PRC was not necessarily illicit. Given lack of clarity about the rules and motives for windfall profit, however, it shaded easily into gray and black areas. And, given the previous norms and rules of the system, an influx of money would not have to be enormous in monetary terms to represent extraordinary stakes. Below, we examine some of the emergent activities in the postreform environment that might be labeled crisis corruption.

Market reforms gave state enterprises broad freedom to contract among themselves, set prices, and expand into new profit-making activities. The new policies also seemed to permit government bureaus and corporations to diversify operations and set up profitmaking companies. In the context of the hybrid (part plan, part market) economy, such permissiveness encouraged various forms of profiteering and speculation. Cadres or entire state organizations could acquire scarce commodities at low state prices and resell them at inflated prices.[23] By mid-1988 the problem of profiteering had intensified and was contributing to runaway inflation. (Inflation at that time reached the highest level since 1949: prices in June 1988 rose 19 percent and possibly more over the previous June.)[24] By that time there was evident a multiplication of corporations created by ministries and bureaus and a diversification of administrative corporations. For example, in 1988 one province created 56 provincial-level corporations, while one city created as many as 106.[25] The new corporations were closely linked with profiteering. A new term for profiteers (dao ye) emerged in China and a variant form (guandao) was coined to apply to officials, or even whole units, who profiteer.[26]

The sheer number of state firms reported to be engaged in profiteering was staggering. According to China Daily, 250,000 of 360,000 new companies organized under the reforms by mid-1987 were involved in the sale and resale of scarce commodities and production materials, profiting from the disparities between state-fixed and market prices.[27] Their representatives traveled all over China, searching for products to buy low and sell high. They benefited from low-cost state loans to companies they set up under the reforms (e.g., materials supply and trading corporations and technology development centers). Sheer numbers, however, were not the only change. There was a qualitative departure from the past as well. The new phenomena differed from old practices of factories searching out and hoarding materials to ensure their supplies in that the main purpose of the new activity was simply to make a financial killing.[28]

The operations of profiteering companies were facilitated by their employment of retired cadres who could take advantage of their connections and influence to help them resell scarce merchandise and capital goods and raise prices.[29] In 1986, then-Premier Zhao Ziyang and CCP General Secretary Hu Yaobang reportedly advocated rules to forbid cadres from starting firms and taking a revolving door into private companies. This had little effect.[30] In 1988 there were reports that Guangdong businessmen were saying that the secret to getting wealthy was "notes, bills, and face." *Face* referred to favors and connections, which provided the means to obtain *notes* (i.e., official documents and instructions), which in turn allowed the bearer to collect "up to a difference of RMB 30,000 yuan over the original." *Bills* were the various middlemen's fees and bribes.[31] Retired cadres could influence people in responsible positions with informal notes (*tiaozi*) peddled for a fee (*piaozi*) to help the bearer get some "consideration."[32]

These activites bred increased resentment among the populace and concern among state and party leaders, who nonetheless proved incapable of making an effective response. Many managers reportedly began protesting against state-run companies set up directly by CCP and government institutions who were striving for "money as well as power." The managers complained that the new companies were even worse than the old meddling administrators because, by taking advantage of their authority and of differences between state-set and market prices, they could competely destroy the businesses of others. In July 1988, a vice-minister of the State Economic Restructuring Commission advocated introduction of a genuine market order to cool excessive price hikes, complaining that "power abuse for personal gain, illegal reselling at exorbitant prices, graft and bribery are seriously hampering normal operations." State-run companies, he pointed out, were profiting by reselling marketable commodities.[33] The path of introducing a genuine market was of course not taken. New rules were announced in July 1988 to close down profiteering companies and to prohibit the employment of retired officials who peddle influence, but results were negligible.[34]

Corruption after the reforms more often took the form of plunder than of greasing the wheels. Clearly the stakes were now higher than in the days of the grain bureau driver's petty corruption (though such petty corruption continued to occur). In addition to profiteering, bribery after the reforms also moved in the direction of higher stakes. One foreign businessmen in 1989 complained that whereas a decade ago "a Cross ballpoint pen was sufficient to open many doors," of late factory managers and officials had begun to demand color TVs and VCRs as their price for doing business. In addition to these luxury items, some officials and managers reportedly wanted cash delivered in person or deposited in their Hong Kong bank accounts. Increasingly, bribes took the form of U.S. college tuition for the offspring of an official—or even sponsorship for the official himself to emigrate.[35]

All this forms one part of the picture of crisis corruption: new high stakes, the transformation of existing cadre networks into money-making operations, the scramble among elites for money, and the consequent disruption of state functions.[36] PRC economists began to refer to this phenomenon as the "monetisation or commercialisation of administrative power."[37] Already serious, the problem was further compounded by an influx of overseas Chinese money and influence.

The Influx of Overseas Chinese Money and Influence

A significant portion of China's opening to the outside world involved commercial relations with Hong Kong and Taiwan. In late 1987 the PRC began a policy of encouraging Taiwan businessmen to invest and set up production lines on the mainland, as opposed to encouraging import of consumer goods from Taiwan.[38] Taiwan's government since mid-1988 has officially permitted its businessmen to invest in the mainland through Hong Kong agents.[39] In November 1987, the PRC organized an investment seminar in Hong Kong for the agents of Taiwan businessmen.[40] As of February 1988, forty-six Taiwan-based companies had established production lines in Fujian province through Hong Kong agents, and reportedly there were altogether eighty wholly or partly Taiwan-owned factories on the mainland, mostly in Fujian and Guangdong.[41] The PRC offered special treatment for Taiwan investors in its SEZs and in 1988 the government announced plans to set up a special industrial zone just for Taiwan investors, near Shenzhen.[42] Investment from Taiwan has been additionally facilitated since 1987 by the Taiwan government's policy of permitting its citizens to visit relatives on the mainland. Many visitors from Taiwan reportedly rushed to take advantage of visits to relatives to tap the investment climate on the mainland.[43]

A widely publicized case in 1986 suggested some of the unintended effects of China's opening to Hong Kong and Taiwan. It concerned a Chinese citizen known as "Du, the god of fortune" because of his legendary money-making powers. In a period of only a few months, Du allegedly made more than RMB 100 million yuan through swindling and 120 million through profiteering and speculation; he also smuggled more than 20 million yuan worth of goods. In the course of his operations, he was said to have used large sums of money and high quality consumer goods to bribe cadres in party and government organs, financial and commercial departments, traffic departments, customs areas, and political and legal departments to the point where "some of our party and government institutions . . . even became the working bodies of the swindler." Du reportedly had bribed more than twenty cadres and signed more than seventy fraudulent contracts with the province of Fujian and other regions, as well as smuggling out of the country US $108,000 and HK $619,000 that he had purchased on the black market.[44]

It seems that Du began his career as a humble office clerk; he was able to draw numerous people into his deal by boasting that he had a "background" in Taiwan and Hong Kong. A commentator publicizing the case noted that in the past,

> some cadres were very enthusiastic in following the "leftist" line and despised those who had relatives in Taiwan, Hong Kong, or foreign countries . . . but now they have an insatiable desire for these relations and try in every way to make connections with people who have these relations. That is why they so easily got hooked . . .
>
> Whenever [cadres] find someone who has "an enormous amount of money," who is the "shareholder and manager of a certain corporation of a certain country," and who is "a friend of a certain wealthy businessman," and who is "the son of a cadre with relatives in Hong Kong and Taiwan;" and whenever they learn of somebody who has a "financial channel," who will "invest," provide "free assistance" and "foreign goods or popular commodities in short supply" and the like, they regard such people as guests of honor, call them brothers, and even spend large sums to establish relations with them, hoping that they would "invest," or "reciprocate with gifts."[45]

The story of Du further illustrates themes introduced in the previous section: the appropriation of the party organization by cadres scrambling to make money, and the commercialization of administrators. It also indicates the rising influence of overseas Chinese conenctions (real or bogus): it was Du's alleged background in Hong Kong and Taiwan that gave him his entrée to corruptible cadres.

In the spring of 1988, the central authorities in Beijing announced that trade between local governments and individuals with relatives in Taiwan would be prohibited; henceforth, only trade and economic agencies in Beijing would be permitted to contact Taiwan businessmen.[46] Problems continued, however. Reports linking corruption to overseas Chinese money and connections were rife as 1989 dawned. Reports suggested that the economic activities and influence of Hong Kong and Taiwan Chinese and their mainland connections were of increasing concern to authorities in Beijing. A practice of evading customs duties under the guise of donations from overseas Chinese and compatriots from Hong Kong, Macao, and Taiwan prompted the government to issue new regulations to "improve management" of such donations.[47] An official in charge of donations from abroad in Guangxi's regional office for overseas Chinese affairs was charged with collaboration in a major auto smuggling scheme.[48]

Another report in January 1989 concerned the banning of twenty-nine economic entities which had used the lure of foreign investment capital as bait for illegal money-making schemes. They had reportedly engaged in swindling, profiteering, and speculation by means of forging various approval documents, letters of introduction, notices, letters of guarantee, checks, bills of exchange, and fund-affirming certificates. A count showed that fourteen of the 29 banned firms had been formed by the All-China Federation of Returned Overseas Chinese, three more by the Federation of Chinese Returned from Hong Kong, Macao, and Taiwan, and one each by the China Nationality Industrial Associated Group and the Federation of Chinese Returned from All Parts of the World.[49]

In the same month, a report described a new trend in Guangdong province, where people who had embezzled public funds were able to flee to Hong Kong after having made elaborate—and illegal—plans for a retreat. According to a Guangdong procuracy official, a new characteristic of recent economic malfeasance is the trend toward more crimes being committed with the assistance of outside connections. Such cases, he said, constituted more than one-third of the total economic crimes committed in Guangdong province and 40 to 50 percent in border areas such as Shenzhen.[50]

These reports no doubt had a political motivation: conservatives could highlight the nefarious effects of overenthusiastic reform and the unhealthy tendencies rampant in get-rich-quick provinces such as Guangdong. Taking exaggeration into account, the reports do suggest a situation (in southeastern coastal China in particular) not unlike the sudden influx of money typical of crisis corruption: stakes are raised and existing networks are transformed by a flood of new resources and players.

Disintegrative Corruption: Nepotism

Officials in China historically have passed on their accumulated power by placing their offspring, or proteges, on the bureaucratic ladder below them.[51] Nepotism in the PRC of the 1980s became more visible, and more important as a resource, because of the entrée it provided to prestigious, money-making activities (higher stakes). The Hong Kong journal *Zheng Ming* in early 1986 commented on the trend of senior cadres' children engaging in trade (legally and illegally) and holding important posts in trade-related offices. The hereditary advantage enjoyed by this privileged group reportedly led to their becoming known as the "princes' party."[52]The "princes" were allegedly involved in a variety of shady activities. One report complained that some cadres and cadres' children had become "chips" or "good luck charms" used by speculators and swindlers.[53] One such case involved a Taiwan man who entered China in 1984 with a fake passport and only HK $900 (US $115).

Protected by the children of a few leading cadres, he reportedly duped state enterprises into signing 8 billion dollars worth of bogus import contracts.[54]

Children of many top party and government leaders figured prominently in this trend. Zhao Dajun, son of deposed Premier Zhao Ziyang, at one point served as honorary chairman of an allegedly fraudulent technology development company run by a former convict who reportedly swindled agencies out of more than 19.7 million yuan by signing phony joint operation agreements and marketing contracts with various provinces and municipalities.[55] The younger Zhao was also reportedly involved in color TV imports and other lucrative businesses in Shenzhen.[56] Deng Xiaoping's son, Deng Pufang, was involved with the Kang Hua Development Corporation, which became an object of criticism and was eventually shut down for engaging in profiteering in coal and other raw materials. Other noteworthy examples include Deng Xiaoping's son-in-law, who became head of PolyTechnologies Inc. (a government enterprise that buys and sells arms), and a son of President Yang Shangkun, employed by a Beijing business enterprise under the the control of the Central Military Commission.[57]

Top officials have long been sending their offspring to study abroad in preparation for official careers. In the 1950s the Soviet Union was the foreign destination of choice. Soviet-trained children of high-level leaders who have risen to prominence in contemporary China include Premier Li Peng (the adoptive son of the late Premier Zhou Enlai) and Guangdong governor Ye Xuanping (son of the late Marshal Ye Jianying). Both Li and Ye studied engineering in the Soviet Union. Reportedly, Deng Xiaoping induced the old marshal to retire as head of the National People's Congress a few years ago by promising to make his son mayor of Canton and later governor.

In the 1980s, the United States has replaced the Soviet Union as the educational destination of choice for the children of senior leaders. The list of U.S.-trained offspring includes children of former party General Secretary Hu Yaobang and Politburo Standing Committee member Qiao Shi. One observer has argued that the freewheeling economic climate of the reforms in fact serves to motivate sons and daughters of senior cadres to urge their fathers to hang on to power because "the old men's influence is easily converted into that ultimate perk—cash."[58]

Nepotism in the 1980s added to the public perception that reforms had merely provided cadres and bureaucrats with new opportunities to gain influence and material benefit while excluding or discriminating against aspiring entrepreneurs and managers. While opportunities for both legitimate and illegitimate benefit increased substantially, nepotistic practices skewed the distribution of benefits in favor of those people with family connections. As a result, there was a widespread perception that ordinary people were being excluded from enjoying the fruits of reform. Johnston's description of mid-sixteenth-century England affords an interesting comparison. There, as in postreform China, a rapid increase in the number of opportunity seekers undermined the stability/legitimacy of an established system of cronyism and nepotism—despite a substantial net expansion of economic opportunities.[59]

We have suggested that highly disintegrative forms of corruption—crisis corruption and nepotism—tranformed a pattern of relatively more stable and routine forms of market corruption and clientelism. One would expect this to have some effect on system legitimacy under any circumstances. Although Johnston only intends the term *disintegrative* to refer to the effect on the participants—i.e., whether it links more or less persons in more or less stable relationships—he acknowledges that the two disintegrative forms tend to be politically destabilizing.[60] System destabilization further depends on popular beliefs about right and wrong and the degree to which exclusionary practices produced by corruption tend to overlap with, and exacerbate, existing group cleavages, thereby becoming infused with potency as a political issue.

With respect to popular beliefs about right and wrong, corruption has perennially been politically problematic in the PRC, due in part to contradictions inherent in Leninist systems in general. Paradoxically, these systems structurally generate clientelism and market corruption while constantly delegitimizing them politically. Clientelism and networks of particularistic relationships create special kinds of legitimacy problems for Leninist systems. Particularistic loyalties and networks of personal ties contradict the official norms of communist systems, which are universalistic. Unlike full-fledged patron-client-based societies, such relationships are never accepted as legitimate.[61] Leninism calls for devotion of cadres to the party as an organization, not to individual patrons within it, and for relations between party cadres and the masses to be governed by universal norms, not by particularistic considerations. Recruitment and promotion within party and state, which the party controls, are supposed to be on the basis of performance and commitment to the cadre role, not on the basis of patronage and personal considerations. Anticorruption campaigns repeatedly call public attention to contradictions between the party's ethos and cadres' actual behavior. In the case of China, the CCP's original popular legitimacy and cadre *esprit* based on its pre-1949 reputation for honesty and integrity (as contrasted with the generally corrupt image of the KMT) rendered this kind of contradiction particularly damaging politically.

A second element affecting beliefs about right and wrong in the case of China is the heritage of Confucianism. This heritage compounds the contradiction between universalistic and particularistic values inherent in Leninism. Scholars of China's history and culture point to the contradiction between the Confucian ideal of officials as virtuous representatives of central authority versus their actual identity as gentry with local roots and members of clans with a duty to advance family fortunes. This structural contradiction within the traditional system bred corruption even as Confucian morality assured its place as a central and perennial political issue.[62] It remained so in the democracy movements of 1979 and the 1980s, very much as a legacy of this cultural heritage.[63] Thus the values and behaviors associated with China's political culture both in its Leninist and Confucian/traditional aspects made corruption politically explosive.

The political effects of disintegrative corruption are further enhanced if they reinforce existing social-historical cleavages. China's urban reform policies tapped coastal cities, particularly in Guangdong and Fujian, to "get rich first" as the leading edge of nationwide economic growth. The subsequent explosion of wealth in these areas, which seemed to have the effect of consigning poorer interior provinces to a perennial backwater status vis-à-vis the coast, fueled an outbreak of inter-regional rivalries and hostilities.[64] Crisis corruption simply reinforced these cleavages.

Chinese history is marked by strong, recurrent tendencies toward regional fragmentation and loss of central control. The reduction of central planning and control after the reforms brought an increase in the powers of local officials vis-à-vis the central government.[65] In January 1989, the *Guangming Daily* noted that reform and the opening to the outside world had fostered the rise of a "closed door mentality" on the part of newly mobilized regional interests and interest groups; such groups were said to have engaged in "feudalistic" rivalries, causing a predicament in central-local relations.[66] The commercialization of administration and the consequent scramble for local advantage served to further reinforce these reform-related tendencies toward regional fragmentation.

Conclusion

In the 1980s China introduced limited competition into its economy while retaining a state sector and a system in which officeholding remained the most important gateway to material reward and status. Such an institutional structure generated personal networks that were able to use their political connections and access to state goods to benefit from economic activities legalized under the reforms. Cadres and their children, relatives, friends, and followers were well situated to take advantage of new opportunities for material gain.

A change in the postreform relationship between officeholding, power, and opportunities for material gain was already well underway by 1989, however. Although one still needed good relations with officials to prosper, or even to operate, one no longer had to actually *be* an official. Money— and the ability to manipulate it for profit—played a role not seen in four previous decades of communist rule. Money could now help an individual create a network of accomplices, instead of being merely a reflection of one's connections. Since one could now legitimately acquire wealth (and spend it as well), economic competition partially replaced political competition as a focus of upward mobility, and the stakes rose precipitously. But, while market reform created new opportunities to make money, differential access to these opportunities heavily favored party cadres and their networks of connections and families. This produced more contenders and higher stakes while retaining the old system of privileged access, thus creating a perception of greater exclusion. Whether or not corruption was statistically more rampant after the reforms, there were undoubtedly greater gains to be captured. And this, in turn, generated an acute legitimacy problem with the public because the abuses in question closely resembled what China's leaders had criticized as the "feudal remnants" of the Maoist era. One might generalize this observation to hypothesize that market reform in a Leninist state without concomitant political reform tends to create new, informal opportunities for cadres to enrich themselves and their networks while weakening the formal control of the party-state.

After the introduction of urban reform, familial and/or business connections in Hong Kong or Taiwan that once constituted a political liability emerged as a resource. This amounted to a new (or renewed) set of connections that provided not only money but status, giving some people preferential access to do business and to initiate dealings with party officials. With continued expansion of economic linkages with Taiwan and Hong Kong, this trend will be difficult to stem—notwithstanding the post-Tiananmen tightening of the entrepreneurial screws in China.

The tendency of China to fragment into local "independent kingdoms" reasserted itself with a vengeance following the advent of market reforms. Strong regionalist and localist tendencies plus the influence of Hong Kong and Taiwan Chinese and their mainland family and business connections reinforced the operational autonomy of clientelist groupings and *guanxi* networks, rendering them less susceptible to central control. In this manner, disintegrative corruption engendered increasing disaffection among the populace, while at the same time rendering the regime incapable of effective response.

Notes and References

1. See "Full Text of the CCP Central Committee Decision on Reform of the Economic Structure," *Xinhua*, October 10, 1984, in *Foreign Broadcast Information Service—China* (hereafter, *FBIS*), October 22, 1984, pp. K1-K19.

2. See Constance Squires Meaney, *Stability and the Industrial Elite in China and the Soviet Union,* University of California, Berkeley, Institute of East Asian Studies China Research Monograph no. 34 (1988).

3. See discussion of this factor in Nina Halpern's essay in the present volume.

4. Thomas Gold, "Neo-Authoritarianism Won't Create Economic Miracle," *Los Angeles Times,* June 30, 1989, II, p. 9.

5. See James T. Myers, "Modernization and 'Unhealthy Tendencies,' " *Comparative Politics* 21, no. 2 (January 1989), pp. 193–214.

6. Michael Johnston, "The Political Consequences of Corruption: A Reassessment," *Comparative Politics* 18, no. 4 (July 1986), pp. 464–65.

7. *Ibid.*

8. *Ibid.*

9. I will apply this proposition only to behavior connected with the urban reforms and the opening to the outside world. For analysis of the effects of reform on corruption and clientelism in the agricultural sector, see Jean C. Oi's chapter in the present volume.

10. *China News Analysis* (hereafter CNA) 1366a (August 15, 1988), p. 4.

11. For discussion of this point see Dorothy J. Solinger's chapter in the present volume.

12. Johnston, note 6, p. 466. See also discussion in Oi, note 9.

13. For an extended development of this point see Kenneth Jowitt, "Soviet Neotraditionalism: The Political Corruption of a Leninist Regime," *Soviet Studies* 35, no. 3 (July 1983), pp. 275–97; also Jowitt, "An Organizational Approach to the Study of Political Culture in Marxist-Leninist Systems," *American Political Science Review* 68, no. 4 (1974), esp. pp. 1176–78. For an interpretation of corruption in the PRC, see Alan P. Liu, "The Politics of Corruption in the People's Republic of China," *American Political Science Review* 77, no. 3 (1983), pp. 602–23; and Myers, note 5.

14. See Andrew Walder, *Communist Neotraditionalism: Work and Authority in Chinese Industry* (Berkeley, Los Angeles, and London: University of California Press, 1986); and Jean C. Oi, "Communism and Clientelism: Rural Politics in China," World Politics 37 (January 1985), pp. 238–66. See also *China Daily* (hereafter, *CD*), January 11, 1989, p. 4.

15. John Burns, "China's *Nomenklatura* System," *Problems of Communism* 36, no. 5 (September–October 1987), pp. 36–51.

16. See discussion in Walder, note 14, pp. 26–27. See also Gregory Grossman, "The 'Second Economy' of the USSR," *Problems of Communism* 26, no. 5 (September–October) 1977.

17. Liu Binyan and Liu Guosheng, "An Invisible Machine—A Negative Example of Perfunctorily Carrying out Party Rectification," *Renmin Ribao* (hereafter, *RMRB*), February 8, 1984, p. 4, in *FBIS,* February 10, 1984, pp. K5-K9.

18. Liu and Liu, note 17.

19. *Ibid.*

20. *Ibid.*

21. See Samuel P. Huntington, *Political Order in Changing Societies* (New Haven: Yale University Press, 1968).

22. Johnston, note 6, p. 472.

23. A famous case involving buying, selling, and reselling by a state firm was that of the Hubei Tobacco Monopoly Corporation, which sold 5,000 cartons of a popular brand of cigarettes to a retailer, requiring the latter to take 5,000 cartons of a less popular brand at an inflated price. The corporation then bought back the unpopular brand at the lower, state-set price, while the retailer made up the loss by raising the price of the popular batch (*CNA*, note 10, p. 5). A number of profiteering schemes involving fertilizer needed by peasants were reported recently. In one case, fertilizer was resold three times resulting in a 94.4 percent markup. (*Ibid.*) In Guangxi, fertilizer was sold and resold eight times by various state firms while the legitimate farming materials companies were unable to purchase any, because, they complained, they were unable to afford the money for gifts and entertainment involved in these transactions. (*CD*, July 22, 1988, p. 3.) Profiteering in coal by taking advantage of the double-track price system is yet another featured example. (*CD*, September 8, 1988, p. 3.)

24. *Asian Wall Street Journal*, July 25, 1988, p. 5. The report attributed inflation not only to inability of factories to meet overheated demand but also to hoarding by middlemen who control distribution and who each "tack on a premium to the ultimate retail price."

25. *CNA*, note 10 (quoting from *Gongren Ribao*, June 11, 1988).

26. *Ibid.*

27. *CD*, July 28, 1988, p. 3.

28. "China's Price Pirates," *Far Eastern Economic Review*, October 13, 1988, pp. 96–97. The report notes that regional governments set up road blocks and internal tariffs to control such activity, which has produced "warring economic fiefdoms."

29. *CD*, July 22, 1988, p. 1.

30. See Lynn T. White, "Changing Concepts of Corruption in Communist China," in *Issues and Studies* (Taipei) 24, no. 1 (January 1988), pp. 49–95.

31. *Inside China Mainland* 10, no. 9, issue 117 (September 1988), p. 8, translation of an article from the CCP Central Committee's *Lilun Yuekan*, June 1988.

32. *CNA*, note 10, p. 6.

33. *CD*, July 18, 1988, p. 4.

34. *CD*, note 29.

35. *Wall Street Journal*, July 20, 1989, A10.

36. Compare Johnston's comment about Bolivia after 1980, note 6, p. 472.

37. "Eternal Mandarins," *Far Eastern Economic Review*, November 9, 1989, p. 33.

38. *China Post* (Taiwan) (hereafter, *CP*), March 15, 1988.

39. *San Francisco Chronicle,* July 18, 1988, p. A15.

40. *CP,* November 22, 1987.

41. *CP,* March 27, 1988.

42. *CP,* March 15 and 27, 1988.

43. *CP,* January 5, 1988.

44. *Xinhua,* January 14, 1986, in *FBIS,* January 15, 1986, p. K1. Myers (note 5) comments that the corruption of party cadres, not the amounts involved, appeared to be the real reson why the case received so much publicity as a bad example.

45. "What Is Shown by the Career Rise and Arrest of 'Du, the God of Fortune'?", *RMRB,* December 30, 1985, p. 1, in *FBIS,* January 7, 1986, pp. K1–2.

46. *CP,* March 15, 1988.

47. *Zhongguo Tongxian* (Hong Kong), January 24, 1989, in *FBIS,* January 27, 1989, p. 14. The report also noted a smuggling problem involving unauthorized marketing of materials imported duty-free for processing. With more opening of the economy to the West, smuggling has been extended to inland customs offices, such as Chongqing. See also *Xinhua,* January 27, 1989, in *FBIS,* January 27, 1989, p. 19.

48. *CD,* January 20, 1989. The report notes that another Guangxi official was executed in August 1988 for accepting a bribe of RMB 130,000 yuan.

49. *RMRB,* January 19, 1989, p. 1, in *FBIS,* January 25, 1989, pp. 21–23.

50. *Zhongguo Xinwen She,* January 19, 1989, in *FBIS,* January 25, 1989, p. 49.

51. See *Wall Street Journal,* June 2, 1989, A10.

52. *Zheng Ming* 99 (January 1, 1986), pp. 6–8, in *FBIS,* January 6, 1986, pp. W3–8.

53. *Xinhua,* January 14, 1986, in *FBIS,* January 15, 1986, pp. K1–3.

54. *Ibid.,* also *Agence France Presse* (Hong Kong), January 15, 1986, in *FBIS* (January 15, 1986), p. K3.

55. *Zheng Ming,* note 52.

56. *New York Times,* July 2, 1989, p. 1.

57. *Ibid.,* note 56; also *South China Morning Post,* January 19, 1989, p. 1.

58. *New York Times,* note 56; *Wall Street Journal,* note 51.

59. Johnson, note 6, p. 471.

60. *Ibid.,* note 6, pp. 471, 473.

61. For discussion of the nature of patron-client relations in modern, universalistic societies (pluralistic or monolithic) and of countervailing forces to their development, specifically in the USSR and USA, see S. N. Eisenstadt and L. Roniger, *Patrons, Clients, and Friends: Interpersonal Relations and the Structure of*

Trust in Society (Cambridge, London, and New York: Cambridge University Press, 1984), pp. 184–95.

62. See, *inter alia*, Lucian Pye, *Asian Power and Politics* (Cambridge and London: The Belknap Press of Harvard University Press, 1985), pp. 56–57.

63. For discussion of this phenomenon see Andrew Nathan, *Chinese Democracy* (Berkeley and Los Angeles: University of California Press, 1986), Chapter 4.

64. *San Francisco Chronicle*, June 9, 1989, p. 1. In this article, a reporter relates his conversation with a waiter in Xian who, when asked for his feelings about the Cantonese managers of the joint-venture hotel in which he worked, responded, "We hate them."

65. See "China's Economy," *The Economist*, August 1–7, 1987, pp. 15–17.

66. *Guangming Ribao*, January 19, 1989, p. 3, in *FBIS*, January 27, 1989, p. 21.

8

Partial Market Reform and Corruption In Rural China

Jean C. Oi

At the end of 1978 China embarked on a radical program to loosen central planning and restructure the rural economy. Collective farming was abolished, markets were reopened, and the agricultural sector was geared to commodity production. Household farming ended the power of grass-roots cadres (production team leaders) to decide where, when, and for how much pay peasants would work. The individual peasant household, rather than the collective, became the unit of work and accounting. After paying the state tax and selling a certain amount of their harvest to the government, households were now free to consume or sell the remainder on the newly legalized free market. Taken together these reforms freed the peasants from the confines of the collective, opened new doors of opportunity, and altered the distribution of power. As the state began to extricate itself from agricultural production, as the public sector declined, as individuals and markets became more important in the economy, and as peasants gained greater control over their work, one might have expected peasants to become increasingly free from cadre abuse and corruption. Yet this has not been the case in China. The official Chinese press has been filled with reports of cadre corruption and peasant abuse in the countryside after the reforms. The following list includes but a few examples of the more commonly cited problems:[1]

1. Peasants are unable to obtain their legal allotments of chemical fertilizer and gasoline.
2. There is inequitable distribution of state-supplied goods, such as chemical fertilizer, and state and collective jobs and sales contracts.
3. Market inspectors confiscate goods from peasants on illegal pretexts.
4. Tractors stand idle because their owners are refused licenses by county cadres.

The author would like to thank Richard Baum, Kathy Hartford, Michael Johnston, Lewis Putterman, Jonathan Unger, Ezra Vogel, David Zweig, Brewer Stone, and the reviewer for Routledge Press for useful comments on earlier versions of this paper.

5. Cadres illegally block peasant attempts to leave the village to pursue nonagricultural work.

6. Cadres force peasants to make them partners in enterprises without having to either pay for the shares or put in appropriate labor.

7. Toll collectors demand illegal payments before letting peasants pass with their goods on their way to market.

8. Cadres illegally withhold portions of peasant receipts from sales to the state on various pretexts.

9. Granary cadres and cotton purchasing station cadres cheat peasants out of a fair price for their goods.

10. There is preferential enforcement of the government's birth control policy in return for suitable gifts.

11. There is preferential handling of contracts for enterprises, sales, and land.

12. Collective land is appropriated for private house building.

13. Specialized households and "ten thousand yuan households" are pressured to make "donations."

14. Counterfeit goods are sold, e.g., fake fertilizer, and peasants are made to buy unwanted and sometimes defective goods in order to secure needed commodities.

15. Reports are falsified to get bonuses.

16. Signed rental contracts are arbitrarily raised when profits unexpectedly increase.

17. *Ad hoc* local surcharges are imposed.

What causes such behavior? How can these problems be explained? Some observers point to cultural factors.[2] Liu, in examining rural corruption, stresses the existence of a "traditional peasant ethos" and attributes certain types of corruption to "acts peculiar to the Chinese Communist system."[3] Myers lays the blame on a "spiritual" or value crisis, i.e., the incoherence of values exhibited by the regime.[4] Such cultural explanations, while insightful, fail adequately to probe what I believe to be the more important structural and systemic causes of corruption in communist and reforming communist systems. The persistence of cadre corruption in the face of major structural changes is in itself an insufficient test of cultural theories and does not disprove structural explanations.[5] It is quite possible that the systemic sources of corruption may persist despite structural reform. Indeed, reforms may even create new systemic incentives and opportunities for corruption. In this paper I will argue that much of the corruption that has occurred in rural China since the launching of reforms has resulted not from the introduction of market reforms *per se,* but from the *incompleteness* of the reforms, resulting in a system that is doubly plagued by problems attributable both to the plan and to the market. These problems reflect a system that has failed to remove all the sources of corruption inherent in the socialist planned economy while opening new opportunities for malfeasance with the addition of a partial market. James Scott, in his comparative study of corruption, suggests that "the larger . . . the size and scope of the public sector, the greater will be the proportion of certain acts that will meet our criteria of corruption."[6] The problem in China is that the public sector is still sufficiently large to allow public officials (cadres) to manipulate their control over scarce and necessary resources to their advantage.

In this paper I will limit my discussion to rural China, but I hope the present study will also provide some insights into the larger problem of corruption that has come to the fore in urban China (as evidenced in the protests that marked the short-lived Beijing Spring of 1989) as well as in other communist systems such as the Soviet Union, Vietnam, and Eastern Europe. My findings will not settle the debate over the usefulness of cultural vs. structural explanations, nor can they explain all occurrences of corruption, but they will provide a clearer picture of the opportunities and incentives for corruption within reforming Communist systems.

Corruption and Communist Systems

There is considerable evidence to support the view, advanced here, that communist systems foster acts that most would call corruption, not because their citizens are more greedy or lack moral principles, but because of the very *structure* of the state and economy. Studies have shown that communist systems tend to display structural properties that constrain their members to engage in illegal actions to survive and to promote their basic self-interest.[7]

The most well known of these behaviors involve circumvention or manipulation of official regulations by officials or agents of the state in the routine performance of their duties. This includes the activity of factory managers and their *tolkach* or *caigouyuan* (purchasing and sales agents), who illegally barter for needed goods and services or submit false reports that exaggerate production and costs; it also includes the actions of rural cadres who either over- or underreport output, conceal production, or illegally keep extra grain in villages. This category of illegality also includes participation in what Unger and Chan have called the "hidden economy,"[8] known as the "second economy" in the USSR.[9]

One need not invoke any longstanding "tradition" of corruption or any supposed uniqueness of China to explain this behavior;[10] it is simply a rational response to the communist system itself.[11] For example, in the

Chinese countryside during the Maoist era, team leaders falsified reports,[12] hid production, and manipulated existing regulations on the division of the harvest. The reason lay in the state's overly harsh policies that left both officials and peasants with little alternative but to take from the state to provide for their own needs, which included routine production costs, demands from brigade and commune officials for administrative expenses, and sufficient food grain for team members.[13]

A less rigorously studied but oft-mentioned set of acts is the common practice in socialist system of using connections, whether these be the casual use of *blat* or *guanxi* or the formation of more long-term clientelist relationships, to get ahead in the system.[14] These latter forms of behavior do not necessarily violate any clear rules or regulations; as such they are not technically corrupt, in the narrow definition of the term. However, because of the preferential treatment accorded some people and not others, they violate conventional as well as socialist norms of equal access and fairness.

For those who study noncommunist systems, the existence of such particularistic relationships will hardly come as a surprise. Clientelism has been a familiar concept in the study of elite-mass relations. This has not been the case for the study of communist systems, however, even though factionalist and even clientelist models are often used in the study of political elites.[15] It has often been assumed that communist rule is impersonal, impartial, and effective. This was in part, no doubt, due to the influence of the totalitarian image of communist rule.[16] Only recently have studies shown that clientelism is not an aberration but rather an outgrowth of the communist system.[17]

In practice, neither the communist commitment to equality nor the rationing of scarce commodities has precluded inequality of access and distribution. It is true that communist officials cannot easily deny a citizen his minimum rations. In this respect there is little room for maneuver, particularly in Maoist China where almost all essential commodities and opportunities were rationed or centrally allocated. But officials do have it in their power to provide the few available goods to one person *before* another. Preferential access and "cutting to the front of the line" is how one gets ahead in communist systems characterized by scarcity and rationing. Moreover, and perhaps most importantly, officials have discretionary power to allocate the "slack" in the system, which exists in spite of scarcity. There are always better jobs, housing, commodities, and extra ration tickets to be had. In this context, particularistic relationships are used to maximize one's interest, not merely to subsist.

During the Maoist period, each peasant was assigned work to do and received a share of the harvest along with a private plot. But some jobs were more desirable than others, some plots more fertile and better situated than others, and some scoops of grain more rounded than others. The favor of the team leader was not essential to guarantee basic entitlement, but he could make life easier for some than for others.[18]

For the cadre (patron), the rewards were both material and political. In absolute terms, what cadres received was not particularly valuable economically. During the Maoist period, both cadres and peasants barely kept ahead of subsistence. But it was precisely because of this poverty that clientelism took on added value. Goods that we might consider inconsequential—e.g., a piece of pork or a dinner invitation—were for China's rural inhabitants significant.

Perhaps even more important than material rewards, cadres engaged in clientelist relationships for political reasons. In a highly politicized system such as Maoist China, loyalty and political support, along with enthusiasm and assistance in carrying out policies, were invaluable for weathering the many political campaigns, for staying in office, and for maintaining one's basis of patronage.[19]

To sum up, the structure of the Maoist system facilitated the development of two different types of corruption. One was the adoption of evasive and illegal actions on the part of cadres to survive the strictures and inadequacies of the system; the other was the adoption of particularistic relationships, pursued by peasants and cadres alike, to get ahead in the system. For purposes of analytical clarity the former can be termed bureaucratic corruption, the latter, clientelism.[20]

The first can be understood as corruption that costs the state—it takes resources away from the government or violates rules of the government. The relationship is not one of exchange; implied is a more one-sided flow of goods or resources, from the state to the cadre or local level. In contrast, clientelism implies a reciprocal flow of private benefits between cadre and peasant.

This distinction is far from absolute, however. In practice, corruption and clientelism represent two sides of a single coin; one often shades into the other. Clientelism, and other forms of particularistic exchange, guide the flow of goods and opportunities that are gained as a result of bureaucratic corruption. For example, when a team leader withholds grain from the state to keep more at the local level, he also puts more resources at his own disposal to benefit himself, his family, or his friends, all of which increase his power. Ambitious peasants, in turn, try to cultivate a clientelist relationship with those who control such resources.

Despite their mutual affinity, I distinguish between these two types of corruption to facilitate my discussion of the effects of reform upon the opportunities and incentives for corruption. As I will show, the reforms have had differing effects on these two types of corruption. I begin with a discussion of the impact of the reforms on bureaucratic corruption, i.e., on those corrupt forms of behavior adopted by officials to facilitate the execution of their duties.

Bureaucratic Corruption and the
Postreform Communist System

Reforms have brought about a marked change in the "necessity of evasion" encountered by rural cadres during the Maoist period. Most significantly, the reforms have reduced, if not eliminated, the need for cadres to engage in bureaucratic corruption with regard to the grain harvest, around which much of the evasive action centered during the Maoist period. The role of village officials is now limited to ensuring that the households under their jurisdiction comply with the rules and regulations, but the ultimate responsibility for production, sales, and consumption of grain now lies completely with each individual household rather than the collective. This is not to say it would not reflect poorly on a cadre if his peasants did not pay their tax, but the consequences are vastly different from before. The amount of grain sold to the state is no longer the major measure of cadre performance;[21] the village official will not suffer a shortage of funds if a harvest of a certain size is not produced. In short, this aspect of the communist structure has changed sufficiently to make it less necessary for cadres to engage in falsification of reports to the upper levels.

The reforms have not eliminated all incentives for false reporting by local cadres, however.[22] Cadres will always be under pressure to meet policy objectives, but the state has now taken a much lower profile. The pressure from above is far less than that experienced by cadres in the Great Leap Forward or during the Cultural Revolution decade, when selling grain to the state was directly linked to political loyalty. The fear of being sent to "study classes," or being attacked in a political campaign, is greatly diminished. Perhaps most important, their actions will not affect whether members of the village will go hungry. At most, a cadre who is caught transgressing official regulations will have his bonus pay docked, or perhaps lose his job, but even that is unclear now that officials are actually elected by the village.[23] Cadres who now falsify reports on the local development of a commodity economy, the creation of specialized households, or trends in peasant income do so less out of collective necessity than out of individual interest. Since good results bring personal rewards, when a cadre engages in false reporting he is serving his own rather than the village's needs; he will be the one to receive the bonus given to leaders of advanced units.[24]

Some villages use a point system, paying cadres according to how well policies have been carried out.[25] Cadres may receive higher-level recognition not just for satisfying state demands for more grain, but also for promoting the largest number of specialized households or for doubling peasant incomes. Cadre careers still hinge on good reports, but their achievements now bring lucrative financial rewards, rather than mere titles, as before.[26]

The Institutional Basis of Particularistic
Exchange in the Postreform System

The reforms did not remove either the institutional causes of clientelism or the use of particularistic relationships to get ahead in the system. Rather, the reforms redistributed power—taking it away from certain cadres, most notably team level cadres, but leaving in tact, and in some cases adding to, the power of higher-level cadres. As the following section will document, structural reforms made the peasants less dependent on cadres; but they were not wholly independent, either. For example, while the reopening of markets provided the peasants a way out from the closed corporate village of the commune, peasants still relied on cadres to get ahead in the new market-oriented economy.

Students of noncommunist agrarian systems have used the term "incomplete rationalization of the market" to explain the continuance of clientelist politics in systems where the economy changes into a seemingly modern one, where markets are an established fact of life, but where traditional elites have been able to maintain their hold on local society using clientelist ties.[27] The phrase is quite apt as a description of the situation in post-Mao China. The structure of production has changed, and markets afford new opportunities; and though the identity of the patrons, their bases of power, as well as the terms of exchange may change, the dynamics of politics remain strikingly clientelist.[28]

The examples of cadre wrongdoing cited earlier can be divided into three categories, according to the type of resources involved and keyed to the routine spheres of peasant life over which cadres have administrative control: (1) enforcement of state regulations; (2) distribution and management of public goods and resources; and (3) treatment of successful specialized households.

Enforcement of State Regulations

The first category of cadre misconduct centers on the implementation of government policies. Many examples could be included here, but I have created separate categories to provide a differentiated typology that highlights the areas of cadre responsibility and the goods and resources involved. This first category focuses on the cadres' power to interpret and implement higher-level policy directives and to perform routine bureaucratic procedures such as conducting inspections, paying fixed procurement prices for state purchases, and granting licenses.[29] It excludes the management and distribution of physical material inputs.

Cadres who have such bureaucratic power engage in activities ranging from illegally withholding portions of peasant receipts from sales to the state, to imposing *ad hoc* surcharges, to extorting money from peasants at purchasing stations.[30] For example, granary cadres or cotton purchasing station cadres may illegally lower the price given to peasants for their goods on the pretext that they are of low quality, a practice known as *yaji yajia* (to suppress grade in order to suppress price).[31] In other cases, cadres can preferentially enforce policies, including the government's one-child policy.[32]

Their positions also allow cadres to falsify reports to get bonuses and praise from higher levels. Cadres receive upper-level recognition for promoting state policy to their advantage. Here one sees the gap that exists, even in strong states such as China, between the intended effect and the reality of state policies.

Distribution and Management of
Public Goods and Resources

The second category of cadre misconduct centers on administrative responsibility over those productive resources that are scarce, rationed, or centrally allocated. This encompasses all land, including orchards and fishponds, as well as collective properties such as factories and large capital equipment, and such items as chemical fertilizer, diesel fuel, and insecticide. This is the category of cadre power one might have thought would most likely be reduced with the advent of structural reforms and the reopening of the market. Yet corruption of this type persists—not because of the reforms *per se* but because of the incompleteness of reform.

Peasants may now procure most, if not all, of their needed inputs on the free market. The problem is that not everyone goes to the market, and therefore not everyone pays (relatively high) market prices. The government re-introduced the market, but the government also retained central distribution and rationing of many key inputs. The result, as I have described in greater detail elsewhere, is a hierarchy of prices for key commodities which the Chinese term the "double-track" price system.[33]

The difference between the market price and the rationed price for key inputs is at least twofold, if not greater. Thus, those who are able to procure their inputs from the state at the rationed price will be able to earn much higher profits. Consequently, the economically rational peasant will try to secure as many of his inputs as possible through the rationing system. In such a context, contrary to popular expectation, markets are sometimes the *last* rather than the first choice for the purchase (and often for the sale) of goods and services. In a situation of continued scarcity, when the state still retains portions of the central resource allocation system that allows for the provision of below-market-priced inputs, the market is not cost-efficient.

How does this lead to cadre corruption? Each peasant is allotted a certain number of ration coupons. Until recently, in most areas peasants have had to go through their village cadres to get these coupons. The cadres are responsible for distributing coupons to each village household on an equitable basis—usually the amount of land contracted. The problem for the peasant is that he only knows the minimum number of ration coupons he should receive; he is unaware of the total number of coupons provided the whole village. Village cadres are thus able to withhold or preferentially distribute a portion of the state-allocated ration coupons.

A second problem is that the state continues to allocate only the ration coupons, not the actual items. Once he obtains the coupon, a peasant has to go, usually on his own, to procure the needed items at the supply and marketing cooperative (*gongxiao she*).[34] This creates yet another opportunity for corruption, this time by the cadres who actually handle the goods, both at the cooperative store and at the higher levels that supply these stores. Not surprisingly, one frequently finds these supply and marketing cadres illegally charging higher prices for rationed goods. One also finds store cadres selling counterfeit goods, i.e., fake fertilizer, or forcing peasants to buy unwanted and sometimes defective goods in order to obtain needed goods at the rationed price. Cadres at various levels of the distribution system also skim off state supplies for sale on the free/black market at high prices, which results in empty shelves when peasants go to redeem their ration coupons.[35]

A variation of this type of corruption stems from the new role of the village cadre as keeper of collective lands and property. Since the return to household farming under the responsibility system, peasants have become independent of team-level cadres in their work and payment for work. But peasants under the responsibility system do not own their land. Land is still collectively owned; peasants only have a right to lease the land from the collective. Because it is the responsibility of village cadres to oversee the division and apportionment of collective land and property, they have it in their power to appropriate these key resources for private use. The result in some cases has been the preferential granting of house-building permits to friends and relatives as well as preferential allocation of lease contracts for collective enterprises, orchards, fishponds, and equipment.

To a lesser degree, cadres retain a valuable resource in the form of control over the administration of state procurement contracts. Although peasants are now free to sell their surplus product on the open market, state procurement remains an alternative to free-market sales. In situations where there is an oversupply of a particular commodity, and where the market price is lower than the guaranteed state procurement price, or where the peasants simply want the security of a guaranteed market for their goods, a government contract can be a valuable resource.[36]

A related problem faced by peasants under the reforms is the need for market information. Lacking experience in a market-based system, and lacking access to relevant market information, peasants, particularly in the early stages of reform, tend to rely on those with greater information and expertise than themselves; and these are generally the local officials.[37] This cadre advantage is likely to fade, however, as the marketing infrastructure becomes more developed, as information and transportation flows improve, and as peasants become more experienced in the ways of the market.[38]

Another advantage enjoyed by local cadres stems from their influence over the selection of peasants for factory work, where the highest rural incomes are now earned. Those who hold lease contracts for the factories have a say in who will be hired, but local cadres continue to wield considerable influence through recommendations; in some cases, they have denied permission for a peasant to leave the home village for a more lucrative factory job in another village.[39] The degree of cadre control depends, *inter alia*, on the number of factories and the competition for jobs. The more jobs are available, the less competition there will be, and hence the less control any local official will be able to exercise.

One area where local cadres, particularly party secretaries, clearly exercise direct control is in the selection of peasants to contract and manage local enterprises.[40] Bids are often taken in this process, but the highest bidder does not always obtain the right to contract a factory. From interviews in various villages, it is apparent that local officials make the final decision on who is to run a local collective enterprise, whether it be a factory, a fishpond, or an orchard.[41] Local cadres also have the power to declare such contracts null and void.[42]

Treatment of Specialized Households

I treat this as a separate category to highlight the problem of what the Chinese often call "red-eye disease" (*yanhong*), loosely translated as envy of successful entrepreneurs. The symptoms usually include various means of extortion applied against successful peasants who have taken advantage of the official policy allowing some peasants to "get rich first." Here one sees clearly how cadres can either sabotage government attempts to enliven the economy and encourage entrepreneurial spirit or, conversely, benefit from it, depending upon whether the specialized household prefers to be a victim of cadre corruption or a client of a still-powerful cadre.

Using their designated role as agents of the state who have authority to implement and interpret the government's policies, local cadres can close down the businesses of successful peasant entrepreneurs and confiscate goods on various pretexts if they refuse to pay them off with gifts in kind or with a share of the profits. For example, peasant entrepreneurs who have left farming to open up restaurants and foodstalls must contend with unscrupulous inspectors who seek bribes and unnecessarily harass and threaten to close them down on false pretenses, such as unsanitary conditions. Sometimes cadres force peasants to make them partners in a business without the cadres having to make an investment or provide labor.[43] Cadres have also pressured specialized households and "ten-thousand-yuan households" for "donations."[44] Finally, there have been numerous incidents where cadres arbitrarily voided signed rental contracts when peasant profits unexpectedly increased beyond the originally agreed upon rent.[45] To prevent such exploitation, peasants often try to understate their wealth lest they become victims of those with red-eye disease—both cadres and less successful villagers.

Cadres on occasion have also hindered peasant entrepreneurs from receiving necessary licenses to operate their business or machinery. In one such case, 258 tractors stood idle because their owners were refused licenses by county cadres.[46] Even petty clerks such as toll collectors are in a position to extort money from specialized households. Cadres at weighing stations and roadway collection stations can demand arbitrary "highway fees" before letting peasants pass with their goods on their way to market.

Peasant entrepreneurs who have become factory managers are also heavily dependent on cadre support. For them, however, the situation is a bit more complex. On one level, the cadres on whom they depend are often at the higher levels of administration, at the township or county levels, the bureaus, the economic commissions, and the banks and tax offices where access is provided to scarce production materials and credit. But peasants do not generally directly seek out these higher-level bureaucrats; they go to their local cadre, such as the village party secretary, to have him intervene with the upper level. This is because most of these peasant-run enterprises are in fact still owned by the village or township. The key entrepreneurs are often the local party bosses.[47] At the local levels, the reforms have not taken the party out of running the economy.

The Changing Character of Particularistic Exchange in the Postreform System

While the incompleteness of the reforms has allowed cadres to continue to wield significant power over peasants, there have been important changes in the type of cadre able to hold power, the resources used as a power base, and the impact of that power. Cadres with power over peasants are no longer just team leaders and village cadres. Now, clerks at the cooperative store, at the toll stations, at the gas stations, license bureaus, procurement stations, etc., are all in a position to engage in activities—including illegal ones—that directly affect the well-being of peasants.

I shall now fill in the typology by identifying the functions and positions of those cadres who have the power to commit the various types of abuses mentioned above.

I. Distribution and management of state- or collectively-supplied goods and resources. Type of cadre:
   a. village head/party secretary
   b. supply cadres
      1. cadres in township- and county-level supply and marketing cooperatives
      2. gas station attendants at various levels
      3. personnel at supply and marketing cooperative distribution centers
II. Enforcement of state regulations. Type of cadre:
   a. village head/party secretary
   b. granary cadres working at procurement stations
   c. cadres in charge of licensing and inspection in township- and county-level bureaus
III. Treatment of successful specialized households. Type of cadre:
   a. all officials, from village to county levels, with whom entrepreneurs must deal in the production and sale of their product, including tax officials.

It is important to note that for the most part, these cadres did not obtain their power because of the reforms. They have always had power; indeed, most of the examples of abuse cited above are quite familiar to students of prereform China. Granary officials, for example, always had power to determine the grade of grain delivered to the state and to allocate payment accordingly; similarly, peasants have always had problems securing sufficient amounts of chemical fertilizer and diesel fuel. The reforms only changed the unit affected. In the collectivization period, the unit affected was the production team, not individual households within the team. Now corruption by procurement agents and supply and marketing coop personnel affects individual households. Now one peasant from a village can lose profits while another gains, depending on their respective relationships with those in power. The reforms clearly have made peasants more vulnerable as *individuals* to a *wider variety* of arbitrary or discriminatory behavior by officials and petty clerks than during the Maoist period.

Because of the increased number of officials with whom a peasant must routinely deal, the particularistic relationships that exist in the countryside are likely to be more casual—what may be fittingly described as a one-time passage "through the back door"—without any long-term expectations of mutuality on the part of either party to the exchange. In this respect they are unlike clientelistic ties, and are more akin to what one scholar has called "market corruption," where there exists a large number of suppliers and the where stakes or goods exchanged are routine.[48]

The reforms have also affected the type of pressure that cadres can exert on peasants. For example, during the Maoist period, cadres could openly withhold various types of authorization; the state indirectly sanctioned their actions in both ideological and economic terms. Then, cadres could use state policies that forbade "capitalist activities" and required all peasants to stay in the teams and grow grain as a pretext for refusing to let a peasant engage in sideline work. Now, cadres who keep peasants from leaving are in fact acting against state directives that encourage specialization and entrepreneurship. Consequently, cadres who hold up licensing in order to extract gifts from peasants have to be more subtle and more devious than before.

A further effect of rural reform has been to raise the stakes of clientelism for both peasant and cadre. For the peasant, it is no longer a matter of a few work points or a slightly better private plot, but the opportunity to operate a factory or orchard that may result in profits of thousands of yuan. Moreover, for the cadre it is no longer just political support that is important; now cadres can demand and get lucrative financial rewards, including a share in the profits of successful entrepreneurs.

Whether one should treat these peasant entrepreneurs as "victims" of cadre corruption or as "clients" of cadres in a mutually beneficial relationship is difficult to assess. Here one is again faced with the fuzziness of the distinction between corruption and clientelism. What is clear is that cadre support in China's new market-oriented economy is an invaluable asset for peasants, in exchange for which they are willing to give cadres a cut of the profits. Cadres can steer contracts toward certain enterprises; more important, particularly for those peasant entrepreneurs who have ambitious plans for expansion, cadre support remains the key to securing loans, foreign currency and technology, and scarce raw materials.[49]

The Rise of Cronyism and Nepotism

Lastly, the reforms have allowed cadres greater autonomy in selecting the recipients of their favor. The removal of "political hats" has lifted the political stigma from that small group of peasants with problematic class backgrounds. It is no longer politically suspect for a cadre to help a peasant from a landlord family. The calculating cadre can now use economic rather than political criteria and seek out those peasants who can offer the most lucrative return, including specialized households and families that manage collectively owned enterprises, fishponds, or fruit orchards as clients, particularly those newly rich, much-publicized ten-thousand-yuan households.

One emergent problem, not so much for the parties involved as for the larger polity, is the widespread perception that the most lucrative contracts are disproportionately falling into the hands of party members, cadres, former cadres, and their families and closest friends.[50] This further fuels the cynicism that already exists concerning corruption among Communist party members.

The fear that structural reform would lead to substantially increased income inequalities has, in fact, been actualized; some families are clearly wealthier than others. The large number of successful entrepreneurs who are of cadre background or who have close links with officials further raises questions about the kinds of class distinctions that are emerging as a result of reform. It is one thing to have social divisions between those who are rich in monetary terms and those who are not, so long as people feel that the determining factors are hard work and entrepreneurial skill. It is quite another matter, however, if economic success depends primarily on political position or patronage. In this connection, it should be noted that public outrage against such preferential, ill-gotten gains on the part of the sons and daughters of the country's top leaders—a phenomenon known as *guandao* (official profiteering)—played a major role in the Tiananmen demonstrations of spring 1989.

Corruption and clientelism, at whatever level, are more likely to be tolerated if the ordinary citizen thinks that someday he too may profit; but that same person is likely to harbor resentment if he believes there is no chance for him to prosper. Michael Johnston has argued that the development of nepotism and cronyism often have more politically disintegrative effects than clientelism.[51] The anger and accusations levelled against top PRC leaders suggest that this may be the case in China. It may be that whereas corruption was previously seen as "necessary grease," now it is perceived as a by-product of an inefficient, inequitable state run by and for the benefit of a small, privileged group of cadres.

Moreover, where ten-thousand-yuan households and entrepreneurs are predominantly former cadres, the regulation of policies and the collection of fees and rents are most likely to be carried out by "cronies." This has in some cases resulted in significant financial losses for the state. Because those being regulated are former colleagues, friends, and relatives of the regulators, the regulators, particularly at the village level, have had a difficult time collecting the owed dues and contract fees—a problem the Chinese press refers to as "petticoat influence."[52] The result in some villages has been empty collective coffers.[53]

Conclusion

What does the Chinese case suggest about structural reform and cadre (mis)behavior in socialist states? The most obvious conclusion is that a freer market environment does not necessarily lead either to the end of bureaucratic control or to the demise of cadre power. Somewhat less obvious is the fact that the introduction of market reforms is not the direct cause of many of the types of corruption discussed above. Rather, it is the incompleteness of the institutional reforms that has bred new forms of malfeasance.

The policy *context* is at least as important as policy *content* in determining the outcome of attempts at reform.[54] Restructuring the economy and re-opening markets offer peasants more opportunities than before and put new limits on cadre power; but they have not removed many of the sources of corruption. Indeed, the policy context in post-Mao China has actually undermined the regime's reform policies. One cannot expect market mechanisms to work smoothly or to develop efficiently in a context in which alternative allocational mechanisms are available for the procurement of necessary goods and services. The continued existence of such mechanisms provides local cadres with resources which they can manipulate to their own advantage. Local cadres may not be as politically potent as before; but they remain the primary economic fulcrum[55] of the new system, and their actions will ultimately determine the fate of the reforms.

What is interesting about the Chinese case is the way local cadres have reacted to the reforms. Grossman, writing about the prospects for reform in the Soviet Union, has argued that those most heavily involved in illegal behavior are most likely to resist and even sabotage efforts at reform.[56] The Chinese case certainly contains many examples where cadre self-interest has worked at cross purposes with the intent of the reforms; but the Chinese case also suggests that resistance is not necessarily the dominant strategy of choice for local cadres.[57] Rather than obstructing reform, Chinese rural cadres have taken advantage of the reforms, both directly and indirectly. One manifestation of this has been the proliferation of corrupt forms of behavior in the period of post-Mao reform.

In the wake of the crackdown at Tiananmen Square, conservatives in the Chinese leadership sought to freeze, and in some cases roll back, the economic reforms. In doing so, one important consideration was the regime's desire to curb the rampant growth of corruption and inflation, and thereby to disarm an issue that had generated substantial public support for student demontrations. It will be interesting to see whether, by whom, and how intensely such curbs are resisted in China's villages, where the reforms have served to provide local rural officials with new opportunities to substantially improve their fortunes.

Notes and References

1. This list is drawn from the national press, particularly from newspapers such as *Zhongguo Nongmin Bao,* that specialize on rural affairs. Similar examples have come out in my interviews with cadres and peasants in Hong Kong and China. Unlike Alan Liu ("The Politics of Corruption in the People's Republic of China," *American Political Science Review* 77, no. 3 [1983], pp. 602–23), I have not undertaken statistical surveys of the Chinese press. I can thus make no quantitative statements about the frequency of such corruption. For more detailed documentation of different types of offenses, see Oi, *State and Peasant in Contemporary China* (Berkeley: University of California Press, 1989), chapters 8 and 9.

2. See, for example, Liu, note 1; and James T. Myers, "China: Modernization and 'Unhealthy Tendencies,' " *Comparative Politics* 21, no. 2 (January 1989), pp. 193–214.

3. This list would include illegal feasting, feudal rites, false models, and illegal imprisonment and torture. See Liu, note 1.

4. Myers, note 2.

5. Gabriel Almond writes that "The success or failure of communist regimes in transforming the attitudes and behavior of populations may constitute a test of the explanatory power of political culture theory." See Almond, "Communism and Political Culture Theory," *Comparative Politics* 15, no. 2 (January 1983), pp. 127–38.

6. James Scott, *Comparative Political Corruption* (Englewood Cliffs: Prentice-Hall, 1972), p. 9.

7. On the Soviet case see, for example, Gregory Grossman, "The 'Second Economy' of the USSR," *Problems of Communism* 26, no. 5 (September–October 1977), pp. 25–40.; John M. Kramer, "Political Corruption in the USSR," *Western Political Quarterly* 30, no. 2 (June 1977), pp. 213–24; Steven J. Staats, "Corruption in the Soviet System," in *Problems of Communism* 21, no. 1 (January–February 1972), pp. 40–47; also Jerry Hough, *The Soviet Prefects: The Local Party Organs in Industrial Decision Making* (Cambridge: Harvard University Press, 1969); and Joseph Berliner, *Factory and Manager in the USSR* (Cambridge: Harvard University Press, 1957). On the Chinese case see, *inter alia,* Anita Chan and Jonathan Unger, "Grey and Black: The Hidden Economy of Rural China," *Pacific Affairs* 55, no. 3 (Fall 1982), pp. 452–71; and Oi, note 1.

8. Chan and Unger, note 7.

9. See, for example, Grossman, note 7.

10. Liu, note 1.

11. Liu, in contrast, argues that corruption was due to a breakdown of the system.

12. This would also include false reporting resulting in false models. Contrary to Liu, I would argue that the phenomenon of false models is not unique to China,

but occurs in any system that is highly politicized, including countries such as Zambia, where the fate of local officials is closely tied to their ability to enthusiastically carry out central directives. See Stephen A. Quick, "The Paradox of Popularity: 'Ideological' Program Implementation in Zambia," in Merilee Grindle, ed., *Politics and Policy Implementation in the Third World* (Princeton: Princeton University Press, 1980), pp. 40–63.

13. For other examples on China, see Chan and Unger, note 7. Similar behavior, stemming not from grain policies but from general bureaucratic red tape, is found in noncommunist developing states. See, for example, James Scott, "Patron-Client Politics and Political Change in Southeast Asia," in Steffen W. Schmidt, James C. Scott, Carl Lande, and Laura Guasti, eds., *Friends, Followers, and Factions* (Berkeley: University of California Press, 1977), pp. 123–46.

14. Kramer (note 7) seems to regard such behavior as a form of bureaucratic corruption, which he sees as not necessarily designed to get ahead but simply to *survive* in the system, i.e., to obtain vital supplies. Both forms exist; moreover, not all use of connections should be regarded as clientelism. See Jean C. Oi, "Communism and Clientelism: Rural Politics in China," *World Politics* 37, no. 2 (January 1985), pp. 238–66.

15. See, for example, Andrew Nathan, "A Factionalism Model for CCP Politics," in Schmidt, et al., note 13, pp. 382–401.

16. Because of the influence of the group politics model, students of communist systems have tended to focus on formal channels for political expression. Little attention has been given to the intersection of state and society, to the relationship between the bureaucratic actors who carry out the state's policies and those they are assigned to govern; it is in this latter nexus that one would expect to encounter a prevalence of clientelist ties.

17. Such studies suggest that Kramer (note 7) may have understated his case when he noted that communist systems are just as susceptible to corruption as any other. Kramer, *ibid.* See Oi, note 1; and Andrew Walder, *Communist Neo-Traditionalism* (Berkeley: University of California Press, 1986).

18. See Oi, note 1.

19. *Ibid.*

20. Not all particularistic relationships are clientelist in nature. For a discussion of the differences, see Oi, note 14.

21. At least until the post-Tiananmen crackdown of 1989, cadres were being evaluated according to their degree of success in developing rural industry, specialized households, etc. For details of the new measure see Oi, note 1, chapter 9.

22. There are a few exceptions to this generalization. See, for example, *Guangdong Nongmin Bao* (hereafter, GDNMB), April 7, 1985, p. 4.

23. China interviews, 1988.

24. *Nongmin Ribao* (hereafter, NMRB), February 26, 1985, p. 2; *Joint Publications Research Service* (hereafter, JPRS) CPS–85–105 (October 15, 1985), p. 62.

25. China interviews, 1986 and 1988; also *Gongshe Caiwu* 2 (1983), pp. 9–12.

26. See, for example, *JPRS*, note 24; *JPRS* CPS–85–100 (September 26, 1985), p. 29; *JPRS* CPS–85–121 (December 19, 1985), pp. 101–04; *NMRB*, February 26, 1985, p. 2.

27. Luigi Graziano, "Patron-Client Relationships in Southern Italy," in Schmidt, et al., note 13, pp. 360–77.

28. Judith Chubb, *Patronage, Power, and Poverty in Southern Italy: A Tale of Two Cities* (Cambridge: Cambridge University Press, 1982); also Graziano, note 27.

29. This is similar to a situation that Chubb describes (note 28) concerning officials in Italy who use bureaucratic power, such as licensing, as a new basis of clientelism.

30. See, for example, *Jingji Cankao* April 23, 1985, p. 2; *GDNMB*, May 4, 1983, p. 3; *Renmin Ribao* (hereafter, *RMRB*), March 16, 1985, p. 5; *Zhongguo Nongmin Bao* (hereafter, *ZGNMB*), July 14, 1983, p. 3; January 12, 1984, p. 2; and August 14, 1984, p. 4.

31. *RMRB*, note 30; *ZGNMB*, note 30.

32. Hong Kong interviews, 1984.

33. I use the term *hierarchy* rather than *double track* because in practice there are three, not two, prices for goods. The third is an intermediary price that is higher than the rationed price, but lower than the market price. See Jean C. Oi, "Peasant Households between Plan and Market: Cadre Control over Agricultural Inputs," *Modern China* 12, no. 2 (April 1986), pp. 230–51.

34. To alleviate such problems, some villages collectively procure in bulk the allotted fertilizer from the cooperative.

35. See, for example, *ZGNMB*, July 7, 1983; *Shanxi Nongmin*, October 29, 1983. For further examples see Oi, note 33. As of the summer of 1988 procuring fertilizer was still a major problem meriting front page coverage in *NMRB* (June 7, 1988), and was identified as a problem in interviews with officials and peasants.

36. See Jean Oi, "Peasant Grain Marketing and State Procurement: China's Grain Contracting System," *China Quarterly* 106 (June 1986), pp. 272–90.

37. On problems in the implementation of the new grain sales contracts, see Oi, note 36.

38. This is reminiscent of Migdal's discussion of the advantages elites have over peasants as capitalism develops in traditional settings. See Joel S. Migdal, *Peasants, Politics, and Revolution: Pressures toward Political and Social Change in the Third World* (Princeton: Princeton University Press, 1974).

39. Factory managers must have the village head's approval before a peasant is hired. Interviews with factory managers in China, 1988.

40. China interviews, 1988.

41. *Ibid.*

42. See Oi, note 1, chapter 9, for details of this process.

43. See, for example, *RMRB*, July 7, 1984, p. 3.

44. This may take the form of donations for schools, temples, etc., i.e., for collective welfare.

45. For a detailed discussion of the problem with "contracts," see David Zweig, Kathy Hartford, James Feinerman, and Deng Jianxu, "Law, Contracts, and Economic Modernization: Lessons from the Recent Chinese Rural Reforms," *Stanford Journal of International Law* 23, no. 2 (1987), pp. 319–64.

46. *ZGNMB*, May 26, 1983, p. 1.

47. See Jean C. Oi, "The Fate of the Collective after the Commune," in Deborah Davis and Ezra Vogel, eds., *Chinese Society on the Eve of Tiananmen: The Impact of Reform* (Cambridge: Harvard University Council on East Asian Studies, 1990).

48. It will be interesting to see if this type of market corruption becomes so pervasive and routine that it develops into a system similar to that found in the Qing dynasty, where petty officials demanded a set bribe known as a "customary fee" before a service would be performed.

49. China interviews, 1988. See Oi, note 47, for a more detailed discuss of this point. The situation I describe is apparently also the case in areas of model entrepreneurship such as Wenzhou. See the fascinating discussion by Liu Yialing, "The Private Economy and Local Politics in Rural Industrialization—The Case of Wenzhou in the Post-Mao Period" (unpublished manuscript).

50. For a published report see, *GDNMB*, January 27, 1984, p. 4; this also appeared to be the case from my interviews in both 1986 and 1988.

51. Michael Johnston, "The Political Consequences of Corruption: A Reassessment," *Comparative Politics* 18, no. 4 (July 1986), pp. 459–77.

52. *JPRS* CPS–85–121, December 19, 1985, pp. 101–04.

53. Interview with village cadre, 1987.

54. On the difference between content and context in policy implementation, see Grindle, ed., note 12.

55. I would like to thank Richard Baum for suggesting this term.

56. Grossman, note 7.

57. There is evidence that resistance was encountered among some rural cadres. But this was an *initial* reaction, most likely from those cadres who felt they could not adapt to the new market situation.

9

Permanent Technological Revolution and China's Tortuous Path to Democratizing Leninism

Edward Friedman

Prior to the 1989–90 political transformations in East and Central Europe, many analysts found it inconceivable that Leninist states could become democratic.[1] This essay argues not only that democratization is possible, but that, in an era of rapid and continuous global technological revolution, democratization can facilitate the modernization of Leninist systems. Unlike early theories of once-and-for-all modernity, which ordained a singular transition to universalistic values and thereby condemned the familistic Confucian societies of East Asia to perpetual backwardness,[2] this essay views modernization as an ongoing process of institutional adaptation to technological change—change that periodically produces new economic lead sectors and shifting world market logics.[3]

Viewed from this perspective, the contemporary drive for basic reform in Leninist states emerges as a consequence of the declining efficacy of the centralized command economy's hierarchical mass production system, which was originally designed to compete with the great steel-based economies of Germany and America at the start of the twentieth century. This system was supported by an inordinately rigid institutional framework unsuited to an international era that demanded increasingly flexible institutions and competitive trade as conditions of economic progress.[4]

Social theorists in Leninist states speak to the same point when they find that late twentieth-century developments in science and technology cannot be exploited by Leninist-Stalinist institutions developed for an earlier age of steam, railroads, and heavy steel. Leninism, they argue, is increasingly incompatible with the imperatives of post-steel modernization.[5] This outdatedness opens (or reopens) the question of democracy as an integral part of a particular historical moment in the ongoing process of technological revolution.

The Crisis of Leninism

Once the original charismatic, state-building leader of a Leninist system dies or is discredited, the regime, which cannot deliver on its promise of post-steel modernity, requires a new mode of legitimation. Democratization, as a response to systemic crisis, is an attempt to relegitimate the system and its temporary need for shared sacrifice in order to retool economically.[6] Such illegitimacy is explained in Leninist systems in terms of a generally accepted finding that the country is more backward than democratic market societies, leading to a Marxist labeling of the Leninist system as feudal, that is, precapitalist—and thence to a (misdirected) attack on traditional culture as a presumed source of continuing backwardness.

In focusing primarily on the issue of a ruling group's capacity to deliver the material blessings of a changing form of modernity, no slight is intended to the notion that democracy is a human universal. It is well known that from ancient China to precolonial Africa, diverse societies have embraced elements of civil rights and community participation. That the theory and practice of democracy developed most fully in the West does not make democracy a culturally peculiar Western product any more than the fact that penicillin was discovered in Britain means that it cannot be used in Beijing or Moscow.[7] The desire to have institutions which reduce the likelihood of arbitrary power and human degradation is not a passion unique to a rising bourgeoisie. People in Leninist systems suffer the daily humiliations of fawning before the powerful and dissembling in front of their children. A healthy polity is democratic. As science, medicine, and technology are universal human achievements, so are toleration, human rights, and democracy.

Nonetheless, democracy has spread most rapidly at particular moments in history. Certain challenges to state power more readily facilitate democracy as a solution. Democracy first rose in western Europe as an open, participatory response to a crisis of late medieval absolutism and religious intolerance when trade and technology expanded to offer new wealth-creating opportunities.[8] Absolutist, mercantilist states with their narrow monopolies came to be seen as corrupt and privileged parasites, denying to too many people the blessings offered by new economic opportunities.[9] It is possible that in the post-steel world of rapidly changing technologies, global forces act in a similar way to discredit privileged, statist, mercantilist dictatorships of the Leninist type that fail to win or spread the benefits of new technological and international economic opportunities. In China the Leninist party dictatorship is increasingly (albeit unofficially) blamed for leaving the Chinese people ever farther behind their East Asian neighbors.[10]

Democrats in Leninist states challenge the very legitimacy of the system in their redefinition of self-styled advanced socialist states as relatively backward, feudalistic, or traditional entities. The hidden corruption of the ruling groups, who channel foreign exchange to their friends and families for purchase of foreign cars, delicacies, and electronic goods, is experienced in much the same way as a venal monarchy monopolizing all economic benefits for itself and its courtiers—at the expense of the country. In a world of nationalism, the economic polarization of Leninism, pitting state against society, redefines the rulers as parasites. Their unearned, sometimes secret, always readily gossiped-about privileges discredit the ruling groups as less than modern.

There are major social science traditions which take seriously Stalin's identification with the earlier and only partially successful Russian modernizers such as Peter the Great and which understand the dynamics of Leninist systems as more traditional than rational, in the Weberian sense of modernization.[11] Analytic categories which conceptualize Leninist systems as based on traditions of fealty and hierarchy rather than competence and contract[12] have been utilized by social scientists to decode the political language of China as feudal,[13] neofeudal,[14] or neotraditional.[15] Nonetheless, rulers in the Soviet Union, as in China and other Leninist systems, did—as in modernizing Japan—put in place institutions designed to improve on the impressive economic record of Bismarck's nineteenth-century, rapidly rising Germany in protecting steel and grain, and delivering military autarky, state strength, and national power.

Lenin and the German Experience

Like Japan's Meiji oligarchs, Lenin and his colleagues looked to the most rapidly industrializing countries of the West for clues as to how to build a yet stronger, more prosperous nation. In 1920, Lenin found Germany to be "a country that is able to set gigantic productive forces in motion . . . Her technical level [in electrification] is even higher than America's."[16] For Lenin, "The electrical industry is the most typical of the modern technical achievements of capitalism."[17]

Lenin was deeply impressed by "the younger and stronger" Germany.[18] He found that "Bismarck accomplished a progressive historical task . . . Bismarck promoted economic development."[19] In *State and Revolution*, Lenin cited Engels to argue that what socialists must do is to change the political logic of Bismarck's achievement so that the wealth produced would serve socialist purposes (by raising the great mass of people), rather than serve purportedly capitalist purposes (by only enriching the few wealthiest exploiters). In short, Lenin argued that Bismarck's " 'revolution from above' . . . must not be reversed, but supplemented by a 'movement from below.' "[20]

In his essay *Imperialism*, Lenin described contemporary Germany as the epitome of modern development. No longer was it "a miserable, insignificant country."[21] By concentrating economic power in the few largest monopolies, trusts and cartels—a concentration that permitted coordination among banks, industries, and government so that large investments "can accelerate technical progress in a way that cannot possibly be compared with the past"[22]—Germany emerged "younger, stronger and better organized." Finding that those new economic organizations which concentrated and centralized command of the economy must dominate modern life "regardless of the form of government,"[23] Lenin argued that "[t]he result is immense progress in the socialization of production . . . Production becomes social, but appropriation remains private."[24] Capitalism thus paves the way for socialism, since "state-monopoly capitalism is a complete material preparation for socialism . . . a rung in the ladder of history between which and the rung called socialism there are no intermediate rungs."[25] Calling Germany the "most concrete example of state capitalism," Lenin referred to the German experiment as the " 'last word' in modern large-scale capitalist engineering and planned organization . . . [Substitute] a proletarian state, and you will have the sum total of the conditions necessary for socialism."[26]

Just "remove the top" of the German system so that it serves "the interests of the whole people" and, for Lenin, the result would be a modern socialist state.[27] History, for Lenin, had constructed in Germany and his Bolshevik party "two unconnected halves of socialism." "Germany and Russia had become the most striking embodiment of, on the one hand, the economic, the productive, and the socio-economic conditions for socialism, and, on the other hand, the political conditions."[28]

In Japan, the Meiji oligarchs found other lessons in the rise of Germany and the West. They focused on how private savings could be increased and institutions could funnel funds into industrial investments, how universal and technical education facilitated advanced technology and salable products, how crucial were protected home markets turning out exportable products which earned foreign exchange, how the state helped private businesses stay profitable if they proved internationally competitive, and how a militarily won colonial empire over the backward peoples was a prerequisite of joining the advanced nations. In contrast to Lenin and the Bolsheviks, the Meiji oligarchs institutionalized the expansion of wealth inherent in technological dynamism and trade expansion.

Both Lenin and the Meiji oligarchs saw agriculture as a weakness in Germany. Japan would end that weakness through imperialism: taking rice from Korea, soybeans from Manchuria, wheat from North China, and fruit and sugar from Taiwan. Lenin believed that capitalism's successes were unbalanced and inhuman, causing a disparity between success in steel and failure in agriculture. "The privileged position of the most highly cartelised industry, so-called *heavy* industry, especially coal and iron, causes 'a still greater lack of concerted organization' " in agriculture.[29] While other agricultural policies were, in theory, possible for socialists, in practice—building on Marx's condemnation of the French peasantry under capitalism as counter-revolutionary, on Marx's declaration of a need to industrialize agriculture, and on Lenin's commitment to a "concerted organization" of producers in a statist manner to permit a mobilization for war against counter-revolutionaries—Stalin's class-struggle justification of coerced collectivization[30] was one logical, catastrophic consequence of a Leninist misunderstanding of the lessons of capitalist agricultural development. It was, moreover, one not easily reversed.[31]

"Fordism" and Soviet Gigantomania

Seeing the large, the organized, and the statist as progressive, while seeing the small, the spontaneous, and the market-based as backward, ruling groups in the Soviet Union pressed forward with a gargantuan centralized form of modernity. Whereas Japan adopted a flexible, somewhat decentralized approach to production that stressed technical education,[32] in the Soviet Union Henry Ford's mass-production techniques were praised, imported, and expanded. The result was a Leninist-Stalinist caricature of late nineteenth- and early twentieth-century Germany and America, acknowledged as the world's two most economically advanced societies. Automation lines were set up with deskilled tasks so the jobs could be filled by peasant illiterates. But lacking the discipline of competitive capitalist markets, Stalin carried Fordist principles of mass production and an unskilled division of labor far beyond the point of economic irrationality (a point at which the Ford Motor Company virtually became bankrupted in the 1930s, in the face of competition from General Motors).[33] With innovation impossibly expensive because of oversized units of production, and with no spur from international competitiveness because of his preference for autarky, Stalin's gargantuan, heavy-steel, mass-production Fordism stagnated technologically. These obstacles to technological innovation were intensified by a secret police apparatus and a *nomenklatura* system for cadre selection and promotion which rewarded the loyal and obsequious and penalized the creative and innovative.

The successful space flight of the Soviet Sputnik in 1957 called attention away from Hungary's 1956 democratic revolution and obscured the fact that the rapid spread of innovations in science, technology, communications, finance, and trade were rendering Stalin's unchanging Bismarck-Ford model ever more wasteful and ever further behind new, fast-moving lead technologies. While Americans argued about an alleged Soviet missile gap, the Soviets in the 1960s tried to use spies to steal computers and information technology.[34] The humiliating fact for the Soviet Union was that the Leninist state—with its command economy, collectivized agriculture, maximization of import substitution and self-reliance, with its secret police, closed society, and appointments premised on networks of political loyalty rather than competence—was becoming ever further outmoded, yet ever more deeply entrenched.

The Democratic Impulse

It was so obvious to Soviet physicist Andrei Sakharov that Soviet-type systems would stagnate and decline if they did not open up and democratize that (watching President Lyndon Johnson act on his Great Society agenda) Sakharov predicted that capitalist societies would emulate socialist ones in guaranteeing all citizens basic minimums and that Leninist dictatorships would go democratic as had the West. The two worlds would converge.[35] Detente and democracy were predictable because inevitable.[36] If the Soviet Union did not open up, encourage creativity, rely on professionals, democratize, allow public mobility and freedom of information, then the economy would stagnate, incomes would fall, morality would decline, alcoholism, crime, and drugs would spread, and the Soviet Union would "fall behind the capitalist countries in the course of the second industrial revolution and be gradually transformed into a second-rate provincial power."[37]

A similar anxiety has motivated nationalistic reformers among ruling groups in post-Mao China.[38] In their view, either China modernizes or it will stagnate as a second-rate power and continue to lose legitimacy among an increasingly cynical and privatized population. While modernization requires democratic openness, virtually no democratic theorist in China or any other Leninist state has in recent times imagined democratization in terms of harmonies with the dominant thrust of the policies of Mao Zedong or the writings of Karl Marx. For Mao, democratization had little to do with legal due process, civil liberties, the right of an opposition to organize and win state power in competitive elections, or checks on arbitrary power. For Mao, true democracy meant using state power to smash the sources of class distinction. While he could mobilize people to attack hated officials, the result of what Mao called class struggle—as with Stalin's purges—was the use of state coercion and terror against factional and personal opponents at all levels of society.[39] Nothing democratic was achieved.

Strikingly, democrats in reforming Leninist systems do not hark back to Marx's notion of all power to the associated laborers. While there is among Chinese reformers some interest in codetermination in the workplace, and while there has been some discussion of worker-owned enterprises and democratized labor unions, there is virtually no theorizing about workers seizing power. Mao totally discredited that Marxist notion in the Cultural Revolution's vigilante brutalities against technocrats, managers, and professionals—indeed, against all educated people.

In Leninist states, a major factor delegitimating the notion of democratization as power to manual laborers is the perception that, in order to move up the technological ladder, to improve economic efficiency, and to become competitive in the world economy, it is necessary to rely on knowledge, not brawn, on white-collar, not blue-collar workers, on the skilled, not the unskilled, on leaders who understand modern technology, not on political hacks.[40] The proletariat as a vanguard class (not as powerless individual workers) is experienced as being at one with the parasitic party-state officials who serve themselves first and thereby force the powerless within the na-tion—and the nation within the world economy—to fall further behind.

Openness to the international world of advanced science and technology is a prerequisite of democracy and development in general. And for China, it is also a prerequisite of integration in, competition with, and growth within, the dynamic Pacific Rim.[41] Such international openness cannot be long sustained without a concurrent opening to democratization. As Franco's Spain opened to democracy when it gradually integrated with a democratic European Economic Community,[42] similar tendencies will predictably be unleashed in Leninist states as they seek to become integrated into a world market dominated by political democracies.[43]

Theoretical Perspectives on the Democratic Prospect

Democratization of Leninist regimes has suddenly emerged as an issue—seemingly from nowhere—because the three major contending approaches to Leninist systems essentially preclude the prospect of democratization. In totalitarian theory, which highlights the inhumanities inherent in Soviet-style regimes, there are no internal, dynamic contradictions which permit transcendence or transformation of tyranny.[44] From the theoretical perspec-tive of orthodox Leninist-Stalinism, on the other hand, the nominally social-ist state is already a functioning democracy—albeit a "people's democ-racy."[45] Finally, in the third major approach to Leninist systems, which stresses analysis of factions, interest groups and bureaucratic politics, consid-erable insight is generated into key short-run issues—much as neoclassical economics sheds light on the relationships among prices, wages, and interest rates. However, the approach does not lend itself to addressing long-run questions about regime change—just as neoclassical economists cannot fore-see changes in technological lead sectors and hegemons.

Many theories of modernization similarly tend to bracket the issue of democratization. Neither of the two dominant modernist schools, the Marx-ist and the Weberian, conceives of democracy as part of the solution to the postfeudal crisis.[46] Instead, solutions are sought in terms of negating the evils of capitalism or building efficient organizations or mobilizing the masses behind charismatic leadership. In both the Marxist and Weberian traditions, democracy is at best epiphenomenal and more likely an obstacle to progress. Indeed, even at the end of the 1980s, Leninist rulers who thought in Marxist terms about emulating Pacific Rim economies assumed that all that was needed was economic readjustment. Analysts in the Weberian tradition conceived of Pacific Rim success in terms of the efficient institutional adaptations of soft, authoritarian developmental states.[47] In neither case was democracy part of the solution.[48] The categories of established social scientific comprehension slighted the democratic agenda.

There are, of course, ways to think of the rise of the East Asian economies which do focus on the issue of democracy. Japan's post-World War II success was made possible by the legalization of unions and the legitimation of interest groups and competitive parties. This constrained Japanese planners to pay careful attention to rising socioeconomic expectations at home—which became the basis of Japan's successful export drive. Democratization and development were similarly facilitated by land reform, which destroyed concentrated landlord power. As the cases of England, Sweden, and post-World War II Japan demonstrate, democratization is more solid when based on a broad alliance that includes an independent peasantry.[49] Decollectivizing the Leninist system may thus be seen as a prerequisite of democratization.

Authoritarian industrialization, wherein labor cannot demand a fair share and capital is not democratically competitive, invariably rests on a fragile and volatile foundation, as revealed in the cases of South Korea in the 1970's, prewar Japan, and Bismarck's Germany.[50] While authoritarian industrialization involving great popular sacrifice is no doubt possible, equitably shared sacrifice—made easier by democracy—can best provide the necessary social tranquility and a successful path through the painful retooling and restructuring of the economy, both requisites for modernization in the post-steel era.[51]

Recent theories of political change, rather than taking a long and comparative view of large scale democratization in earlier eras, tend to focus narrowly on the present moment.[52] Attracted by an extraordinary series of post-1973 political developments from Greece to Argentina, much of the current writing on democratization treats the process as one of redemocratization. Tellingly, this category comfortably includes a democratizing Czechoslovakia (conquered by Soviet forces in 1948 and crushed by those same forces in 1968), but excludes a China which has never known democracy and has never gone through Renaissance, Reformation, or Enlightenment.

Restructuring the Leninist Leviathan

An issue that is missing in a focus on redemocratization is how aging, steel-based, uncompetitive, gargantuan, labor-intensive industries such as Poland's Lenin Shipyard must be restructured as part of a larger undoing of the command economy,[53] accompanied by a redoing of the Leninist system to replace the *nomenklatura* with competitively elected officials and professional civil servants, replacing the lawless, pervasive police with an independent judiciary and individual rights, and replacing the party's monopoly on truth with a democratic equity pact.

To theorize about democracy in terms of the discrediting of a feudal-like state incapable of managing a more modern economy, as this essay does, leads to a focus on the earlier democratizations of Holland and England rather than on Greece and Argentina in the late twentieth century. This approach directs our attention to the striking similarities between contemporary Leninist state quandaries and those experienced in an earlier democratizing epoch.

China's modernization process will undoubtedly find its own particular way of negating its premodern inheritance, just as the Netherlands, England, and France were shaped by their rooted particularities. Traditional norms have been reinforced by Leninist forms. The key point, as stated by China's noted democratic writer Liu Binyan, is that not only had China's initial May 4th (1919) drive to win democracy by destroying feudalism failed, but that the Leninist system, far from burying the corpse of feudalism, had carried on its spirit and breathed into it new life.[54] Its "management principles modeled on the feudal patriarchal system are a step backward from capitalism."[55] Its use of marriage as a way of cementing political obligations and networks made in-law relationships "twice as important as they ever were in feudal society."[56] The result of the system was that a leader, "though he lives in a socialist society in the eighth decade of the twentieth century, dreams the dreams of an eighteenth century feudal monarch."[57] So manifest and palpable is the analogy with the vicissitudes of reform in the late absolutist monarchies of Europe that the government of China in the early 1980s censored writings premised on this analogy.

Even in the cases of the Netherlands and Britain, historians tend to agree that political democracy is not the immediate consequence of a rising bourgeoisie and its revolution. Instead, democratization reflects a political seizure of opportunities and openings, a grasping of particular contingencies and conjunctions—as, for example, when the need to raise taxes for public purposes or to mobilize for war constrains elites to permit greater political access on the part of a larger portion of the citizenry. As part of the costly restructuring of wasteful and inefficient Leninist systems, the challenge of shared sacrifice to meet contemporary global, technical, and economic competition may offer just such a conjunctural possibility. In a situation of systemic crisis, Leninist ruling groups cannot succeed with half-way reforms; the center loses money, taxes seem inequitable if not corrupt, and the only alternative to democracy is more inflation. In order to mobilize popular action or sacrifice from citizens, Leninist elites, acting in their own interest, may thus be compelled to consider including the citizenry in the political process.[58]

Reactionary Alternatives to Democratization

Yet it is possible for reactionary Leninist rulers, in their desire to maintain power at any price, to substitute a populist, ersatz democracy of nativistic scapegoating for the real thing—as was done by the German Kaiser and the Russian Czar. The implicit nativism of Chinese leaders, who treated violent student riots against Africans in December 1988 much more gently than they treated peaceful demonstrations for democracy a few months later, offers an instructive comparison. Something dangerous is at work when frustrated male Chinese students and young workers in Nanjing, anxious about marriage, money, and housing, become enraged at the sight of supposedly inferior Africans, amply supplied by the Chinese government with money and living space, also dating Chinese women. The whole system seems illegitimate when native virtue goes unrewarded while foreigners cavort at Chinese government expense.

Chinese tell stories of their officials allowing African students to get away with bullying, berating, or beating up Chinese. They view Chinese women involved with African men not as dates but as prostitutes lacking patriotic dignity, selling out national pride for a fistful of money.

Patriarchy and patriotism, gender chauvinism and national chauvinism are emotional forces that fuel explosive passions. The scarcities and inequities of daily life in China, while foreigners are pampered in luxury hotels and air-conditioned buses serve to reinforce a militant chauvinist perception that foreigners routinely exploit Chinese—who must then fight back to regain their dignity. When the Chinese government abjectly apologized for a 1988 train crash in central China that killed several Japanese high school students on a graduation trip, the government of Japan nonetheless demanded indemnification. Chinese were insulted. Victims of Japanese aggression in World War II, proud but poor Chinese were now seemingly reduced to having to beg for aid, investment, and indulgence from rich, arrogant Japan.

Such perceptions of repeated humiliation at the hands of foreigners fan the flames of populist xenophobia. When Indonesia, Vietnam, and Albania turned against China in the 1960s and 1970s after having been recipients of Chinese foreign aid, it reinforced the experience of many ordinary Chinese that their country's leaders had rewarded undeserving foreigners and slighted long-suffering Chinese. In a similar vein, student demonstrators in 1986 ridiculed China's rulers for failing to take the Diaoyutai Islands back from Japan,[59] and in 1988 criticized those same rulers for failing to block the continued separate existence of a rival "Republic of China" on Taiwan.[60]

Populist scapegoating hurts the democratizers. While pro-democratic activists have sought to mobilize popular sentiments to discredit the excessive patriotism of China's rulers, opponents of reform have found it convenient to turn populist xenophobia against reformers, accusing them of selling out the nation to "polluting" foreigners.[61] Reformers usually retreat in the face of such scapegoating tactics, thus further legitimating a reactionary chauvinism which threatens to undermine reform, openness, and democracy. Democracy demonstrators in Beijing in spring 1989 almost never identified themselves that way. Instead they called their struggle a patriotic movement. The same populist nativism which presents the disease AIDS as yet another evil foreign import that kills innocent Chinese also renders it extremely difficult to challenge the view that excessive permissiveness and liberalization are the root causes of pro-independence riots in an ungrateful Tibet, requiring harsh martial law. Chauvinism pervades China.

Populist Movements and the Search for Dignity

As they struggle to regain their lost dignity, the Chinese people find little evidence—except in the military sphere—that they have actually stood up, as Mao claimed at the time of the founding of the People's Republic.[62] The perception that China's Leninist state system has not permitted the people to stand up is strikingly put in Zhang Jie's novella, "The Ark." She writes:

> It has started all over again, this life of pleading and begging. Whether you wanted to get a divorce, an apartment to live in or a suitable job, it always involved grovelling at the feet of others in the hope that they would show pity and understanding. What was so extraordinary about such requests? They were not asking for more than their fair share. When would Liu Quan at last know what it felt like to stand up proud and straight? She was not yet old, but she felt as if her back had been bent for a whole long lifetime.[63]

In the months preceding the Tiananmen crisis of 1989, people gossiped openly about a corrupt and hypocritical elite that feathered its own nest at the expense of the bent-over people. Tales spread of children of rulers residing in cushy foreign posts or growing rich as middlemen in trading companies, grabbing superprofits without contributing any real productive labor, and thereby contributing to spiraling retail prices paid by hard-working, innocent Chinese on the supposedly "free" market. In 1988, Deng Xiaoping, China's paramount leader, had to reprimand his own son who was running a firm said to be imposing monopoly prices on imported television sets.

The Nanjing anti-African riots of December 1988 showed the explosiveness of the conflict between Leninist rulers who refuse to concede to genuine democratic demands and an outraged people who insist on a right to articulate their own interests. Mistrust of government officials helped spark the outburst in Nanjing. Similar frustrations had earlier fueled a riotous celebration in Beijing after the defeat of Japan's volleyball team[64] and an angry riot in Beijing upon China's being defeated by Hong Kong in soccer.

In 1985 and 1986, populist xenophobia took a more political turn. Demonstrations against Japanese merchants, portrayed as venal, dishonest, and corrupting of Chinese officials, provided a thin mask for naked contempt toward hypocritical, parasitical powerholders, conceived as betraying their own people by imposing high prices while grabbing unearned, speculative profits for themselves through foreign connections.[65] This widespread contempt for corrupt, self-serving officials erupted briefly—but powerfully—in the massive anti-government demonstrations of April and May 1989. This contempt has deep roots and long branches.

Viewing the democratic reform movement through the prism of their own struggles, in 1986 democratic intellectuals sought to memorialize the victims of the cruel, massive purge of educated people in 1957, only to find their path blocked by Deng Xiaoping, who had played a key role in the 1957 repression. As a sign of his displeasure, Deng assented to a purge of reformist party Secretary Hu Yaobang, and launched a campaign against bourgeois liberalization, threatening to spill the blood of future proponents of democracy.

The Democracy Movement of 1989

In the light of such events, China's democrats concluded by the spring of 1989 that if they did not act to change China's direction, then, as had been the case for generations, once again reactionary rulers would drag the Chinese people away from the changes required to win them the blessings of the modern world. Among educated people, this feeling was intensified by a series of debates in 1988–89. Party General Secretary Zhao Ziyang made a desperate attempt to woo paramount leader Deng Xiaoping away from reactionary party elders by embracing the notion of a neo-authoritarian transition to modernity which did not require democratic political reforms and which could be built on the foundation of China's traditional Confucian culture—much as (supposedly) had occurred in Japan, South Korea, Taiwan, and Singapore. The Chinese gerontocracy remained unmoved, however. Represented by General Wang Zhen, who reportedly prides himself on his illiteracy, they led the successful campaign against reform leader Hu Yaobang, banned the film *River Elegy*, which traced China's downfall as a world power to its nativistic feudal culture, and put the brakes on all further structural reform.[66]

Muckraking journalists like Liu Binyan were silenced when they wrote that nationalism had to be tempered. Democratizers who called attention to the privilege, corruption, and tyranny of the conservative military were likewise silenced.[67] Meanwhile, China's post-Mao rulers continued to embrace as supreme symbols of legitimation successes with atomic bombs, hydrogen bombs, and intercontinental missiles.[68]

By early 1989 students and democrats realized that immediate action was needed to reverse a reactionary chauvinism pulling the Chinese people back toward the nineteenth century instead of pushing them forward to the twenty-first. A nascent civil society emerged as citizens began to organize in their own interest. Official preparations for the celebration of the seventieth anniversary of the May 4th movement, which had in 1919 embraced democracy and science, produced convoluted claims by conservative party propagandists that victory had already been won and that therefore people who attacked feudalism today were actually traitors demeaning China's glorious culture. This direct, frontal challenge provoked many more students to openly embrace democratic values as practiced in the West. They ridiculed the Confucianism of senior leaders as a self-serving national betrayal similar to that of earlier reactionary rulers such as Yuan Shikai and the Empress Dowager. And they concluded that China needed a more powerful May 4th student/citizen movement for democracy. With reactionary rulers fearful of losing everything and democrats believing that all would be lost if they did not risk themselves, the two forces moved inexorably toward a clash.

Much remains unknown about top-level maneuverings and divisions within the party and military during the spring 1989 flowering of democracy. It seems that Deng himself, as in 1957, played a key role in carrying out the conservative agenda. One wonders what might have happened had some top Politburo leaders been willing to publicly oppose Deng and his senior allies, or had party Secretary Zhao Ziyang early on turned to embrace the hundreds of thousands of demonstrators. Perhaps a democratic opening might have been won. But the Leninist system which kept those higher-ups in power would have had to go. For whatever reason, reform leaders within the party, government, and military vacillated at the critical moment, allowing Deng to unite with the reactionary gerontocrats and their allies within the government and military to kill the flower of democracy.

Conclusion: The Future of Leninism

Notwithstanding the brutal Chinese crackdown of June 1989, the crisis of the permanent technological revolution cannot be solved by reactionary Leninism. There are some remaining state leaders whose hands are not bloodied who could seize another opportunity to join the citizenry against the delegitimized Leninist state. Meanwhile, Deng and his allies can appeal to superpatriotism and traditional values to woo those harmed or placed under stress by the effects of modernizing reforms. There are in contemporary Leninist states large numbers of people who, as in late feudal times, fear losing their small guild protections. The transition from a traditional, feudal-style autocracy to a dynamic society capable of technologically competing in the world market inevitably causes painful stresses, losses, and frictions. Without genuine democratization, Leninist rulers face an increasingly difficult and complex political problem—how to hold on to the levers of power while continuing modernizing reforms. Enlightenment aristocrats in late eighteenth-century France failed; revolution ensued. Bismarck in late nineteenth-century Germany succeeded in holding on to power and continuing with modernization—but only by not alienating traditional rural and military bases of power, i.e., by not continuing with political reforms. Instead, Bismarck and his conservative successors displayed military toughness abroad while conceding to racist populism at home by scapegoating some of the new domestic rich as not real Germans.

Similar historical dynamics are at work in China. Caught on the sharp horns of an insoluble dilemma, China's rulers—like Bismarck in Germany—have embraced much that is reactionary and chauvinistic. It is a dangerous path. The crisis is systemic, but the question of which way to turn is clearly political. The struggle continues between revolutionary democracy and reactionary Leninism.

As with post-Bismarck Germany, Taisho Japan, or post-1905 Russia, what the crisis of Leninism reveals is not that democracy *must* win but that it *may* win. Economic challenges offer an opening. Politics determine if the opening will evolve into democratic political forms. Consequently, as in post-French Revolution Europe, conservatives may win for a while. Likewise, military force may temporarily gain the upper hand. As demonstrated at Tiananmen and Timisoara, naked coercion can be employed to suppress democrats. Neighboring countries may suffer. Nonetheless, the historical forces that gave rise to the democratic impulse are undiminished; and the issue of democratization cannot but remain high on a basic and continuing political agenda.[69]

Notes and References

1. William H. Luers, "Don't Humiliate Gorbachev," *New York Times,* January 30, 1989; Shaomin Li, "The Road to Freedom: Can Communist Societies Evolve into Democracies?" *Issues and Studies* (Taiwan) 24, no. 6 (June 1988), pp. 92–104. The scholarly editors of a three-volume study of democratization decided not to include any communist countries because "there is little prospect among them of a transition to democracy." (Larry Diamond, Juan Linz, and Seymour Martin Lipset, eds., *Democracy in Developing Countries: Asia* [Boulder, Col.: Lynne Rienner Pub., 1989], p. xix.) A classic statement of the view that Leninist states cannot be democratized from within is in Jeane Kirkpatrick, *Dictatorships and Double Standards* (New York: Simon and Schuster, 1982).

2. In the late 1940s it was generally assumed that Confucianism blocked modernization; by the 1980s, however, the common view was that Confucianism facilitated modernization. The British historian Maitland has described cultural explanation of historical outcomes as "a sort of *deus ex machina,* which is invoked to settle any problems which cannot readily be solved by ordinary methods of rational investigation." Cited in Peter Geyl, *Debates with Historians* (New York: Meridian Books, 1958), p. 212.

3. Influential theorists adopting this perspective include Schumpeter, Kuznets, Vernon, Rostow, and Kondratieff. That a permanent technological revolution was in place by the eighteenth century and contributed to democratization is argued in Roy Porter and Mikulas Teich, eds., *Revolution in History* (Cambridge: Cambridge University Press, 1986).

4. For a history and theory of flexible production as superior to Fordist production, see Michael Piore and Charles Sabel, *The Second Industrial Divide* (New York: Basic Books, 1984). For an argument that flexible production facilitates democratization in Leninist states, see Edward Friedman, "Theorizing the Democratization of China's Leninist State," in Arif Dirlik and Maurice Meisner, eds., *Marxism and the Chinese Experience* (Boulder: Westview Press, 1989). The relevant problem for Leninist systems is not that mass production is outdated but that a system solely defined by that logic is anachronistic.

5. See Elizabeth Valkenier, *The Soviet Union and the Third World* (New York: Praeger, 1983), pp. 90 ff.; and Richard P. Suttmeier, "Science, Technology and China's Political Future," in Denis Simon and Merle Goldman, eds., *Science and Technology in the Post-Mao Era* (Cambridge: Harvard University Council on East Asian Studies, 1989), pp. 375–96.

6. Hungarian democratic leader Janos Kis finds that, "[R]uling parties are seeking to make room in the power structure for a legal opposition with the design of using its authority to legitimize austerity measures and demobilize social resistance." (J. Kis, "Poland and Hungary in Transition," *Journal of Democracy* 1, no. 1 [Winter 1990], p. 76.) Similarly, Vladimir Bukovsky finds democracy the best way to solve "the problem of converting an extensive and inefficient economy into an 'intensive' and productive one." (V. Bukovsky, "Squaring the Circle," *Journal of Democracy* 1, no. 1 [Winter 1990], p. 87.) Barrington Moore, Jr., highlights the importance of social compact or equity pact among groups as being essential to the democratic route to modernity. See his *Social Origins of Dictatorship and Democracy* (Boston: Beacon Press, 1966), p. 415. For an application of Moore's theory to East Europe, see Gale Stokes, "The Social Origins of East European Politics," *Eastern European Politics and Societies* 1, no. 1 (1987), pp.30–74.

7. The Chinese democrat Fang Lizhi makes this point: "Just as in the case of making the atomic bomb, the first scientist to make one got the Nobel Prize, but now any student of high-energy physics understands the principles . . . It is not too difficult to repeat what someone else has done." *Ming Bao,* July 1988, translated in *Joint Publications Research Service* (hereafter, *JPRS*) CAR–88–061 (October 3, 1988), p. 4.

8. There is much persuasive data on the long crisis of the sixteenth and seventeenth centuries that served to facilitate popular movements—such as creation of the democratic Netherlands —against wasteful courts incapable of organizing for wealth expansion, food delivery, and legitimate taxation. See Geoffrey Parker and Lesley Smith, eds., *The General Crisis of the Seventeenth Century* (London: Routledge and Kegan Paul, 1978).

9. Hernando De Soto, *The Other Path: The Invisible Revolution in the Third World* (New York: Harper and Row, 1989) spells out this historical analogy between the mercantilist states of old and today. The scriptwriters of the Chinese television series *River Elegy* are also aware of this similarity when they speak of "officially sanctioned monopoly rights and a privileged stratum having authority over the distribution of commodities." (The script is translated in *JPRS-CAR–88–002-L* [December 6, 1988].) They equate the promise of China's opening to the world in the late twentieth century with that earlier opening. "The ships that began to sail the open seas in the fifteenth century . . . carried the hope of science and democracy" (p. 34).

10. This experience was consciously heightened in the immediate post-Mao era by the Deng Xiaoping group, which circulated to schools, enterprises, and government agencies videocassettes of travelogues from Taiwan and other similar material. The contrast with Japan is made in the television series *River Elegy*, where it is noted that whereas at the start of Mao's Great Leap "China's gross national product was about the same as Japan's, by 1985 it was only one-fifth of Japan's." *JPRS*, note 9, p.24.

11. Alec Nove, *Political Economy and Soviet Socialism* (London: George Allen and Unwin, 1979), chapter 2; Robert C. Tucker, "Stalinism as Revolution from Above," in Robert C. Tucker, ed., *Stalinism* (New York: W. W. Norton, 1977), esp. pp. 97–100. A classic statement of this equivalence of Leninist socialism with backward, feudal absolutism is Ryszard Kapuscinski, *Emperor* (New York: Vintage Books, 1983 [1978]).

12. Kenneth Jowitt, *The Leninist Response to National Dependency* (Berkeley: Institute of International Studies, 1978).

13. Tang Tsou, *The Cultural Revolution and Post-Mao Reforms* (Chicago: University of Chicago Press, 1986), chapter 5. Chinese political philosopher Wang Ruoshui argues that the habit of blaming corrupt, arbitrary power and privilege on class enemies, so common in the Maoist era, made sense to Chinese because feudal culture led Chinese to assume that democracy meant benevolent despots rather than public servants: "Due to the deep influence of feudal ideology, our discussion of democracy has been limited to how leaders should understand the people. An upright feudal official and a good emperor could be democratic if they accepted others' advice . . . We have to correct this misunderstanding. First, democracy is the system of a country under which the people have the right not only to criticize but also to supervise, vote, recall, etc." (Wang Ruoshui, *Wei rendaozhuyi bianhu* [Beijing: Sanlien Publishers, 1983], in *JPRS-CAR–88–056* [September 19, 1988], p. 15.) Earlier moments in this democratic critique of socialist feudalism are explicated in Friedman, "The Societal Obsta-

cle to China's Socialist Transition: State Capitalism or Feudal Fascism?" in Victor Nee and David Mozingo, eds., *State and Society in Contemporary China* (Ithaca: Cornell University Press, 1983), pp. 148–71.

14. Lowell Dittmer, *China's Continuous Revolution* (Berkeley: University of California Press, 1987), pp. 58, 79, 245.

15. Andrew Walder, *Communist Neo-traditionalism* (Berkeley: University of California Press, 1986).

16. Included in Robert C. Tucker, ed., *The Lenin Anthology* (New York: W.W. Norton, 1975), p. 632. Nikolai Schmelev and Vladimir Popov similarly cite Lenin's concept of socialism as, "Soviet power plus the Prussian railway system plus American technology and organization of trusts plus American public education." N. Schmelev and V. Popov, *Revitalizing the Soviet Economy* (New York: Doubleday, 1989), p. 4.

17. V. I. Lenin, *Imperialism* (New York: International Publishers, 1939), p. 68.

18. Tucker, note 16, p. 187.

19. *Ibid.*, p. 199.

20. *Ibid.*, p. 361.

21. Lenin, note 17, p. 119.

22. *Ibid.*, p. 39.

23. *Ibid.*, p. 58.

24. *Ibid.*, p. 25.

25. Cited in Ulysses Santamaria and Alain Manville, "Lenin and the Problem of the Transition," *Telos* 27 (Spring 1976), p. 80.

26. *Ibid.*, p. 81.

27. *Ibid.*, p. 83.

28. *Ibid.*, p. 82. It was democratic socialists in Germany, arguing for an electoral path to power, who first contended that, given the socialized economy created by state capitalism, their party's democratic conquest of state power would guarantee the full victory of socialism.

29. Lenin, note 17, p. 28.

30. Robert Conquest, *The Harvest of Sorrow* (New York: Oxford University Press, 1986). Shmelev and Popov, note 16, find war mobilization to be the essence of the Leninist system.

31. See Edward Friedman, "Decollectivization and Democratization in China," *Problems of Communism* 38, no. 5 (September–October 1989), pp. 103–07. This centralized "war communism" attack on the peasantry was carried yet further, first by Mao and then by Pol Pot. See Friedman, "After Mao," *Telos* 65 (Fall 1985), pp. 23–46.

32. David Friedman, *The Misunderstood Miracle* (Ithaca: Cornell University Press, 1988).

33. David Halberstam, *The Reckoning* (New York: Avon Books, 1986), chapter 5.

34. Jay Tuck, *The T Directorate* (New York: St. Martin's Press, 1986). KGB defector Stanislav Levchenko reports the organization's mission in Japan as "getting our hands on as many high technology items as possible." (*On the Wrong Side* [New York: Pergamon-Brassey's, 1988], p. 102.)

35. Andrei Sakharov, *Sakharov Speaks* (New York: Vintage Books, 1974), pp. 54, 105.

36. *Ibid.*, p. 100.

37. *Ibid.*, p. 132. In contrast, C. B. McPherson (*The Real World of Democracy* [New York: Oxford University Press, 1972], p.17) found Soviet rulers "within sight of their goal of a classless society."

38. Edward Friedman, "Maoist and Post-Mao Conceptualizations of World Capitalism: Opportunities and/or Dangers," in Samuel Kim, ed., *China and the World,* 2d ed. (Boulder: Westview Press, 1989).

39. J. Arthur Getty, *Origins of the Great Purges* (Cambridge: Cambridge University Press, 1985) argues that Stalin predated Mao in unleashing the rank and file against the established bureaucracy in the name of political purity, democracy, and the rights of the party rank and file (pp. 242, 105, 195, 206). Only in the subsequent wartime need of the Soviet Union for national unity did Stalin protect the corrupt, privileged bureaucracy and become the precursor of the Brezhnev era.

40. The script for *River Elegy* reflects this view in its comment: " 'Those who operate on skulls make less than those who shave heads, and those who play the piano make less than those who move pianos.' Payment for mental labor and physical labor is turned upside down." (*JPRS*, note 9, p. 24.)

41. In this perspective, the key citation from Karl Marx is the following: "The Pacific Ocean will have the same role as the Atlantic has now and the Mediterranean had in antiquity and in the Middle Ages—that of the great water highway of world commerce; and the Atlantic will decline to the status of an inland sea, like the Mediterranean nowadays." (Cited in B. Klyuchnikov, "The Soviet Far East in the Pacific Century," *Far Eastern Affairs* 4 [1988], p. 7.)

42. See Edward Malefakis, "Spain and Its Francoist Heritage," in John Herz, ed., *From Dictatorship to Democracy* (Westport, Conn.: Greenwood Press, 1982), pp. 215–30.

43. Democrats in Taiwan and Hong Kong have long argued this larger significance for their local efforts. Deng Xiaoping and his allies condemn the conspiracy of democratic reformers in China and world market integrationists in the industrialized democracies for trying to roll back communism. The threat to China's dictatorship from the new moment in modernization is palpable.

44. Consequently, many analysts focused on the Hungarian revolution of 1956 as if it were mainly a nationalistic struggle. General Bela Kiraly, leader of Hungary's freedom fighters, responded that their struggle was *"for* democracy" and

"against the secret police." The goal was "reform within the Party . . . internal democracy in the Communist Party." (Michael Charlton, *The Eagle and the Small Birds* [Chicago: University of Chicago Press, 1984], pp. 124, 125.)

45. It is symbolic of the delegitimation of this tradition that Samir Amin writes, "The dogma of a single and monolithic party is, therefore, antithetical to socialist democracy." The "absence of even bourgeois democracy signals that the Soviet state is oppressive and exploitive." "Democracy, which is an historical product of the bourgeois revolutions in the West, represents a decisively progressive step in the evolution of human society." (*The Future of Maoism* [New York: Monthly Review Press, 1981], pp. 121, 99, 98.)

46. Ira J. Cohen, "The Underemphasis on Democracy in Marx and Weber," in Antonio and Glassman, eds., *A Weber-Marx Dialogue* (1985), pp. 274–95.

47. Koji Taira, "Japan's Modern Economic Growth: Capitalist Development under Absolutism," in Harry Wray and Hilary Conroy, eds., *Japan Examined* (Honolulu: University of Hawaii Press, 1983), pp. 34–41; Chalmers Johnson, "Political Institutions and Economic Performance," in Frederick Deyo, ed., *The Political Economy of the New Asian Industrialism* (Ithaca: Cornell University Press, 1987), pp. 136–64. For the social science literature on whether dictatorial states facilitate economic development, see E. William Dick, "Authoritarian versus Nonauthoritarian Approaches to Economic Development," *Journal of Political Economy,* July–August 1974, pp. 817–28; Erich Weede, "The Impact of Democracy on Economic Growth," *Kylos* 36 (1983), pp. 21–39.

48. But since, as David Friedman (note 32) shows, militarist Japan's economy was one of flexible production, one cannot argue that in itself flexible production leads to democracy. The post-steel new technologies which require instantaneous, horizontal communication and coordination help erode dictatorship. But political action is still required at the state center. Barrington Moore, Jr., concludes that with respect to both freedom and prosperity, "it was the atomic bomb and MacArthur's occupation . . . that broke the shackles of Japan's ancient regime." ("Japanese Peasant Protests and Revolts in Comparative Perspective," *International Review of Social History* 33 [1988], pp. 327, 328.)

49. See Joseph Femia, "Barrington Moore and the Preconditions for Democracy," *British Journal of Political Science* 2, no. 1 (January 1972), pp. 21–46; Jonathan Tumin, "The Theory of Democratic Development," *Theory and Society* 11 (1982), pp. 143–64; D. A. Rustow, "Transitions to Democracy," *Comparative Politics* 2 (1970), pp. 337–63; Franklin Castles, "Barrington Moore's Thesis and Swedish Political Development," *Government and Opposition* 8, no. 3 (1973), pp. 313–31.

50. Ralf Dahrendorf, *Society and Democracy in Germany* (New York: W. W. Norton, 1979). Anti-democrats in both the Soviet Union and China romanticize South Korea's experience as an iron fist or neo-authoritarian path to wealth and power, ignoring the explosive fragility of Korea in the 1970s.

51. The problem for noninsulated rulers is that mutually beneficial international openness can appear to vulnerable sectors of the society as a betrayal and sellout of the nation to foreigners.

52. See Guillermo O'Donnell et al., eds., *Transitions from Authoritarian Rule* (Baltimore: The Johns Hopkins University Press, 1986).

53. This is argued in detail in Roman Laba's Ph.D. dissertation on Poland's Solidarity (University of Wisconsin, Department of Political Science, 1989), to be published by Princeton University Press.

54. Personal conversation, December 1988.

55. Liu Binyan, *People or Monsters?* (Bloomington: Indiana University Press, 1983), p. 8.

56. *Ibid.*, p. 52.

57. *Ibid.*, p. 61.

58. David Mason, cited in Gregory Flynn, "Problems in Paradigm," *Foreign Policy* 74 (Spring 1989), p. 67. Cf. the articles by Kis and Bukovsky, note 6.

59. Allen S. Whiting, "The Politics of Sino-Japanese Relations," in June Teufel Dreyer and Ilpyong J. Kim, eds., *Chinese Defense and Foreign Policy* (New York: Professors World Peace Academy, 1989), p. 143.

60. Personal report from Nanjing.

61. Since the Communist party's official historians of the Mao era denounced reformers as traitors, reform democrats in the post-Mao era not only legitimate earlier reformers such as Yan Fu and Liang Qichao who struggled for "civil rights," "ruler . . . chosen by the public and dismissed by the public," and "constitutionalism," but these democrats also equate today's opponents of reform with earlier reactionaries protecting vested interests. (See Li Honglin, "Looking at the Reform Movement of 1898 Ninety Years Afterward," *Xin Guancha,* Nov. 25, 1988, in *JPRS-CAR–89–014* [February 15, 1989], pp. 7–9.)

62. Patriotic Chinese take pleasure therefore in selling expensive weapons to foreign nations to the displeasure of U.S. Government officials.

63. Zhang Jie, *Love Must Not Be Forgotten* (Beijing: Panda Books, 1986), p. 159.

64. On anti-Japanese sentiment see Whiting, note 59, pp. 135–65.

65. Debates in China on Japanese brutality are explosive. Writer Bai Hua said of the Nanjing massacre, "Nanjing had a defense force two and a half times the size of the Japanese army . . . [But] the commander-in-chief . . . panicked and fled; the people were left without a leader and Nanjing was lost. Within six weeks, the Japanese took 300,000 lives. Even the Japanese could not believe it. Once 135 Japanese soldiers even managed to capture 13,000 Chinese soldiers, and tied them up, ten to a bundle . . . and slaughtered them all. Just by sheer number of bodies, these 13,000 men could have overwhelmed the Japanese, but they were full of cowardly hope, and nobody resisted. In the end, they were all killed." Bai Hua's point is that a narrow, materialistic, and fatalistic culture of survival, as in the days of Japan's occupation, still threatens China today when rulers "resemble serf owners," because people still try to get by rather than sacrifice themselves for democracy. (*Jiushi Niandai,* November 1988, in *JPRS-CAR–89–005* [January 13, 1989], pp. 59, 60.) Bai Hua's vision of a

culture which leads Chinese to be "thankful for being able to survive for one more hour" was criticized as an apology for the murderous Japanese, equivalent to a Jew apologizing for Nazi genocide. (*Jiushi Niandai,* January 1989, in *JPRS-CAR*–89–014 [February 15, 1989], pp. 51–53.)

66. For a study which focuses on the reactionary role of the gerentocracy, see Liu Binyan, "*Tell The World*" (New York: Pantheon, 1989).

67. These exposés of the military include "What if I Were Real?" in Perry Link, ed., *Stubborn Weeds* (Bloomington: Indiana University Press, 1983), pp. 198–250; "General, You Can't Do This!" in Helen Siu and Zelda Stern, eds., *Mao's Harvest* (New York: Oxford University Press, 1983), pp. 158–71.

68. See John Wilson Lewis and Xue Litai, *China Builds the Bomb* (Stanford: Stanford University Press, 1988).

69. With the Leninist-Stalinist path to modernity discredited, the clash between traditionalist chauvinists and democratic reformers resembles similar struggles in the era before World War I and the Bolshevik Revolution, whose outcomes were not invariably favorable to the democrats. See, e.g., Ervand Abrahamian, *Iran between Two Revolutions* (Princeton: Princeton University Press, 1982).

10

Epilogue:
Communism, Convergence, and
China's Political Convulsion

Richard Baum

More than a quarter of a century has passed since Zbigniew Brzezinski and Samuel P. Huntington first published their celebrated rebuttal of the theory of postindustrial convergence.[1] In that work they drew a sharp distinction between the universal socioeconomic attributes of modernization—including technical rationalization, functional specialization, and organizational complexity—and its more problematic Western political by-products, e.g., interest group pluralism and democratization. Examining the postrevolutionary development of the Soviet Union, Brzezinski and Huntington found little evidence to support the notion that industrial modernization in the USSR had led to the imposition of greater restraints on the exercise of political power by the monolithic Soviet party-state, greater political autonomy for emergent Soviet social forces and functional groups (including professionals and technical intellectuals), or greater tolerance for political dissent and deviancy.

Finding little cause for optimism in the post-Stalinist bureaucratization of one-party rule, or in Nikita Khrushchev's advocacy of a more humane, consumer-oriented "goulash communism," Brzezinski and Huntington held out scant hope for the emergence of Western-style pluralism or democratizaton behind the iron curtain. So long as the Leninist party-state, through its *nomenklatura*, maintained near-total control over the allocation of social rewards, ranks, positions, and perquisites, nonparty groups and special interests could not hope to exercise significant political influence or aspire to organizational autonomy—two essential preconditions of classical Western-style pluralism.[2] On this basis, they concluded that barring some "unforeseen paralysis" of the system—the result, e.g., of a prolonged, debilitating succession crisis—the Soviet future (and by implication, the future of Leninist regimes everywhere) would be marked by an underlying "continuity in the pattern of political control and indoctrination on the basis of growing collectivist consensus."[3]

For over two decades, Brzezinski and Huntington's prognosis of essential communist continuity successfully resisted a series of scholarly challenges, modifications, and emendations.[4] Then, in the late 1980s, a new and unprecedented series of events in the Communist world called sharply into question the core assumption of the Brzezinski-Huntington thesis, *viz.*, the "iron law" of Leninist monocracy. These events raised anew the issue of communism's mutability, compelling students of comparative communism to take a second, less jaundiced look at the emergence of fundamentally new pathways of post-Leninist development—including that of democratic-pluralist convergence.

Convergence Revisited

As the 1990s began, it was no longer possible to speak of reforms in the Communist world as essentially cosmetic, marginal, or epiphenomenal—or as mere passing phases in a recurrent cycle of totalitarian relaxation and control. Nor was it possible to speak simply of changes of *degree*. Changes of *kind*—some well advanced, others only incipient—were everywhere in evidence. The visible spectrum of qualitative changes included, *inter alia,* the growing marketization (and privatization) of socialist commerce; the opening of socialist economies to foreign investment (and socialist borders to foreign emigration); the emergence of consumer-oriented "revolutions of rising expectation"; the proliferation of open public and private information channels—signifying the Leninist regime's tacit acknowledgment of society's "right to know"; the political legitimation and articulation of group interests and interest groups; and even, in some cases, the open contesting of elections by noncommunist parties and groups. All these developments represented significant changes of kind, rather than mere variations on old, familiar totalitarian themes.

By the dawn of the 1990s the iron curtain and the Berlin Wall, prime symbols of communist insularity, had been rendered irreversibly porous and permeable by the electronic information revolution—as well as by investment capital seeking high returns, by intellectuals seeking enlightenment, and by divided families seeking reunification. Bolstered by enormous increases in the cross-national flow of people, money, commodities, and ideas, ordinary citizens throughout the Communist world—spearheaded, predictably, by "critical intellectuals"[5]—had asserted an unprecedented claim to empowerment, demanding freer mobility, more abundant consumer goods, greater access to ideas and information, and a higher quotient of truth from their governments.[6]

Viewed against these radical developments, Brzezinski and Huntington's 1963 prognosis of unbroken "continuity in the pattern of political control and indoctrination on the basis of growing collectivist consensus" seems quaintly anachronistic. Throughout the Communist world the pattern of centralized political control has been greatly (though not uniformly) attenuated; indoctrination in the ideology of Marxism-Leninism has lost much of its social relevance and effectiveness—particularly among young people; and the collectivist consensus on socialist economic institutions and values has been shaken by the spread of free markets, private enterprise, and the pursuit of personal wealth. The result has been a profound shift in the traditional relationship between strong Leninist states and their weak, captive societies.[7] Notwithstanding the obvious potency and near-universality of this emergent shift, the reform process has nowhere been smooth, continuous, or trouble-free. On the contrary, the process has been marked by the appearance of extraordinary frictions, discontinuities, and contradictions. At every turn, and with each new attempted relaxation of control or innovation in policy, would-be reformers have confronted both the entrenched, vested interests of a conservative party *apparat* and the aroused expectations—and heightened anxieties—of ordinary citizens. In some cases moderate liberal reformers have been upstaged by radical populists seeking to capture easy gains from the process of mass political mobilization. In other cases centrifugal forces unleashed by reform have threatened to overwhelm and nullify the authority of the central government.

Troublesome Consequences of Reform

Everywhere, the effects (real or anticipated) of reform have been highly unsettling. Widespread fears of uncontrolled inflation have stopped price reform in its tracks in several countries. Militant demonstrations (including mob violence) by long-suppressed ethnic minorities have accelerated the movement toward regional autonomy, separatism, and fragmentation in others. Fearing the wrath of unchained, angry masses, conservatives in two countries initiated coercive crackdowns, temporarily halting—or even reversing—the movement toward liberalization and reform. Meanwhile, gross inequalities (and inequities) in income and resource distribution, exacerbated by the advent of market reforms, have called into question the viability of the traditional socialist social compact that guaranteed, *inter alia,* lifetime job security and heavy state subsidization of food, housing, education, and health care costs for workers and their families. The threatened removal of this fundamental safety net (known in China as the "iron rice bowl") has left hundreds of millions of people throughout the Communist world anxious and insecure about the future.[8] Finally, wherever centralized command economies have undergone substantial structural reform, permitting the increased play of individual and group entrepreneurship, the incidence of economic crime—including speculation, profiteering, and various forms of corruption—has also risen dramatically, resulting in widespread public cynicism and demoralization.[9]

These are only a few of the more troublesome unintended consequences of reform to date. So new and without precedent are the policies associated with *glasnost* and *perestroika,* so volatile and unpredictable have been their effects, and so uncertain their future, that few analysts have ventured to make bold predictions concerning the ultimate viability or permanence of reform. Though all but the most hard-nosed defenders of the totalitarian model have now conceded the radical innovativeness of *glasnost, perestroika,* and *demokratizatsia,* there is little agreement on either the probable limits of reform, the long-term (ir)reversibility of the reform process, or its ultimate political consequences.[10]

The Chinese Case:
Convergence or Refeudalization?

A recurrent thematic thread running through this volume has been the question of whether China's Marxist-Leninist elites, institutions, and values can successfully endure and adapt to the intense pressures and turbulent currents set in motion (or accelerated) by the process of reform. At the very least, ongoing developments in the Soviet Union and Central and Eastern Europe suggest that China's future remains highly unsettled.

If communism does not collapse altogether in China—as it has already done in other parts of the erstwhile Soviet empire—what will it look like five, ten, or twenty years from now? Will it be recognizable? Will a resurgent, neofeudalistic variant of the Leninist "iron law" reassert itself in the Middle Kingdom, relegating structural reform and the open policy to the same historical museum of short-lived liberalization experiments as the "hundred days of reform" or the "hundred flowers" campaign? Under duress, will China turn inward once again, as it has so often in the past? Will hardliners succeed in turning back the clock, placing "politics in command" and reviving previously discarded techniques of ideological exhortation and mass mobilization?

Notwithstanding either the tragedy at Tiananmen or its legacy of political repression, we are strongly inclined to think not. Globalized markets, information flows, and cries for popular empowerment have already conspired to render autarky, self-reliance, and neo-Maoist ideological mobilization obsolescent as development strategies. Confronting the same dynamic global forces that have operated to radically alter the political environments of Eastern Europe and the Soviet Union, China's chaos-fearing leaders will, we believe, eventually fail in their bid to achieve order without opposition, affluence without openness, modernity without pluralism.[11]

A major basis for our prognosis lies in the observed effects of the information revolution on the events of 1989–90. During and after the Tiananmen crisis, the Chinese government attempted first to sharply curtail and then to rigidly contour the flow of ideas and information into and out of the country. A nationwide news blackout was imposed; satellite transmissions were interrupted; and Voice of America radio broadcasts were jammed on several (but not all) shortwave frequencies; meanwhile, pro-government propaganda flooded the mass media. In the past, such measures would have succeeded in preventing—or at least minimizing—the diffusion of potentially damaging, dissonant information and feedback. This time the effort demonstrably failed.

In the aftermath of the June crackdown, regime attempts to sanitize and apply "spin control" to the Tiananmen massacre were severely undermined by the presence in Beijing of too many foreign journalists, video cameras, and fax machines; too many open telephone lines; too many shortwave radios tuned to BBC and to the few remaining, mysteriously unjammed frequencies of VOA.[12] The result was a dramatic loss of governmental power to effectively redefine and politically "frame" the events of June 3–4—at least in Beijing and other major metropolitan areas.[13]

Painfully aware of its diminished credibility both at home and abroad, the Chinese government was quickly forced onto the defensive by a cascading wave of popular unrest that overtook Leninist regimes in East and Central Europe in the second half of 1989. There was considerable irony in this situation: By employing massive, deadly force to repulse the challenge of "bourgeois liberalism" in Beijing, more or less in full view of a global television audience, China's leaders brought down upon themselves a tidal wave of condemnation that made it demonstrably more problematic for other communist regimes to follow suit in the weeks and months that followed.[14] With the threat of state coercion substantially diminished (though not ruled out entirely) by the prospect of a televised holocaust, when push came to shove in East Europe, communist regimes generally reversed the Chinese pattern and—with the singular exception of Romania—chose to concede rather than confront. Perforce, the information revolution played a major role in shaping this outcome.[15]

A second and related irony emerged from the wave of extraordinary political concessions made by European Leninist regimes in the months following the Beijing massacre. The cascade of communist compromises served to strengthen the conviction of China's hardliners that they had accurately assessed the situation back in June, when they concluded that only two alternatives were available—either to retake Tiananmen Square by force or to stand aside and capitulate to the counterrevolutionary forces of "bourgeois liberalization" and "peaceful evolution." Throughout the autumn of 1989, Chinese government spokesmen thus congratulated themselves on their prescience and their political firmness—in the process hardening the lines of ideological demarcation between friend and foe.[16]

From Tiananmen to Timisoara:
The "Gentle Revolution" Hardens

The Chinese government's veneer of self-confidence suffered a damaging blow when the "gentle revolution" swept into Romania in December. Unlike other European communist regimes, Romania's hardliners defied the mobilized masses, drew a line in the sand, and invoked military force to underline their determination to resist change. When scores of unarmed civilians were shot by Romanian security forces in Timisoara in mid-December, Chinese leaders became visibly anxious. For the architects of the assault on Tiananmen Square, the Timisoara massacre must have seemed, in the immortal words of Yogi Berra, a case of "*déjà vu* all over again"—until the Romanian people dramatically altered the script. Instead of retreating in the face of overwhelming force (as the dazed populace of Beijing had done after the June 4 massacre), the citizens of Bucharest confronted the regime, chiding and challenging it. In a critical encounter between heavily armed units of the Romanian military and defiant, unarmed civilians, army officers refused to order their troops to fire on the crowd. Within days of the officers' mutiny, the Romanian government was overthrown, the dictator Ceausescu hunted down and executed.

In the aftermath of Ceausescu's demise, Chinese nervousness turned to outright alarm. Already facing a massive credibility gap at home and abroad, China's leaders quickly erected a wall of defiance to shield them against fallout from the Romanian upheaval. Dismissing out of hand all hints of similarity between conditions in Bucharest and Beijing, they quietly reinforced security forces in the nation's capital, placing them on standby alert.[17] At the same time, government spokesmen were dispatched to college campuses in Beijing to calm down restive students and to propagate the party's line on Romania—a line that contained a curious mix of political condemnation and diplomatic neutrality.[18]

As Beijing's leaders wrestled uncomfortably with the implications of the Romanian revolution, it became abundantly clear that they could no longer seal their country off from the impact of events transpiring in far-off places. Within two days of Ceausescu's ouster, posters appeared on a building at Peking University calling the Romanian dictator (who had not yet been executed) a "lost dog," and suggesting that he might soon be on his way to China to join four other dogs—a clear, if deliberately oblique, reference to Beijing's unpopular ruling quartet of Deng Xiaoping, Yang Shangkun, Li Peng, and Jiang Zemin.[19] In similar fashion, when the Soviet Communist Party Central Committee voted in early February 1990 to eliminate Article 6 from the Soviet constitution—ending thereby the CPSU's monopoly on political power—the news was withheld by China's government-controlled mass media; nevertheless, within forty-eight hours Beijing's intellectual community had been fully apprised of the latest Soviet constitutional developments—including the final distribution of votes in the CPSU Central Committee.[20]

Alarmed by the Romanian army's role in the collapse of the Ceausescu regime, the Chinese government in February replaced the entire leadership of the People's Armed Police, a 600,000-member security force charged with maintaining public order.[21] At the same time, the government began to tighten its political controls over—and to step up political education within—the People's Liberation Army; these measures were accompanied by the reported reassignment of certain local and regional military commanders whose loyalty to the regime was suspect.[22]

Thus forced onto the defensive, China's embattled leaders struggled throughout the winter of 1989–90 to regain the political initiative. Anticipating a popular outcry in favor of multiparty political reform in the wake of the CPSU's decision to abolish Article 6, Chinese party leaders quickly sought to preempt any such demands, sternly warning, in a *People's Daily* editorial, that "without the strong leadership of the Chinese Communist Party, new turmoil and [civil] wars would surely arise, the nation would be split, and the people . . . would suffer."[23] Seeking to counter the spread of multiparty pluralism and democratization in the Soviet Union and East Europe, China's leaders hastily revived the old Maoist model of political consultation, which involved "mutual cooperation and supervision" between communist and noncommunist parties—but no electoral competition.[24]

On the ideological front, the CCP sought to inject new life into a long-dormant, Mao-inspired mass campaign to "emulate Lei Feng." Intended to counteract the moral aimlessness and "bourgeois individualism" that ostensibly afflicted Chinese young people, this throwback to traditional Maoist methods of moral exhortation and self-cultivation reportedly met with widespread cynicism and apathy among young people in China.[25]

With the Chinese government on the defensive, with cynicism—sometimes bordering on nihilism—rampant among the nation's educated youth, and with the loyalties of the Chinese army in some doubt, it was unclear whether, or for how long, the political situation could remain quiescent. While many observers anticipated renewed turbulence (perhaps precipitated by the passing of Deng Xiaoping), none could predict just how or when the next crisis would emerge, or what its outcome would be; consequently, no strong consensus emerged on the question, "Whither China?"[26]

The Political Outlook

Although we cannot provide a definitive answer to this question, it is nevertheless possible to identify certain developmental trends that may be expected to affect the outcome of China's current political travails. First, it should be noted that although the Chinese Communist Party remains firmly and monopolistically entrenched in power, having permitted no significant organized opposition to gain a foothold, the nature and complexion of the party itself have changed appreciably over the past decade. In response to Deng Xiaoping's call to recruit well-educated younger men and women of talent to replace superannuated leading cadres, by the mid-1980s an elite group of approximately one thousand college-educated, technically proficient cadres in their forties and fifties had been promoted to positions of political and administrative responsibility in central and provincial party and state organs. Below this top-level group another thirty thousand talented young and middle-aged cadres were selected for special grooming at the prefectural and municipal levels, with another hundred thousand chosen at the county level. Collectively, these new elites are known as the "third echelon." In training, talent, and outlook, members of this group are considerably more cosmopolitan than the elderly, insular revolutionaries they replaced; and they are thus unlikely to respond enthusiastically to recent ultraconservative, neo-Maoist attempts to turn back the political and ideological clock in China.

Nevertheless, and despite their relative youth, education, and sophistication, third echelon cadres are not necessarily overwhelmingly pro-democratic or pro-Western in their political outlook. Most members of this middle-aged generation received advanced training in the Soviet Union (or in Chinese polytechnical institutes modelled along Soviet lines), rather than in the West; and most were trained as engineers and applied scientists, rather than as critical intellectuals. Members of this group—especially those in their 50s—thus tend to display the characteristics of "bureaucratic technocrats" rather than liberal democrats; for this reason, some analysts regard them as unlikely to comprise a strong force spearheading the promotion of radical structural reform or Western-style pluralism when they attain power.[27] In the absence of strong elite-level support for democratization, a more plausible developmental alternative would appear to be that of "neoauthoritarianism," which combines strong, centralized political leadership with decentralized, market-oriented economic activity, a là Singapore, South Korea, and Taiwan. Prior to his dismissal from office in 1989, Zhao Ziyang—himself a member of the second echelon—was widely believed to have been moving in the direction of neoauthoritarianism.[28]

At the outset of the 1990s, the third echelon collectively occupied the pivotal middle ground between the elderly law-and-order conservatives of the party's Central Advisory Committee and the younger, pro-democratic forces of the nascent Chinese fourth echelon, or "New Left." Among this latter group—comprised of young, highly educated party members in their late twenties and thirties, many of whom have traveled or studied in the West—support for liberal reform was quite widespread during the Beijing Spring of 1989, when thousands of their number (and by some accounts tens of thousands) actively participated in massive pro-democracy demonstrations.

Deng Xiaoping's show of support for the party's right wing in May and June 1989, coupled with the purge of reform leader Zhao Ziyang and the subsequent crackdown against "bourgeois liberalization," deprived the fourth echelon of a political voice. Although the silencing of youthful liberals enabled hardliners to dominate the nation's policy agenda at the top, conservatives nonetheless occupied only a minority of leading positions in key Chinese party and government organs. And it could thus be expected that the death or disability of key hard-line octogenarians, if it did not precipitate a chaotic and debilitating power struggle, would tend to shift the political balance back toward the moderate, neoauthoritarian center—or perhaps even left-center—of the reform spectrum.[29]

In this connection it should be noted that despite the widely publicized 1989 crackdown on liberalism, which witnessed the interrogation of tens— perhaps hundreds—of thousands of CCP members and cadres concerning their activities in May and June, no systematic purge of pro-democracy party members took place after the Tiananmen crisis. In fact, large numbers of liberal, reform-oriented party members who participated in (or otherwise openly supported) the "turmoils" of May–June—and thus were politically highly vulnerable to conservative retaliation—were effectively shielded, by sympathetic unit leaders and higher-level cadres, from severe or thoroughgoing political investigation, criticism, and punishment.[30]

Taken together, these factors suggest that China's elderly law-and-order Leninists (and their middle-aged clients and protégés, such as Li Peng) have been unable effectively to consolidate their post-Tiananmen political gains. Although opposition views have clearly been muted through political intimidation, stepped-up surveillance, and the threat of organizational discipline, there has been no systematic purge.[31] The vast majority of people who supported greater political liberalization and openness before June 3–4 remain in place, though they are clearly sobered and subdued, living under a cloud of suspicion—a situation sometimes referred to among Beijing residents as *neijin, waisong* (superficial calm, interior tension).[32]

Paradoxically, but not surprisingly, the persistence of widespread undercurrents of antigovernment hostility in Beijing made it more, rather than less, difficult for China's leaders to adopt conciliatory measures to reduce political tension in the nation's capital. In the immediate aftermath of the Romanian revolution the Chinese government, internally divided and visibly anxious lest any show of reconciliation be interpreted as a sign of weakness or indecision, was unable to respond in timely, affirmative fashion to a series of unilateral tension-reducing initiatives made by U.S. president George Bush.[33] In succeeding months, despite the cosmetic lifting of martial law and the announced release of more than 800 political prisoners arrested in the post-June 4 crackdown, a number of new restrictions were imposed on Chinese citizens and foreign residents in Beijing, including increased surveillance of journalists and intellectual dissidents, stepped-up political study in schools and universities, new limitations on study abroad for Chinese students, and a new round of harrassment that reportedly affected China's Roman Catholic church and other religious groups.[34] Maoist-style ideological clamps were also placed on the arts, literature, and the mass media.[35] And finally, a new drive to re-register party members was initiated in this period, ostensibly designed to weed out "problem" members.[36]

As the first anniversary of the assault on Tiananmen Square approached, security became tighter still in Beijing, with widespread reports of harrassment of journalists, dissidents, and others. Although no major demonstrations broke out in the nation's capital on June 3–4, tensions reportedly ran high both in the vicinity of Tiananmen Square and on college campuses throughout the city.[37]

Throughout the first half of 1990, the CCP's primary prescription for overcoming its credibility gap with the public continued to consist of a strong dose of old-time ideological rhetoric stressing the party's need to wholeheartedly "unite with the masses" in order to effectively combat "corruption, bureaucracy, subjectivism, formalism, passivism, and other serious phenomena."[38] Most observers regarded such neo-Maoist, neofeudal exhortations as implausible surrogates for genuinely enhanced political participation and pluralism, however; and political stability was thus expected to remain a highly elusive goal.

Conclusion

Returning to the theme with which we began this essay, we may now summarize our principal arguments concerning the recently revived question of post-Leninist pluralism and convergence, relating these arguments to China's long-term political development. In our view, Huntington and Brzezinski (along with most other students of communist systems, the present author included) failed to anticipate the tumultuous events of 1989–90 because they did not fully appreciate the potent social and political effects, not of industrial modernization *per se*, but of three critical *post*industrial phenomena: the increased participation of socialist countries in international transactions involving transfers of capital, technology, and manpower (i.e., *global interdependence*); the market-driven, productivity-enhancing decontrol of socialist exchange relations (*commercial marketization*); and the concurrent, technologically driven revolutionization in the means and media of mass communication (the *information revolution*). Together, these three forces have had a profound, catalytic effect on Leninist systems everywhere, driving them toward a series of social, economic, and political reforms virtually undreamed of a scant decade ago.

In almost all of the countries affected by the gentle revolution, trade with—and technology transfers from—the West had increased substantially in the decade before the upheavals of 1989–90. By the time of the Beijing Spring, several East bloc countries already had longstanding joint ventures and other commercial agreements with Western technological and financial partners (with several of them incurring substantial deficits and daunting debt burdens in the process); some had even joined (or applied for membership in) the World Bank and other Western-dominated financial institutions; and one—the People's Republic of China—had become the third world's largest importer of Western capital.[39]

Stimulated by the socialist bloc's increasing global commercial and technological involvement and interdependence, the trend toward marketization—involving the introduction of discretionary economic (as opposed to mandatory administrative) mechanisms of resource allocation—emerged in the late 1980s as a powerful remedial response to endemic problems of bureaucratic stagnation and ossification in Stalinist-type command economies.[40] Indeed, it has been persuasively argued that the economic logic of *market*ization, rather than the organizational logic of industrial *modern*ization (as stressed by an earlier generation of convergence theorists), has been the principal force driving a number of contemporary communist systems toward greater openness—and toward incipient sociopolitical pluralization.[41]

Along with the sharp rise in communist global commercial interactivity and domestic market expansion has come a dramatic increase in the transnational flow of ideas and information. No longer islands unto themselves, socialist systems find themselves enmeshed, willy-nilly, in an emergent global information revolution. Technologically fueled and commercially driven, this revolution has been marked by an exponential increase in the generation, reproduction, and global electronic diffusion of information. Contrary to the predictions of such technological dystopias as George Orwell's *1984*, the coming of the information age has perforce dramatically *reduced* the totalitarian state's capacity to isolate, encapsulate, atomize, manipulate—and thereby dominate—society.[42]

In China, although the Beijing massacre and accompanying crackdown rendered the question of political reform moot for a time, there are, as indicated above, good and compelling reasons, both theoretical and empirical, for anticipating a renewal of societal pressures for greater openness, autonomy, and—ultimately—popular empowerment. This is not to suggest, however, that China's transition to a postfeudal, post-Leninist polity will be smooth or tranquil; on the contrary, the political recalcitrance of Beijing's current law-and-order regime, the unresolved social and economic contradictions of partial reform, and the nagging backwardness and overpopulation of China's vast rural heartland will combine to greatly increase the probability of transitional *luan,* or chaos. Under such circumstances, optimism will be extremely difficult to sustain for some time to come—notwithstanding the long-overdue intellectual revival of a refurbished theory of postindustrial convergence.

Notes and References

1. Zbigniew Brzezinski and Samuel P. Huntington, *Political Power: USA/USSR* (New York: Viking Press, 1964). For a review of the convergence debates of the early 1960s, see Alfred Meyer, "Theories of Convergence," in Chalmers A. Johnson, ed., *Change in Communist Systems* (Stanford: Stanford University Press, 1970), pp. 313–41.

2. The pluralist model is elaborated in Susan G. Solomon, " 'Pluralism' in Political Science: The Odyssey of a Concept," in Susan G. Solomon, ed., *Pluralism in the Soviet Union* (New York: Macmillan, 1983), pp. 4–36.

3. Brzezinski and Huntington, note 1, p. 430.

4. Among the most important contributions to the "revisionist" debate on totalitarianism and convergence in this period were: Allen Kasoff, "Totalitarianism without Terror," *World Politics* 16, no. 4 (July 1964), pp. 558–75; Alfred G. Meyer, "USSR Incorporated," in Donald W. Treadgold, ed., *The Development of the USSR* (Seattle: University of Washington Press, 1964), pp. 21–28; G. Gordon Skilling, "Interest Groups and Communist Politics," *World Politics* 18, no. 3 (April 1966), pp. 435–51; Richard Lowenthal, "Development vs. Utopia in Communist Policy," in Johnson, note 1, pp. 33–116; Jerry Hough, "The Soviet System: Petrification or Pluralism?" *Problems of Communism* 21, no. 2 (March–April 1972), pp. 25–45; R.V. Burks, "The Political Implications of Economic Reform," in Morris Bornstein, ed., *Plan and Market* (New Haven: Yale University Press, 1973), pp. 373–402; Kenneth Jowitt, "Inclusion and Mobilization in European Leninist Regimes," *World Politics* 28, no. 1 (October 1975), pp. 69–95; and Valerie Bunce and John Echols, "Soviet Politics in the Brezhnev Era: Pluralism or Corporatism?" in Donald Kelley, ed., *Soviet Politics in the Brezhnev Era* (New York: Praeger, 1980), pp. 1–26.

5. This term is borrowed from Merle Goldman, "Intellectuals and Culture" (paper presented to the conference "State and Society in China: The Consequences of Reform," Claremont McKenna College, February 16–17, 1990).

6. For a comprehensive account of these trends and developments, see Bernard Gwertzman and Michael T. Kaufman, eds., *The Collapse of Communism* (New York: Random House, 1989).

7. For different views of the shifting balance between state and society in the process of reform in communist systems, see, *inter alia*, Tang Tsou, "Back from the Brink of Revolutionary-'Feudal' Totalitarianism," in Victor Nee and David Mozingo, eds., *State and Society in Contemporary China* (Ithaca: Cornell University Press, 1983), pp. 77–78; Vivienne Shue, *The Reach of the State: Sketches of the Chinese Body Politic* (Stanford: Stanford University Press,

1988); Mihaly Vajda, "East-Central European Perspectives," in John Keane, ed., *Civil Society and the State* (London: Verson, 1988); Gail Lapidus, "State and Society: Toward the Emergence of Civil Society in the Soviet Union," in S. Bialer, ed., *Politics, Society, and Nationality inside Gorbachev's Russia* (Boulder: Westview Press, 1989); and Martin K. Whyte, "Urban China: A Civil Society in the Making?" (paper presented to the conference "State and Society in China: The Consequences of Reform," Claremont McKenna College, February 16–17, 1990).

8. In Hungary, for example, there has been a visible and dramatic rise in the incidence of clinical depression among the population since political reforms were initiated in 1989. This "epidemic" has been traced to the growing sense of insecurity that has accompanied the advent of reforms. See *Los Angeles Times*, March 10, 1990, p. 1. In China, even before the Tiananmen crisis, there was a similar sharp increase in personal anxiety and insecurity, particularly among young people. See Stanley Rosen, "Youth and Society" (paper presented to the conference "State and Society in China: The Consequences of Reform," Claremont McKenna College, February 16–17, 1990).

9. See the chapters by Jean C. Oi and Connie Squires Meaney in the present volume; also James T. Myers, "China: Modernization and 'Unhealthy Tendencies,'" *Comparative Politics* 21, no. 2 (January 1989), pp. 193–214.

10. See, for example, Zbigniew Brzezinski, *The Grand Failure: Communism's Terminal Crisis* (New York: Scribner's, 1989); Gwertzman and Kaufman, note 6; Gail Lapidus and Jonathan Haslam, eds., *Reforming Socialist Systems: The Chinese and Soviet Experiences* (Berkeley: Berkeley-Stanford Program on Soviet International Behavior, 1987); Christopher S. Wren, *The End of the Line: The Failure of Communism in the Soviet Union and China* (New York: Simon and Schuster, 1990); Shaomin Li, "The Road to Freedom: Can Communist Societies Evolve into Democracies?" *Issues and Studies* 24, no. 6 (June 1988), pp. 92–104; and Franz Michael, et al., *China and the Crisis of Marxism-Leninism* (Boulder: Westview, 1990).

11. Along with Edward Friedman, however (*supra*, chapter 9), we remain cognizant of the possibility that China's embattled leaders may, under duress, initiate populistic campaigns to mobilize nativist fears, thus provoking a resurgence of reactionary national chauvinism.

12. It was subsequently disclosed by the official *China Daily* that in the single month of June 1989 an astonishing total of 870,000 shortwave radio sets were sold in China (*Los Angeles Times*, June 18, 1990, p. A11). In another, unrelated manifestation of the information revolution, several telephone lines which had been opened by the Beijing public security bureau in mid–June to facilitate anonymous tips by Chinese citizens wishing to report the whereabouts of political fugitives were rendered inoperable by callers from the United States and other Western countries who used direct-dial access to tie up the phone lines for days on end, thereby effectively sabotaging the government's crack-down effort.

13. In small towns and rural areas, where unofficial sources of information were less readily accessible, and where levels of public attentiveness to the May–

June turmoil in Beijing were generally much lower, government attempts to regulate the flow and content of information were apparently more successful. See *New York Times,* February 22, 1990, p. A3. On media framing effects in politics, see Todd Gitlin, *The Whole World is Watching: Mass Media in the Making and Unmaking of the New Left* (Berkeley and Los Angeles: University of California Press, 1980).

14. In Poland, for example, a potential crisis was averted less than a week after the June 4 massacre, when noncommunist candidates registered a sweeping victory in Poland's first free elections. Debating whether to peremptorily overturn the results of the election—and thereby to risk arousing the wrath of the Polish people—Poland's communist leaders were reliably reported to have been deterred from intervening by the specter of another Tiananmen-type debacle, which would have been widely publicized due to the presence in Poland of large numbers of foreign television cameras, on hand to cover the elections. Similarly, in early October, when East German government forces faced hostile crowds in Leipzig, communist leader Egon Krenz (apparently at the urging of his Soviet military advisor) countermanded Erich Honecker's previous instructions to use force to break up protest demonstrations. Reportedly, the Soviet advisor was acting at Mikhail Gorbachev's personal behest. Gorbachev, it will be remembered, had been in Beijing during the height of the pro-democracy demonstrations of mid-May 1989, departing China one day before the declaration of martial law.

15. Commenting on the extraordinary role played by the electronic media at the time of the Tiananmen debacle, a European observer noted that "events that are seen on [television] screens . . . can upset world opinion and ultimately affect the policies of . . . governments; conversely, . . . whatever has escaped the eyes of the camera is virtually erased from reality . . . It cannot generate emotions or mobilize minds." (Simon Leys, "After the Massacre," *The New York Review of Books,* October 12, 1989, pp. 17–19.) For analysis of information-related linkages between events in China and Eastern Europe, see Gwertzman and Kaufman, note 6. On the effects of the information revolution on communist systems, see Joel C. Moses, "The Political Implications of New Technology for the Soviet Union," in D. L. Bahry and J. C. Moses, eds., *Political Implications of Economic Reform in Communist Systems* (New York: New York University Press, 1990), pp. 225–63; see also Walter Roberts and Harold Engle, "The Global Information Revolution and the Communist World," *The Washington Quarterly* 9, no. 2 (Spring 1986), pp. 141–55; and Roy Malik, "Can the Soviet Union Survive Information Technology?" *Intermedia* 12, no. 3 (1984), pp. 10–23.

16. See, for example, Jiang Zemin's National Day speech of September 29, 1989, in *Beijing Review* (hereafter, *BR*) 32, no. 41 (October 9–15, 1989), pp. 11–24; also Zhang Zhen's three-part article, "Marxism-Leninism Is the Banner of Our Time," *BR* 32, nos. 48–50 (November 27 - December 17, 1989).

17. *New York Times,* December 29, 1989, p. A10.

18. Seeking to place primary blame for Romania's upheaval on Soviet leader Mikhail Gorbachev, Chinese party leaders in late December quietly circulated

documents accusing Gorbachev of recklessly undermining socialism and stirring up political unrest throughout East and Central Europe; at the same time, however, Beijing carefully refrained from publicly condemning either the Romanian revolution or the new Romanian government. See Richard Baum, "Old Men Riding a Tiger and Feeling Paranoid," *Los Angeles Times,* January 8, 1990, p. B7; also *Los Angeles Times,* December 28, 1989, p. A20.

19.   See note 17; also Richard Baum, "Scary Parallels for China's Leaders," *Chicago Tribune,* January 12, 1990, p. 27.

20.   Information provided by an informant in Beijing. See also *Los Angeles Times,* February 8, 1990.

21.   *New York Times,* February 15, 1990, p. A3.

22.   *New York Times,* March 14, 1990, p. A14.

23.   *Renmin Ribao* (hereafter, *RMRB*) (Domestic Edition), February 8, 1990.

24.   The decision to promote multiparty consultation as an alternative to multiparty competition was adopted by the CCP on December 30, 1989. The text of the decision appears in *BR* 33, no. 10 (March 5–11, 1990), pp. 18–22. See also *RMRB* (Overseas Edition), February 8, 9, and 10, 1990, p. 1; *New York Times,* February 11, 1990, p. A11; and *BR* 33, no. 1 (January 1–7, 1990), pp. 21, 27.

25.   On the Lei Feng campaign, see *Foreign Broadcast Information Service—China* (hereafter, *FBIS*), December 21, 1989, pp. 20ff. The indifference of young people was reported by Daniel Sutherland, National Public Radio, *Weekend Edition,* March 10, 1990. On the generally increasing demoralization among educated young people in China, see Rosen, note 8; also Stanley Rosen, "Political Education and Student Response: Some Background Factors Behind the 1989 Beijing Demonstrations," *Issues and Studies* 25, no. 10 (October 1989), pp. 12–39; and *FBIS,* December 26, 1989, pp. 14–17.

26.   For a sampling of views on the long-term effects and implications of the Tiananmen crisis, see the chapters by Lowell Dittmer, Nina Halpern, and Edward Friedman in the present volume; see also John Fincher, "Zhao's Fall and China's Loss," *Foreign Policy,* Fall 1989, pp. 3–25; Leys, note 15; Anita Chan and Jonathan Unger, "China after Tiananmen: It's a Whole New Class Struggle," *The Nation,* January 22, 1990, pp. 79–81; Jonathan Mirsky, "The Empire Strikes Back," *The New York Review of Books,* February 1, 1990, pp. 21–25; and Gerrit W. Gong, "Tiananmen: Causes and Consequences," *The Washington Quarterly* 13 (Winter 1990), pp. 79–90.

27.   See, e.g., Hong Yung Lee, *From Revolutionary Cadres to Bureaucratic Technocrats in Socialist China* (Berkeley and Los Angeles: University of California Press, 1990); also Hong Yung Lee, "China's New Bureaucracy?" (paper presented at the conference "State and Society in China: The Consequences of Reform," Claremont McKenna College, February 16–17, 1990), pp. 29ff.

28.   For an elaboration of the neoauthoritarian model in the context of China's post-Mao development, see *FBIS,* March 24, 1989, pp. 40–43.

29.   One indicator of the minority status of conservatives within the CCP was the unprecedented electoral defeat, at the Thirteenth Party Congress in November

1987, of a leading conservative candidate for the Politburo, Deng Liqun. Deng's bid for a Politburo seat collapsed when he failed to gain election to the Central Committee—the result of an anticonservative revolt by congress delegates, who used the device of a secret ballot to register their disapproval of his candidacy. The Central Committee elected by the Thirteenth Congress contained an unusually high proportion—almost 50 percent—of new members, virtually all of whom were middle-aged, moderate reform-oriented members of the third echelon.

30. Sutherland, note 25. This information has been confirmed to the author by several Chinese informants.

31. Aside from Politburo Standing Committee members Zhao Ziyang and Hu Qili, no other liberal-leaning party leaders were removed from either the Politburo or the Central Committee after June 4; and only one pro-reform member of the State Council (Minister of Culture Wang Meng) was dismissed from office. The fact that criminal charges were never brought against Zhao—who stood accused by CCP hardliners of aiding and abetting a "counterrevolutionary rebellion"—was widely regarded as *prima facie* evidence of continued intra-elite resistance to the conservatives' political agenda.

32. Periodically, the political silence of pro-democracy forces is broken by a poignant statement of defiance. In one such incident, reported in the summer of 1989, over 100 students at Peking University paraded through their campus one night, sardonically singing the lyrics of a local television commercial for pesticide spray: "We are pests! We are pests! Uh oh, here comes the dreaded pest killer . . . Let's get out of here!" On other occasions, college students have been observed tossing small bottles (*xiaoping*, a homophonic reference to Deng Xiaoping) out of their dormitory windows.

33. See Baum, note 19.

34. *New York Times,* March 11, 1990, p. 1.

35. See *New York Times,* March 14, 1990, p. B1; also *BR* 32, no. 50 (December 11–17, 1989), pp. 7–8; and *BR* 33, no. 10 (March 5–11, 1990), pp. 12–13.

36. *New York Times,* March 14, 1990, p. A14.

37. See, e.g., *New York Times,* May 31 and June 4, 1990; *Los Angeles Times,* May 28, June 4, and June 5, 1990.

38. These themes, along with the previously-mentioned revival of the 1950s concept of "multiparty consultation," dominated the political agenda of a Central Committee plenum held in March 1990. See *Los Angeles Times,* March 12, 1990.

39. On the increased global economic involvement and interdependence of communist systems in the 1980s, see "China Today: A Major Player in the World Economy," *The AMEX Bank Review* 14, no. 2 (February 1987), pp. 2–8; Zvi Gitelman, "The World Economy and Elite Political Strategies in Czechoslovakia, Hungary and Poland," in *East-West Relations and the Future of Eastern Europe* (London: George Allen and Unwin, 1981), pp. 127–61; Alex Pravda, "East-West Interdependence and the Social Compact in Eastern Europe," in

ibid., pp. 162–87; and Lynn Turgeon, "The Convergence Hypothesis Revisited" (unpublished paper, 1986).

40. On this point see Alec Nove, *The Economics of Feasible Socialism* (London: George Allen and Unwin, 1983).

41. East European economists have been among the most prescient analysts of marketizing phenomena and their socio-political implications. See, *inter alia*, Wlodzimierz Brus, "Political Pluralism and Markets in Communist Systems," in Solomon, ed., note 2, pp. 108–30; Stanislaw Gomulka, *Growth, Innovation and Reform in Eastern Europe* (London: Harvester Press, 1986); and Jan Winiecki, "Are Soviet-type Economies Entering an Era of Long-term Decline?" *Soviet Studies* 38, no. 3 (July 1986), pp. 325–348.

42. On the effects of the nascent electronic information revolution on China, see Richard Baum, "DOS ex Machina: The Microelectronic Ghost in China's Modernization Machine," in Denis Fred Simon and Merle Goldman, eds., *Science and Technology in Post-Mao China* (Cambridge: Harvard University Council on East Asian Studies, 1989), pp. 347–71. See also Moses, note 15; Roberts and Engle, note 15; and Malik, note 15.

Index

African students, 52, 171–72
Agricultural reform, 20, 41–42, 85–86,
110, 143–145, 150–51, 165, 169. *See
also* Peasants, Production responsibility
system
AIDS (HIV), 172
Albania, 171
All-China Federation of Returned Overseas
Chinese, 134
Argentina, 169, 170
Armenia, 26
Azerbaijan, 26

"Back door," 155. *See also Guanxi*
Baltic republics, 24, 26
Bai Hua, 181n
Baum, R., 14, 18
Beijing Municipal Party Committee, 72
Beijing Municipal People's Congress, 93
Beijing Social and Economic Research Cen-
ter, 8, 77
Beijing Spring, of 1989: 8, 84, 94, 97, 145,
190–93. *See also* Democracy movement,
Tiananmen crisis
Berlin Wall, 184
"Birdcage" theory, 9, 23, 84, 87
Bismarck, O., 164–166, 169, 175
Black market, 98, 133, 151. *See also* "Sec-
ond economy"
"Bourgeois liberalization," 4, 29, 34–35,
48–51, 87, 93–94, 99, 173, 187, 189,
191. *See also* Democracy movement, Lib-
eralization, Tiananmen crisis
Brezhnev, L., 20, 25, 28, 63; Brezhnev Doc-
trine repudiated, 26, 34
Bribery, *see* Corruption
Brodsgaard, K.E., 45
Brzezinski, Z., 183–84, 192
Bugaev, E., 26
Bukharin, N., 26
Bureaucracy, 2, 3, 21, 64, 108, 111, 116,
126, 168, 190: corruption of, 134, 135,
147–48, 159n; obstruction of reform by,

6, 12, 27, 30, 119, 126, 193; power of,
31, 150, 157; and Communist party,
179n, 183. *See also* Cadres, Chinese
Communist Party
Burns, J., 127
Burlatskii, F., 26
Bush, G., 191

Cadres: power of, 151–52; corruption of,
3–4, 12–13, 67, 96–98, 125–128, 134–
38, 143, 148–157, 173; income of, 148;
selection of, 127, 166; *See also* Bureau-
cracy, *Nomenklatura*
Cao Siyuan, 18n, 83n, 97
Capitalism, 9, 19, 22, 25, 84, 89, 155,
164–66, 168, 170; "tails of," 9, 22, 84
Catholic Church, 192
Ceausescu, N., 32, 78, 188
Central Military Commission, 135
Central planning, *see* Planned economy
Chan, A., 145
Chauvinism, 14, 59n, 171–73, 175, 195n.
See also Nationalism
Chen Yizi, 65, 77
Chen Yun, 23, 30, 87
Chen Ziming, 77
Child labor, 10, 98
China Social Survey System 67, 70. *See also*
Chinese Economic System Reform Re-
search Institute (CESRRI)
Chinese Academy of Social Sciences (CASS),
8, 47, 62, 72
Chinese Communist Party (CCP): Central
Advisory Commission of, 190; leadership
and authority of, 20, 85, 186, 189–92;
and corruption, 98, 136; and post-Mao
political reform, 3, 85; and private busi-
ness, 84, 93; and Tiananmen crisis, 190–
92; Fourth Plenum of the Thirteenth Central Committee, 99; Third Plenum of the
Eleventh Central Committee, 20, 41, 44,
50, 84–5, 109; Third Plenum of Twelfth
Central Committee, 86, 91, 110; Third

Zaslavskaia, T., 21, 35n, 80n
Zhang Baoning, 93
Zhang Jie, 172
Zhao Dajun, 135
Zhao Ziyang, 23, 43, 48, 50, 65, 68–69,

70, 73–76, 78, 85, 93, 97, 131, 135,
173–74, 190, 198n
Zhou Enlai, 33, 45, 135
Zou Jiahua, 33
Zou Jinmeng, 33

Contributors

Richard Baum is professor of political science at UCLA. He writes on contemporary Chinese politics, modernization, and societal reform.

Lowell Dittmer is professor of political science at the University of California, Berkeley. His latest book is *China's Continuous Revolution* (University of California Press, 1987). He is currently working on a study of Sino-Soviet Relations.

Edward Friedman is professor of political science and director of the Center for East Asian Studies at the University of Wisconsin. His co-authored book, *Chinese Village, Socialist State*, is being published by Yale University Press.

Thomas B. Gold is associate professor of sociology and chair of the Center for Chinese Studies at the University of California, Berkeley. He is the author of *State and Society in the Taiwan Miracle* (M.E. Sharpe, 1986), and is currently working on a book on the resurgence of private business in post-Mao China.

Nina P. Halpern is assistant professor of political science at Stanford University. She has published several articles on Chinese economic policymaking and the role of experts.

Connie Squires Meaney is assistant professor of government at Mills College and research associate at the Center for Chinese Studies, University of California, Berkeley. She is currently engaged in a study of contrasting patterns of state-private sector relations in Taiwan.

Jean C. Oi is associate professor of government at Harvard University. She is author of *State and Peasant in Contemporary China: The Political Economy of Village Government* (University of California Press, 1989). She is currently working on a book on bureaucratic entrepreneurship in rural China.

Stanley Rosen teaches political science at the University of Southern California. His research interests focus on political and social change in China.

Dorothy J. Solinger is associate professor of politics and society at the University of California, Irvine. She is the author of *Chinese Business under Socialism* (University of California Press, 1984) and *The Pursuit of Industrial Policy in China, 1979–1982* (Stanford University Press, 1991).